READY TO LEARN

Ready to Learn

How to Help Your Preschooler Succeed

STAN GOLDBERG, PH.D.

OXFORD
UNIVERSITY PRESS

2005

OXFORD

UNIVERSITY PRESS

Oxford   New York
Auckland   Bangkok   Buenos Aires   Cape Town   Chennai
Dar es Salaam   Delhi   Hong Kong   Istanbul   Karachi   Kolkata
Kuala Lumpur   Madrid   Melbourne   Mexico City   Mumbai   Nairobi
São Paulo   Shanghai   Taipei   Tokyo   Toronto

Copyright © 2005 by Stan Goldberg

Published by Oxford University Press, Inc.
198 Madison Avenue, New York, New York 10016
www.oup.com

Oxford is a registered trademark of Oxford University Press

Library of Congress Cataloging-in-Publication Data
Goldberg, Stan, 1945–
Ready to learn : how to help your preschooler succeed / Stan Goldberg.
p. cm.
Includes bibliographical references and index.
ISBN-13: 978-0-19-516754-2
ISBN-10: 0-19-516754-6
1. Education, Preschool—Parent participation. I. Title.
LB1140.35.P37G65 2005
649'.68—dc22   2004054714

1 3 5 7 9 8 6 4 2
Printed in the United States of America
on acid-free paper

To

*My daughter Jessica and son Justin who taught me
about children, patience, and life.*

*My wife Wendy whose love, tolerance, and support
allowed me the time necessary to finish this project.*

*The parents who gave me the privilege of
serving them and their children.*

*The children who have been a
constant source of inspiration.*

*The Crystal Springs Creative Writing Group
for constructive suggestions they graciously
provided during the preparation of the book.*

*The residents of Zen Hospice Guest House
who through their courage in the face of
death have taught me about living.*

Acknowledgements

*T*o Jody Rhodes who had the faith to offer representation and continued pushing until I "got it."

To Joan Bossert of Oxford University Press whose belief in the project and support led me on to undertake this book.

To Jessica Sonnenshein of Oxford University Press for her untiring work in preparing the manuscript.

Contents

SEVEN
Understanding   181

EIGHT
Storage, Retrieval, and Usage   201

Part III

Family and Friends

NINE
Getting Others To Help   219

TEN
And What About You?   230

ELEVEN
Your Child's Future   253

Illustrations

Preface: You Have Questions

Y
ou see something in your child's behavior that keeps you up at night. It may be very subtle, or painfully obvious. Only you may notice, or others continually comment on it. Most likely, it involves difficulties in attending, understanding, remembering, or using information appropriately. In spite of helpful advice such as "don't worry, she'll outgrow it," you're still concerned. What if she doesn't?

It's a terrible feeling to see something in your child you suspect will cause problems. You desperately want to help—but don't know what to do. Many of the books you've read were very informative. Although most suggested *what* you should do, few told you *how* to do it. It was as if you were given a manual on how to operate a new complex kitchen appliance, but pages were missing. *Ready to Learn* contains both the *whats* and *hows* of helping children learn. Though written for parents whose children are five years of age or less, most of the material, with little modification, is appropriate for children in elementary school. It's a complete step-by-step guide for parents. My experience with thousands of children, including my own, has convinced me every child has the capacity to learn. Hopefully, this book will provide the key to help unlock your child's potential, whether he or she is a different learner or just has one problem that concerns you.

Every suggestion in this book is based on my 25 years as a university professor, researcher, clinician, and parent. I won't talk about labels, many of which have for decades caused needless anxiety for both parents and children. Instead, we'll take a positive approach. We'll look at behaviors. You'll learn how to teach children as young as two years skills that will ready them for kindergarten and the rest of their life.

In our fast-paced society, there is a tendency to want everything *now*— right here, immediately, quickly, and in a condensed form. That includes how we view our children's problems. No parent wants to wait until next month or even tomorrow for a problem to be corrected. You want it gone yesterday. Yet, that's not how learning works. Although learning how to teach children with differences is not as difficult as you may think, it does require an orderly approach. You can't do it by "leap-frogging" from one section to the next, trying to find the one magic sentence that will allow you to correct your child's problem immediately. Unfortunately, some parenting books encourage this approach with exaggerated claims such as, "Turn to page 16 and find six ways of making your child smarter. " There are few brass rings in life. Believing you'll catch it with little effort can cause both you and your child needless pain.

I can remember my son watching me hastily assemble his first tricycle and noticed after it was completed, there were six nuts and a bracket lying on the floor. I subtly tried to hide them under the assembly instructions.

"Daddy, what's that stuff? Shouldn't they go on the bike?"

"No Justin," I tried to say convincingly. "You use that for another model."

Believing me, he hopped on the bike and began pedaling. With each pedal movement, the tricycle listed severely to the left, almost throwing him off. After going about 20 feet he stopped, got off the bike, turned around, and looked toward the pieces hidden under the paper. His eyes moved from them to me and then, he just shook his head. At three years of age, my son instructed me on the importance of taking my time and not skipping steps.

That's the approach I suggest you take with this book, which is divided into three sections. Think of the first as a foundation for understanding learning and your role as a teaching parent. The second is devoted to explaining numerous strategies you can easily use to eliminate or minimize problems your child currently faces or will face when entering kindergarten. In the final section, we'll look at something many parents of children with learning problems often neglect—the family members' emotional well-being. Effective teaching involves all three—knowing what learning is, how you can help, and dealing with the emotional strain a different learner may place on the family. Jumping in the middle can be as frustrating as coming in 30 minutes late for a movie.

There are examples and stories I use to explain concepts or show how to apply a strategy. Every one is based on a real child or parent I've worked with at the university, in private practice, and during research studies. I've modified their identities to protect their privacy. In all cases, names have been changed. In some examples, gender has been reversed and ages modified. In a few, the characteristics and problems of children have been combined. Throughout the book, you'll find little numbers appearing at the end of some sentences. They're called *endnotes* and refer to research articles supporting a strategy or recommendation. For parents, I would suggest ignoring them unless you would like to investigate the basic research. These references are intended for university training programs and clinical researchers.

Books for parents are written in various ways. The most common ones read as if they were cookbooks—follow the recipe exactly and you turn out a perfect dish. But what happens if the recipe is for four people and you have six coming for dinner? If the butcher doesn't have lamb, how do you substitute another type of meat? Can a Cajun spice be substituted for a hot pepper sauce?

With a cookbook approach, you're stuck. You can only do what's printed on the page. There's no room for modifications. In one television cooking show some-one asked Julia Child whether she strictly relies on recipes. Julia patiently re-sponded, "No, that's what *cooks* do. When you understand how to cook, you're a *chef*, and chefs don't need to always follow recipes." In this book, you'll learn the fundamentals of teaching children. You'll learn how to be a chef, capable of modifying recipes based on the needs of your child. Take your time. You and your child are about to enter a marathon, not a sprint race. Go slow, and enjoy the chapters as if they were gourmet meals, not fast-food burgers.

Part I

The Basics

Change is a very interesting phenomenon. Many of us have a love-hate relationship with it. As much as we like to see new things, like an old slipper, there's something very comfortable about what we have been doing. In this book I may be pushing you to a place that's new and possibly uncomfortable. I'll be presenting a different way of looking at children's problems and your role in helping them. Although I'm a professional, I'm also the parent of two children who are now young adults. As a parent, I've watched our role become marginalized. "Professionals know best"—the unsaid mantra many parents believe—is touted by those whose status it affirms. Having stood on both sides of the parent-professional wall for over 25 years, my view is a little different. I believe with knowledge, "parents know best."

ONE

Learning Differently

T he long brown curls became visible as tear-filled eyes peeked from behind the banjo case. My four-year-old son looked at me and tried to form words, but only quivering movements came from of his little mouth.

"Justin!" I screamed, "I told you not to climb on that cabinet! Can't you ever listen to what I say? Don't you understand how dangerous that was? Look at what you did!"

Around him were broken antiques, some over one hundred years old. I looked on the floor at the rubble and saw cracked plates from Dresden factories mixed in with shattered glass from Czarist Russia and the lid of a mangled Cloisonné vase. Fifty antiques fell from the shelves of a two hundred-pound, seven-foot-high cabinet as it toppled over and landed on the edge of my banjo case. While the case saved my son from any injury, the cabinet destroyed the beautiful $1,200 instrument within it. He stood there with a look every parent sees when their child does something terribly wrong, knows it, and waits to hear the inevitable yelling.

"Why did you do that when I told you not to? Can't you ever listen?"

The prior week I moved the cabinet, but neglected bolting it to the wall. I wanted to think my procrastination wouldn't be a problem, but I should've known better. It wasn't as if this was an isolated incident. I chose to ignore warning messages my son sent me since he was two years old. He would forget things, become easily distracted, and often appear confused. And, as someone who didn't wish to face the obvious, I wrongly and thoughtlessly redirected responsibility for the accident onto him. Tears became sobs and he began to cry uncontrollably. Of course he heard my warning, he always did. He always wanted to please both my wife and me. But for some reason, he continually forgot what I asked him to do, or in this case, *not* to do. I *expected* him to listen and stay away from the cabinet. He stood with mismatched socks and knotted laces in a sea of broken antiques. As I watched him, I realized his pain was not only caused by my anger, but something more basic. As he rhythmically rubbed his fingers back and forth on the edge of the broken banjo case, he finally developed the courage to speak.

"I'm sorry Daddy," he said between sobs. Then in a whisper, "I forgot."

At four years of age, he already knew something about him was different. He didn't know what it was, but he did know it caused people, especially me, to become angry. He was a funny, delightful, sensitive, smart, and intuitive child. But like millions of others, his learning style was different. It took time for me to realize Justin's lack of attention wasn't an act of defiance, or a desire to make my life challenging—he just learned differently. In a world that often doesn't recognize differences as positive and natural, his learning style was creating problems. And if people, myself included, continued reacting to Justin as if he learned like other children, the problems were certain to grow and eventually be viewed as something more ominous, a "disorder." I should have known better by then, since my daughter, who was four years older, also learned in her own unique way. But like many other parents, I tried to pretend this was a behavior issue, not something neurological, not something beyond his control.

"If he would just try a little harder," I would say to my wife, "just make up his mind to do things the right way, everything would be fine."

I was wrong. I eventually came to realize my children's problems had nothing to do with not trying. If anything, they tried harder than other children. Unfortunately, they zigged left when most other children zagged right. From the day of the antique disaster, I began a 20-year journey to help not only my children, but also others with learning differences. For Justin, I needed to do things that would make his memory as solid as concrete. I slowed down my speech when I spoke to him, allowing information to slowly seep in. I gave only one idea or request at a time. When I asked him to do something, I would immediately have him repeat back to me what I had said. I always used visual cues, like lists, rather than relying only on words. Not all of his memory problems were corrected, But 17 years later, Justin still uses the strategies I taught to him. His problems have become manageable, enough so that he is able to succeed in a demanding major at a prestigious university.

Some would maintain all children learn differently. Research shows that at least six million children learn in ways that don't match up with the teaching approach used by many parents and educators.[1] These "mismatches" can lead to problems and distress for both children and parents. Children don't understand why they're having so much difficulty learning. Parents wonder why their child can't learn seemingly simple things. They are anxious about how their child will perform in kindergarten, and more importantly, how their learning difficulties will affect them for the rest of their lives.

IS IT A DIFFERENCE, PROBLEM, DISORDER, OR DISABILITY?

Parents of young children become concerned when they see something in their child that looks different. A child may have difficulty listening to a story for more than a few minutes, or struggles when learning the simplest task, or can't recall something said only minutes ago. When they do remember and try to apply what was taught, they may use it inappropriately, making parents wonder if they ever understood it. Are these examples of differences, problems, disorders, or disabilities? You'd think experts would be able to determine which is which, but they don't. When professionals discuss difficulties in learning, all four terms are interchangeably used.[2] Surprising to parents, each label may be used to describe the same behavior in the same child. The term selected often reflects the professional's viewpoint more so than the inherent behavior.

This became apparent to me with my daughter. As a child, she had, and still does have, an uncanny ability to accurately understand what is occurring around her. I remember reading her *Snow White and the Seven Dwarfs*. As I was about to turn the page with a picture of the dwarfs looking at Snow White, she stopped me.

"Daddy, look at him," she said pointing to Grumpy.

"Yes," I replied, not knowing why she singled out Grumpy.

"He's sad Daddy."

"Yes Jessie. He does look sad." I began turning the page again, but she grabbed my hand and stopped me.

Intently looking at me she asked, "Daddy, why did someone do something bad to the nice little man?"

Not a typical response from a child—or even an adult. Although she was able to identify something in the picture deeply human, she couldn't remember the number of dwarfs or, with the exception of Grumpy, their names. She had difficulty with details. I viewed this as a *difference* in the way she perceived her world. Her preschool teacher, however, viewed it as a *problem*, since Jessie required extra attention. A learning specialist using a standard classification system called it a "disorder" or a "disability." Same behavior, same child, but different perspectives. How we label things often has more to do with our own needs than with the thing being labeled. Jessie, at 4 years of age, displayed an ability many adults never develop. But her teacher couldn't get past Jessie not knowing the number of dwarfs in the story. Now, as an adult, she still has to make an extra effort to remember details, but because of her ability to see "the whole picture" she has developed an amazing artistic eye and a broad vision of the world.

Of the four terms, "disorder" and "disability" have the greatest emotional impact. In the Individuals with Disabilities Education Act (IDEA), the federal law uses a precise definition to describe "learning disabilities." The precision and exclusionary nature of this special education category is intimidating to some parents. In a national survey, 48 percent of parents whose children had a learning problem believed labeling them as "learning disabled" would be more harmful than privately struggling with the problem.[3] Because of their fears, these parents waited a year or more before acknowledging the existence of learning difficulties. Some never sought help. Unfortunately, within the public school system, labeling is necessary. If a child isn't labeled, according to state and federal laws, services can't be provided. Don't let a word or label stop you from asking for assistance. If the only way of receiving services is to have your child identified as having a disorder or disability, accept the word—just not the cubicle into which some people would like your child placed. We don't refer to a talented basketball player who can't hit a fastball as having a "baseball disorder." Yet, these are the distinctions routinely made by some educators when it comes to learning differences. However, change is occurring in people's attitudes towards children with learning differences, especially public school educators. Unfortunately, it's not as fast as some of us would like. Hopefully, both of these words will become as unacceptable as the term "cripple" to describe people with orthopedic problems. But until that happens, don't become too upset with the words. Your child's learning style is different, not disordered.

All of our children are different and each has a unique learning style. The style comes from the way a child's brain is wired. Some are strong visual learners, while others are better listeners. Some children, like Jessie, can grasp "the big picture" immediately, but have difficulty with individual facts. Others can retain an enormous number of facts, but can't see how they connect. These are learning *differences*. "Difference" is a neutral term. When someone says, "this is golf and that's soccer," they are identifying two different sports—no judgments are made. The same applies when we say one child is a visual learner and the other is an auditory learner. Throughout this book I'll try to avoid using labels, but sometimes for convenience, or because a term is widely used, I too will use it. Whenever possible, I'll talk about learning problems—behaviors caused by learning differences. Your child is not his or her problem. The problem is only one of many behaviors, values, and emotions that constitute your child's being.

LEARNING DIFFERENCES AND THE BRAIN

In the past, many researchers looked at learning problems in relationship to levels of motivation, personality, teaching ability, and child-rearing practices.[4] They thought parents, society, school culture, and the environment created the problems. If only we could determine why children were *refusing* to learn, everything would be better. We needed to blame someone for our children's failures. For years, fingers were unjustly pointed at parents, children, and educators. Parents weren't raising their children well. Children weren't trying hard enough. And educators just didn't care. However, with new studies, it became apparent that many of the problems are neurological.[5] That is, certain parts of the brains of some children work differently.

The brain, in many ways, is like a computer. Computers have hardware such as motherboards, disk drives, and CD-ROM players. They can't do anything by themselves. Software, such as a Windows operating system or a word processing program, is needed. The structures of the brain are often referred to as its "hard-wiring."[6] The way components are connected is similar to a computer's software. Learning differences may be related to the brain's hardware or software. For example, when you place a disk into a defective CD-ROM player, the reading device may not move consistently, causing data to be missed. This is an example of a hardware problem. A virus that damaged the software program responsible for reading the CD-ROM files may cause a series of other problems, even if the CD-ROM player is functioning perfectly. Our knowledge of how the brain works has been greatly enhanced by the use of imaging equipment. We've been able to see differences in how the brains of individuals who stutter differ from those who don't.[7] Differences have also been found in the brain functioning of individuals who have reading and listening problems.[8, 9]

These findings unequivocally point to a neurological cause of many learning problems. Even more exciting is some preliminary research showing the brain's functioning changes when certain intervention strategies are used. This was found in the area of auditory training for children with attention problems and reading therapy for dyslexia (reading problems).[10, 11] Following the use of specific intervention strategies, the brain activities of children with attention problems and with dyslexia looked like those of children who had neither problem. This is a truly exciting development. It means intervention can change how the brain functions. There is reason to hope similar results will be found for other types of learning problems. Most neuropsychologists believe the changes occurring in the brain because of intervention involve the development of new connections, not necessarily corrections of the hard-wiring.[12] Regardless of what is being repaired, we've seen neurological changes not only in young people, but also in adults with reading problems, individuals who had strokes, and even geriatric patients.[13, 14, 15] It appears that change occurs as a result of specific learning activities.[16]

Just like a computer, your child's brain has many centers. In order to do one thing well, some of the centers need to function together as if they were on a team. For example, if you ask your child to clean her room, she can only do it if she remembers what each of the words in your sentence mean, the model you showed her of what a clean room looks like, and the explicit instructions you gave her for cleaning. Each of these remembered components may be located in various parts of the brain. In order for your daughter to clean her room, the parts have to communicate and work together. If they don't because of either a hardware or software problem, she may forget parts of the instructions or her memory of what a "clean room" looks like may be distorted. The strategies you will learn to help your child are ones that are effective for dealing with either hardware or software problems. As we move through various activities to help your children accommodate, remediate, or detour around problems, you may think your child's brain is changing and what once was a problem is no longer. However, other than in selected areas, such as reading and certain attention problems, there are not yet findings to support changes in the brain. There may be in the future. A child's brain is a marvelous devise. Its plasticity results in the ability to shift job assignments from a damaged area to one that isn't impaired. As we use various strategies to teach children how to learn, our hope is to create new brain pathways. The strategies, at the very least, will develop detours. If in the process, new circuitry is developed—terrific!

HOW CHILDREN PROCESS INFORMATION

Children are bombarded with information every second of their waking lives. For different learners, some of it may become distorted. Other bits may be prevented from being processed and a few pass through the brain without ever finding a home. It's as if a barrier is erected with an inscription painted in large letters saying, "Trespassers Beware!" You wonder what's going on as you watch your child processing information. Is he deliberately not paying attention? Is he just not interested? Or worse, does he have an intellectual problem? The information was directed at your child in a very simple form. And your other children never seemed to have any problems understanding things like this, so why does he?

In order to understand your child's problem, it's necessary to understand the path information takes. From the time it's generated to the time it's used, it travels through five steps: attention, understanding, storage, retrieval, and usage. Any difficulty along the journey can result in learning problems. Mistakenly educators and parents often don't locate the break in the path—an important first step in fostering your child's learning.

The Steps

Every journey begins with a single step. In learning, that step is attention. To learn, children need to first *attend* to the information presented to them.[17] Attention is related to all the senses: hearing, seeing, smelling, tasting, and touching. Once your child is aware of the information, it can be *understood*. Next, the information needs to find a home in their brains and be *stored* for current and later use. Finally, when they need to use it, the information must be *retrieved* and *used appropriately*. These five steps are important in learning.[18] A hiccup in any one can result in the creation of a "learning problem." If you have observed something in your child's learning that's causing you concern, it will be located in one of these five areas: attention, understanding, storage, retrieval, or appropriate usage. Within each information-processing area there can be many types of problems. In Part II, each group of problems will be examined in separate chapters. For now, we'll do an overview of how each processing area should work, and what happens when it doesn't.

Attention

Imagine going into a noisy restaurant where you have to scream to be heard by the person next to you. The waiter comes to your table and in a soft voice explains the specials of the day. But what you hear is just a jumble of sounds, with a barely audible *lightly sautéed* and *mesquite grilled*. Not wanting to embarrass yourself by asking him to repeat the entire list of specials, you choose one of the regular items from an uninteresting menu. The meal comes and as you're looking at your liver and onions, a waiter delivers one of the specials to the table next to you. It's a perfect rack-of-lamb—which happens to be your favorite food. You realize your wish not to be embarrassed resulted in a meal of liver instead of lamb, and there's nothing you can do now other than watch a stranger savor each delicious morsel of what could have been your meal. You wanted to "learn" what the restaurant was serving as specials, but were unable to because you couldn't hear what the waiter was saying. You weren't able to listen to the message. Listening is the auditory form of attention. Things were preventing you from being aware of what he was saying. Without listening, learning becomes distorted or is stopped dead in its tracks.

Now change the scene. I'm in my kitchen preparing a special dinner for guests. Pots are clanging, my favorite music is blaring on the radio, and my daughter enters.

"Jessie, please go back into the living room and put away your toys, we have company coming in 20 minutes."

"Okay Daddy," she says, smiling and returning to the living room.

I finish preparing the dinner just as guests ring the doorbell. Glancing into the living room, I see my daughter surrounded by every one of her 200 little plastic animals. They're everywhere—peeking from under cushions, hiding in the plate of cheese, and swimming in the guacamole. She looks happy to see me and smiles.

"Okay Daddy," she yells excitedly, "Now are you ready to play?"

The only things she heard were "living room," "play," and "20 minutes." And just as I did with my son, I don't understand why she didn't listen to me. It wasn't that she deliberately ignored my request. I created obstacles preventing her from listening, which was something she wanted to do. It would have been easy to prevent the problem. All I had to do was turn off the radio and stop fussing with the pots. If I did that, she would have heard me, and my guests wouldn't have had to pick dinosaurs out of their appetizers. Sometimes parents don't generate the interfering noise. It can come from the environment. Noise can take on many forms, ranging from the clatter of a jackhammer working on the street to a soft conversation between two people. Even minimal amounts of noise can tax a child's attention system if it's impaired.

If children are to learn, they must be able to attend. Although information can be received from all the senses, the two areas most important in learning are hearing and vision.[19] If there's too much auditory noise, children have trouble attending. What you may view as nothing special, may be just the amount of stimuli that breaks down a different learner's ability to attend. The intended message may be hidden by the noise just as secret pictures are in the *Where's Waldo* books. Or, even though a child can detect the presence of a message, it may appear as a disorganized form, similar to what people unfamiliar with abstract art see when they try to find the theme in a painting. Sometimes, the noise is internal. Things may be going on in your child's brain making it difficult to concentrate. While some children on their own develop wonderful helping strategies to handle challenging situations, others are less fortunate. Just as you did in the restaurant, children may make choices they later regret. But unlike you, they may not know why the choice was made. And just as my daughter couldn't understand why I was annoyed at her, your child may not understand your annoyance at something he or she never heard you say. They were *hearing*, but they couldn't *listen*. Children who have problems listening don't purposely tune out; their brains just can't separate the clang of pots and pans from the intended information.

Just as there are problems in hearing, there are also problems in vision. Children may also be *looking*, but not *seeing*. Children may have perfect eyesight, but the way in which their brain organizes images may be different. There may be too many visual stimuli present, such as when a child is asked to do an activity on a table that's covered with superfluous toys and objects.[20]

Or, when asked to look at something having many visual parts, the brain has difficulty differentiating a part from the whole.[21] In some cases, parts of the visual field are even neglected, as if they weren't there.[22] What may appear as defined units to you might be an unorganized collection of visual "stuff" to your child.

Understanding

The way information is presented may prevent understanding, even when children are paying attention. I chose to learn German in high school. On the first day of class, I sat attentively and waited for the teaching to begin. Frau Miller entered the room and intently stared at each of the 25 faces. After five minutes of excruciating silence she spoke.

"Boys and girls," she slowly said in English with a thick accent. "I know some people in this high school think German should be learned by teaching it in English—I am not one of those foolish people. Today is the only day you will hear me speak English. Tomorrow and forever, only German!"

It was not only the worst class I ever had, but it also was the most frustrating learning experience I can remember. My attention was fine. I listened to what she said, and watched what was written on the blackboard—no one dared create noise in Frau Miller's class. But I still wasn't able to understand German because of the way Frau Miller taught. How to speak German was explained in German—but I only understood English. I felt dumb in class every day for an entire year. Fortunately, Frau Miller retired at the end of the second semester. The following year, German II was taught by one of the "foolish people" who spoke English, and that year we all learned.

Young children face problems similar to the high school students in Frau Miller's class. Although they may be listening or watching, the *form* in which the information is presented may make it incomprehensible.[23] There are many things that can confuse children in ways similar to someone speaking words in a language they don't understand. Two occur significantly more often than others do: information that's beyond a child's ability to understand and the presence of too much information. Both can occur in auditory and visual channels. An example of the information beyond a child's ability to understand would be the response a father gives to the question asked by his three-year-old.

"Daddy, how does the TV work?"

"Well son," the father says, pleased with his son's early interest in electronics. "The camera captures the images digitally, and then amplifies the signal, sending it through lines to an antenna on a high tower, then it travels through the air, it's transformed into electrons, then it activates the phosphorescent elements on the screen."

Looking confused, the son says, "No, Daddy, I want to know how the TV *works*. You know, to make the picture come on."

It's as if the father is speaking German to a child who only understands English. The appropriate answer, and the one the child was looking for, is "We press the *on* button."

The second common way a child misses information is when there's more of it than his or her brain is capable of accepting. It's as if 20 people are trying to get through a narrow door at the same time. Single file works, four abreast doesn't. An example of "four abreast" would be a child trying to do a puzzle, while watching television, picking unwanted vegetables out of her pasta dish, and making sure her little brother isn't pulling the head off her favorite doll. She'll never be able to complete the puzzle; too many other activities are elbowing each other at her brain's entrance. Young minds have limits to the amount of information they can process.[24] And minds that learn differently may have an even smaller capacity, or require that the information be very structured.[25] While she wouldn't have had any problems completing the puzzle after dinner with the TV turned off and her brother safely in his bedroom, too much auditory and visual information crowding her brain's little opening prohibited her from doing so before. Although there are other ways in which information becomes jumbled, these are the two greatest culprits—complicated information and the presence of too much of it.

Storing Information

After attending to and acquiring information, the brain places it in storage. It is either held for immediate, or almost immediate use, or placed somewhere else for later retrieval. In the restaurant, you opened the menu, decided on liver and onions, closed it, and waited for the waiter. When he arrived ten minutes later, without any hesitation you said, "Liver and onions." How did you do that? What occurred between the time you looked at the menu and ordered your entrée that enabled you to remember liver and onions? Although nobody really knows how we retain information, there are many theories. A widely accepted one would explain it as follows: As you read the menu, you understood what the words meant and made decisions about what you wanted. You then took the information and placed it in an area where it could be quickly accessed. While there, three different things could have happened to it. The first, it could have been used when you placed your order, and then disappeared. The second possibility is the information could have vanished without ever being used. When the waiter came for your order, you don't remember what you chose from the menu. The third scenario is you not only remembered your order, but also moved the whole episode from the area of

the brain responsible for short-term memory, to the one responsible for long-term memory. Some researchers believe the placement of these memories can be quite complicated, with bits of them chunked together chemically in various parts of the brain.[26] If you stored your restaurant experience in "long-term" memory, you'll be able to recall this embarrassing incident next week.

In the above example, three types of memory were used: working, short-term, and long-term. Working memory is what you use during an activity.[27] Sometimes it's referred to as the "executive functioning" of the brain. It coordinates, manipulates, and rearranges things as you are doing them. For example, you look at a recipe and using your working memory, decide what you will need. Since you just finished reading the recipe, you can immediately start cooking without looking back at it. This is an example of short-term memory.[28] You now begin combining ingredients for the main course, again using working memory. Ten minutes ago, you read how to mix and combine them. Without looking back at the recipe, you assemble them successfully. You made this same dish last month, and remember to set the oven at 450 degrees and cook the dish for 30 minutes. You retrieved this information from long-term memory.[29]

It may be helpful to think about your working memory as an executive who constantly must make decisions regarding his business. People come into your office and provide information. Some of it is very new, other historic. You take all of the information you've received and use it to make decisions. You are constantly using both new and old information to function. A similar process occurs continually in our brains. We are constantly using our working memory to make sense of incoming information and coordinate it with elements stored in short- and long-term memory.[30] Some neuropsychologists believe instead of dividing memory into working, short-term, and long-term, a better way of understanding how the brain works is to think about the types of things remembered: those that are descriptive (e.g., mozzarella cheese) and things that involve procedures (e.g., turn on the oven to 400 degrees).[31] Still other researchers believe that a combination of the two approaches is more comprehensive.[32]

As interesting as the arguments may be, I believe they're more important to researchers than parents. You're concerned with the problems that occur in working, short-term, or long-term memory. Let's again use the cooking analogy, but this time with two new variables: limited workspace and numerous storage closets. The limited space is analogous to working and short-term memory. The numerous storage closets can be likened to long-term memory. You decided to make a complicated dinner requiring many ingredients. To assure everything is fresh, you purchase all new items. You lay them out on the table, moving the items you'll need for the first dish on to the small counter.

When the first dish is completed, you put the ingredients away, making room on the counter to prepare the second dish. When the counter is too cluttered, you have trouble finding specific items and loose some in the mess. Similarly, when there are too many things cluttering up your child's short-term or working memory, information may get lost, be processed incorrectly, or become distorted. If the amount of information can be kept to a minimum, it's less likely your child will have problems with his working memory or lose information before it goes into short- or long-term storage.

For example, a mother says to her five-year-old daughter: "I would like you to go clean your room, be sure to put your books back on the shelf, make your bed, and before you go outside, put your dishes in the sink." By the time the little girl hears "dishes in the sink," everything preceding it had turned into a stew, books and dishes merging into confusing instructions. The problem could have been avoided if the mother said: "Please go up to your room and put all of your books back on the shelf. When you're done, come back down and I'll tell you what to do next." When instructions are minimized, nothing gets lost behind the blender. But working and short-term memory are not enough for learning. We also need long-term memory.

We are unsure how the brain transfers information from short-term to long-term memory.[33] But despite our lack of knowledge, it's quite marvelous to behold. For most people, the information does appear to be stored in some sort of logical manner. Open your cabinets and inspect how you organize your food. If you don't have a system, you might find three bottles of vanilla extract scattered throughout the cabinets. Each time you needed vanilla and couldn't find it, you purchased a new bottle. It was always there; you just couldn't see it. However, if your cabinets were minimally organized, you probably would have found your original bottle, even if it took a while to retrieve it. You would have known it was on the shelf somewhere with all the baking goods. Some people are so well organized, not only are similar types of ingredients stored together, but each category is in alphabetical order. Vanilla is right behind turmeric and in front of wasabi. Your child's brain can operate like any one of these modes, or variations of them. Obviously, the more organized the storage, the easier it is to retrieve information.[34]

Most neuroscientists believe material destined for storage is first broken down into component parts.[35] For example, the memory of a black car is not stored as a simple picture. Rather, it's divided into name, color, size, shape, et cetera, and then each part is stored in different areas of the brain. On recall, the brain recombines them and produces the memory of a small, black Camry convertible. Some children's memory problems involve an incomplete or incorrect storage. For example, only the name of the car may have been correctly stored, with the

Figure 1.1
Teaching Organization—Toy Boxes

color remembered as red and the model remembered as a hatchback rather than a convertible. Other children may have problems storing information in an organized manner. They often have trouble grouping common elements together into categories such as "vegetables" and "things that move." Intervention can be as simple as providing a visual organization model. One example shown in Figure 1.1 involves placing boxes in a child's room, each with a picture of the type of toys that goes into them. Some children with learning differences may never line up the vanilla, turmeric, and wasabi in perfect alphabetical order, but they can learn how to separate cooking ingredients from vegetables.

Retrieving Information

Although there are many theories on how the brain retrieves information, it appears the way it comes out is related to the way it goes in.[36] In recalling your terrible restaurant experience, you probably retrieved more than just the words necessary for describing the event. You most likely were able to see partial or complete images of the whole embarrassing scene, along with the emotions you had, and maybe even the smell of the liver and onions. What went in came out, not exactly, but in a modified and abbreviated form. The process is the same for most children. They don't learn within a sterile capsule. When something is learned, many of the things occurring during the event are also stored with it. Whatever they are aware of during the learning process may become part of the storage and retrieval process. For example, a child sees a red car race down a street.

"What's that?" she asks her father.

"A Ferrari," he responds with longing in his voice.

The word Ferrari is not just stored as a word used to identify a car. Rather, the entire image of a fast moving red car and the longing voice of her father are stored as a complex picture (Figure 1.2). When she again hears the word, the whole scene or parts of it are retrieved.

Figure 1.2
A Child's Definition of a Ferrari

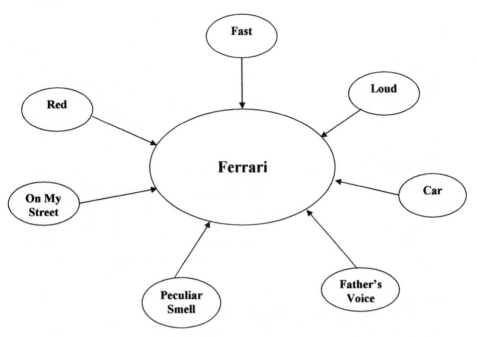

Although we aren't sure how things are stored, we believe visual, auditory, touch, and smell images are involved.[37] In the Ferrari example, the way the child's father said "Ferrari," added something to the word. It could have been the way he elongated the sounds of the word, or the wishful lilt of his voice. In either case, when the child attempts to recall the name of the car, she can hook on to any one element that is now associated with the word "Ferrari"—the sounds her father made as he said it, the image of this thing racing down her street, or even the smell of its exhaust. All were stored along with the name "Ferrari." If the child can grab hold of even one, she probably will be able to recall this unfamiliar and difficult-to-pronounce foreign word. Some sort of memory web, analogous to a spider's, was created. The spider can feel the insect regardless of where it lands on the web. The same seems to be true in the recall of information: Retrieve one part of the scene and all of it may reappear.[38]

However, not all webs are beneficial. In the above example, the child may have incorrectly thought "Ferrari" referred to anything moving fast on wheels. If so, the web will continue triggering incorrect identifications whenever the child sees something on wheels moving fast down the street. Her father probably wouldn't understand why, when she sees an Oldsmobile or an out-of-

control skateboard, she says, "Look Daddy, Ferrari." With some types of learning differences, these inappropriate connections are made. With other children, a more severe problem occurs: Impoverished webs are created forcing the child to use only a few hooks to retrieve learned information.[39] If the child who watched her father say Ferrari was not aware of the richness of things occurring around her when her father said the word, she may have stored the information as a simple graphic image of the car along with its name—nothing else. Children who can't construct webs need to be taught how to do so. The solution is for parents to teach concepts with a variety of things occurring simultaneously, each adding a hook. For example, a mother wants to teach her son how to get ready for preschool by himself. In order for him to be successful, there are three things she would like him to do after he wakes up and before he comes downstairs for breakfast: use the toilet, brush his teeth, and dress. In his room is a colorful card divided into three sections (Figure 1.3). At the top of each section is a number. By looking at the card, the child understands not only that he should do three things, but also what they are, and the order in which they should be done. A card for each morning task appears on location: over the toilet, over the sink, and on top of his dresser. When his mother taught him to do each of these things, she showed him the pictures, had him describe what he saw, and then asked him to do just what was on the picture. Three hooks were created for each activity: sequence, visual image, and auditory description. At the end of the first week, this child, who had both sequencing and memory problems, was able to proudly come to breakfast with everything completed. During the second week, cards with just a circled number (Figure 1.4) replaced the pictures. In the third week, all cards were

Figure 1.3
Early Morning Tasks—First Week

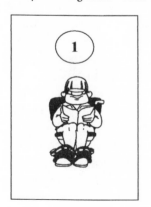
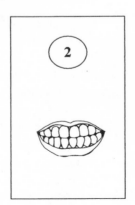

Figure 1.4
Early Morning Tasks—Second Week

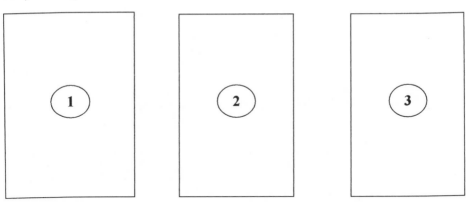

removed, and he remained successful. A simple strategy strengthened both memory and sequencing. This strategy, which will be fully described in Chapter 5, can be applied to many other problems.

Usage

Retrieved information needs to be used at the right *time, place,* and *situation.* When I was first learning to play the guitar, I practiced what are known as "licks"—a series of notes that sound good when played together. They are inserted throughout songs and provide embellishments to basic melodies. Accomplished guitar players know hundreds of them. One of the many differences setting me apart from accomplished guitarists is knowing when to use them. I memorized 15 and could play them fairly well. However, it was a disaster the first time I tried using them in a pickup band at a music festival where nobody had ever played together. Although I was able to retrieve each lick perfectly, I rarely played them at appropriate times. I never learned their rules of usage. Everyone listening still heard the melody, but knew something was wrong—and whatever it was, it was coming from where I stood. It took many months to learn which licks went with each cord, and which licks could be used when cords changed. Children face the same situation when they retrieve information. They not only have to retrieve something they learned, but also use it at the right time, place, and situation.

How often have your children done something *exactly* as you taught them—but used it in the most inappropriate setting you could have imagined? When I was teaching my son to use the toilet, we would go into the bathroom and I would give him as much juice as he wanted. As his little bladder began to fill,

we would talk about the physical pressure he was feeling and I'd asked him to sit on his duck potty.

"No," he said defiantly. "I want to stand up, just like you."

He pulled down his training pants, took aim, and patiently waited to urinate. One day I was talking with a friend on a busy street. My son was standing next to me, and in the middle of our conversation my friend's head turned in the direction of my son. As he laughed hysterically, Justin, with his training pants pulled down around his ankles, was urinating on the sidewalk.

"See Daddy, just like you showed me!" he proudly exclaimed.

The appropriate use of retrieved information is called *pragmatics*. It involves knowing application rules: when to do something and when not to. Most of the time, children can identify what the rules are without being told. They observe how the information is used and then extrapolate on it. However, with some children, the rules need to be explained. For my son, an important new rule I taught him was, "we only pull down our underwear and pee *into the potty*."

Not knowing application rules can have tremendous social implications for children, ranging from negative adult reactions to avoidance by other children.[40] I worked with a five-year-old child who had a wonderful mastery of numbers and letters. He could tell you the number of marbles in his box by just glancing at them. Retrieving his house address, telephone number, and zip code were effortless. He could also read books at a seven-year-old level. In spite of doing all of these things, he didn't know how to play with other children. The rules of play most children use allow them to become good friends in a few minutes.[41] They involve things such as:

- How to start a conversation.
- How to maintain a conversation.
- What to say when someone asks you a question.
- How to ask for something.
- How to share.

This child didn't use any of them. As a result, going to a playground or having children come to his home was a painful experience. Children would quickly abandon him after trying to play for a few minutes. Although he could retrieve vast amounts of information, he didn't know when to apply them. When a child asked him what he would like to do, he responded, "My address is 1426 Myrtle Avenue." When another child began telling him something of importance, he ignored him and kept playing with a toy car. Intervention involved teaching him the rules of play. His parents and I did it through a series of vignettes, just as if he was learning lines in a school show. We would practice

greetings with different simulated children (boys, girls, aggressive children, friendly children, et cetera) and settings (on the street, in parks, classrooms, playgrounds, et cetera). Within a short period of time, his ability to interact with other children improved. Two years after we intervened, his play activity was thought to be appropriate, not only by other adults, but, more importantly, by his newly acquired friends. There were still problems, but all became manageable.

How Learning Differences Cause Learning Problems

The best way to prevent learning problems in school is to deny them the food needed to grow, especially during preschool years. Although some problems, in areas like spelling and reading, may not become evident until a child enters school, they don't materialize out of thin air. There are early warnings—red flags that say "help me." The problems may be subtle in very young children and seem like the types of things all children have trouble with—until they repeatedly occur, or occur in situations in which they shouldn't. I was asked to treat a four-year-old child whose ability to understand far exceeded her ability to use words. She had difficulties retrieving the names of common objects she could easily identify.

"Where's the green pepper?" I asked when we were playing store.

Without any hesitation, she quickly grabbed the plastic green pepper and offered it to me. Each time I requested the pepper, she responded correctly.

"What's this?" I asked holding up the pepper.

"I don't know," she said.

Although it appeared to her pre-school teacher there was just a slight delay between her ability to understand and her ability to express, it was a warning signal—a processing problem was present, probably one involving storing words or their retrieval. There were too many incidences where the names of known objects couldn't be retrieved. Her mother and I began developing strategies for expanding her memory webs to improve both storage and retrieval.

Subtle difficulties like this can indicate children are processing some types of information differently. These differences may lead to problems when certain demands are placed on them. Demands may involve a new task, or one that must be performed under time restraints or performance expectations. It's as if you're driving a car with a tire that has a weakened sidewall. If you're driving at 20 miles per hour, the problem may go unnoticed. However, at 70 miles per hour on a scorching highway, a blowout can occur. That's similar to what happens with some young children. For example, a classification of "hyperactive" may initially have been identified when a six-year-old child is in first

grade, and the teacher noticed she couldn't focus on any activity for longer than a few minutes. Instead of reading from her book, she constantly fidgeted with her dress, moved her legs rhythmically, and looked out the window. Her difficulty in focusing on the lesson arose from a general information-processing (attention) problem she had within the classroom environment. Her mother, however, saw the problem at three years of age. She noticed her daughter became easily distracted when she read a story to her in the living room of her home. Yet, when stories were read in the bedroom, her attention span doubled. The major difference between the two rooms was the amount of noise. The living room faced a busy street. The bedroom, located in the rear of the house, was quiet. By the time the general problem of inattention was identified in school, the child had been experiencing difficulties for three years—half of her life. If the mother had understood how to address her child's focusing difficulties at three, strategies for minimizing the effects of a noisy classroom could have been taught prior to kindergarten.

DIFFERENT LEARNERS AND PARENTAL ANXIETY

Having a young child who learns differently can cause parents a great deal of anxiety. They may stay awake worrying how their children's differences will affect them when they enter school. Will they become a "label" and be treated as having a disorder by teachers and classmates? Will the teacher understand their special needs? I've found parents who understand the potential problems their child's difference can cause deal with their apprehension in one of five ways.

1. Worry about it, but don't know what to do.
2. Ignore it and hope the difference won't cause a problem.
3. Assume the school is prepared to accommodate the difference.
4. Seek professional help.
5. Try to do things now so differences won't become problems.

Worry About It, But Don't Know What to Do

To be a parent means to worry, whether or not there is good cause. We compare how our children learn with others and become concerned when we see differences. Unfortunately, we may not know where to begin helping. I spoke with a woman whose daughter attended kindergarten with my son. Her daughter was perpetually lost in the classroom where the well-meaning teacher didn't know how to help different learners. The teacher's university training emphasized methods of instructing a class of "normal children." Children who showed severe learning or behavior problems were placed in special classes in which "specialists" could be more adequately address their needs. Mary's problems weren't considered to be even close to those of the children in the special education classroom. Yet, some of her behaviors were very different from the children in the regular kindergarten. While other children could attend to the teacher for up to 15 minutes, Mary would last for 5 before she would get up from her seat and wander around the room. When her mother and I spoke, she confided in me that family members were consulted when she started noticing differences in Mary's ability to attend.

"Don't worry about it," Mary's grandmother said. "She's just a little slow developing. You didn't start speaking until you were three."

"You worry too much," her sister said. "Remember when John was two and I had all of those problems with potty training? I just relaxed and everything got better."

"She's a good kid," her husband said. "I'm not worried about it, why should you?"

The advice given by family is almost always well meaning. Unfortunately, it's usually based on experience with only one or two children. And often the person giving advice is too close to the problem to be objective. This mother decided the experience of her family and the rationality of her husband were more important than her intuitive feeling that something was wrong. She worried about her daughter, but following their advice, did nothing. After receiving daily calls from the kindergarten teacher about her child's problems, guilt pervaded her every thought. Together, we devised numerous strategies and convinced the teacher to modify activities, making it easier for Mary to learn and function within a social group. Love your family members and respect their opinions—they're only trying to help. But understand their experience is limited, and so is the time they spend with your child. Trust yourself. If you suspect a problem, don't spend time worrying, act!

Ignore It and Hope the
Difference Won't Cause a Problem

Hoping the difference won't cause a problem is like pretending an elephant in your living room isn't there when you close your eyes. Children who learn differently are at risk for developing problems when they enter school. I saw a mother in the clinic whose 5-year-old was having difficulties adjusting to kindergarten. Although a very bright child, noisy environments made it impossible for Rob to learn. His mother noticed this as early as three. When the TV was on and she asked him to do something, often what was done didn't even vaguely resemble what was asked. Rob rarely misunderstood the request when the noise level was reduced. She believed with maturity, the problem would vanish. After all, this was a very bright child. He knew most of his colors by two, was able to use over a hundred individual words by three and combine them into four-word sentences. His language, according to a speech-language pathologist, was at least two years ahead of his age. How could her child have problems in kindergarten? Impossible! Yet he did. Rob had trouble storing certain types of information and retrieving it. He couldn't remember simple instructions accurately, even for a short amount of time. Tasks, such as putting things away in a specific order, were rarely done correctly. Based on some of Rob's pre-kindergarten behaviors, well-meaning people predicted that he *shouldn't* have any problems in school. His mother, who had the most contact with him, saw the potential for problems.

Most public schools, including the one Rob went to, use a "one-size-fits-all" approach.[42] It's difficult for teachers to individualize instruction for classes of 20 plus children. Kids with learning differences like Rob don't fit the mold. Hoping a regular classroom can accommodate their differences is delusional. It's similar to people who perpetually bet on the 30-1 horse at the races and come home with empty pockets. They never lost hope their horse would win, even when it was 20 lengths behind other horses nearing the finish line. "Hope" is an interesting emotion. While it temporarily soothes, in the long run, it's responsible for many of the problems we face. Rob's mother's hoped he wouldn't have any problems in school and did nothing. Yet, acting when she first noticed the problem could have reduced Rob's troubles when he entered kindergarten. When discussing the negative aspects of hope, the Buddhist nun, Pema Chodron suggested instead of having something like "have a nice day" magnet on your refrigerator, substitute one that says, "Abandon hope."[43] Abandoning hope means you are prepared to do something now that will make your vision materialize. I completely agree with her. Forget hope, substitute action.

Assume the School is Prepared to Accommodate the Difference

I've had the opportunity as a university professor and field supervisor to visit over 100 schools in the past 25 years. During this time I've watched classroom sizes creep upwards, often slowly enough that parents aren't aware what's happening. Nobody notices one or two more children added to the kindergarten roster every year or two. State maximum regulations tend to be bent when "special" circumstances arise. For example, California's 20:1 ratio can be modified to mean 20:1 average *across all kindergarten classes in a district*, or can go beyond 20:1 if there is only one kindergarten in the district.[44] Similar modifications appear in the regulations of many states. Classroom sizes continue to increase in spite of research done over 10 years ago that showed smaller kindergarten classes (13-17) are more effective for learning than large classes (22-25).[45] As important as small classes are for children with a mainstream learning style, they are even more crucial for different learners. During the mid to late nineties, when federal and state funds were more abundant. There was a push to reduce kindergarten class sizes. However, with recent cuts in state and federal budgets, class size reductions have been moved quietly onto the back burner. As class sizes increased and funding decreased, concerned administrators sought ways of alleviating the stress on teachers. As a solution, aides, also known as teaching assistants, were introduced.

The educational requirements for aides vary among states. According to the U.S. Department of Statistics, requirements range from a high school equivalency degree (G.E.D.) to some college courses.[46] As of 2003, only one third of all states had established guidelines or minimum educational standards for the hiring and training of teacher assistants. Where states have not established guidelines, some individual school districts have developed their own. The number of aides will increase as the supply of teachers continues to fall behind demand. In 2003, teaching assistants held over one million jobs in the public school system, mostly in the elementary grades. It's expected the number of teacher aides will grow faster than the average for all occupations across the board through 2010.[47] With lower salaries, part-time work, and limited or no health coverage and other benefits, job commitment becomes questionable for teacher's aides. Often, the aide is a mother of a child in the class. Rarely is there any training, even when minimal hiring standards are used. And when training is required, it doesn't include how to accommodate the needs of children who learn differently.[48] The likelihood your child will receive the individualized attention *you believe* he or she needs is remote.

Seek Professional Help

When things become too painful for either children or parents, professionals are contacted. They can be specialists in speech and language, reading, learning, psychology, child development, or pediatric medicine. When seeking the advice of professionals, care needs to be taken in matching a professional's expertise with the problem. The first person usually consulted is the child's pediatrician. While their training has been extensive in the diagnosis and treatment of physical problems, their understanding of speech, language, emotional, and cognitive problems may be limited. Most may have had only one course in medical school covering non-medical aspects of a pediatric practice. Some rely primarily on their experience with children, which for older physicians may be extensive. There are, however, some exceptional pediatricians whose training and expertise come from other areas. They are usually identified as "developmental pediatricians." Unfortunately, they constitute a very small percentage of pediatricians. Rarely can you find them just by looking through the business section of your phone book. For example, in San Francisco, although there are close to 100 physicians listed under "pediatrician," there are no headings for "developmental pediatricians," yet I know of four. There are three ways of finding them in your area. The first is to do an Internet search for "developmental + pediatrician + (your city)." The second is to start calling pediatricians and asking for referrals. The third is to contact the American Academy of Pediatrics and ask for a member who specializes in developmental pediatrics in your area.

Although many of the nonmedical problems that parents ask pediatricians to examine disappear with age, others don't. Some pediatricians rely on statistics when they recommend to parents whether or not they should be concerned with a problem. Fifty percent of the children I see who have chronic stuttering problems had pediatricians who told their parents, "don't worry; most children grow out of their disfluencies." Yes, the advice is correct, but misleading. Statistically, less than 2 percent of all children who are disfluent at three will become a stutterer.[49] But you can't rely on statistics to make a diagnosis. By differentiating between those children who will grow out of it and those who won't, a problem that becomes resistant at six years of age can be easily corrected at three. The same rule applies to many problems associated with different learners. Once you suspect a problem, seek out the *appropriate* professional. In classified telephone books you'll find various headings related to specific problems, such as "speech therapists," "reading specialists," and "learning specialists." There are also national organizations that may have a list of recommended specialists in your area. Their Websites are provided in Appendix 1 along with parent support sites. Although these sites provide a wealth of information and referrals, you need to take an active role in the selection of professionals who will be helping your child.

When I'm contacted, I always ask parents why they chose me. Although some selected me because of my reputation or a referral from another professional or parent, 80 percent of the answers include ones such as "your Website looked interesting" and "your office is the closest one to where I live." I'm rarely asked questions addressing my competency as a professional. Yet, those are the most important questions for a parent to ask. Many parents feel grateful that someone, anyone is willing to work with their child. Unfortunately, along with gratitude may come compliance. I think that's a mistake. When I work with a child, I feel honored a parent has entrusted me to do things that may have a life-long impact. It's an awesome responsibility for anyone to have and one that shouldn't be given cavalierly. You may get a sense of the professionals' attitudes and level of competency by asking the following 14 questions. If the individual is reluctant to answer, I'd look for someone else.

1. What is your area of specialty?
2. How many children with a problem similar to my child's have you treated?
3. How long have you practiced?
4. What is your highest educational degree? In what area and where did you receive it?
5. Have you done any research in this area?
6. How do you keep up with the latest research?
7. What do you think causes problems like my child's?
8. What is your goal in therapy for my child?
9. How do you determine if therapy is successful?
10. What is the average number of sessions required?
11. How much will each session cost? Will my insurance cover it?
12. How will I be involved in the therapy process?
13. What credentials and licenses do you hold? What do they mean?
14. How will your therapy help my child in kindergarten?

Even if you find a professional with whom you feel comfortable and whose answers are acceptable, the advice given often to parents of preschoolers may be disheartening: "She's too young to diagnose for specific learning problems. Children develop at different rates. Her development is a little slow, but it might be normal. I think we should wait until she is about five and starts kindergarten."

These professionals aren't deliberately disregarding parents' legitimate concerns. They're just reluctant to assess certain types of learning problems in preschool children. Many believe it's too difficult to make an accurate diagnosis until a child's development is more stable.[50] While intellectual and language development progresses through predicable stages in a child, the amount of time it takes to move through each varies, especially before the age of five.[51] Sometimes children move as if on an empty road, while at other times, they appear stuck in rush-hour traffic. Professionals may be right when they suggest waiting until children are older before an accurate diagnosis of specific learning problems is made—but what if a problem is clearly noticeable, whether or not it can be diagnosed or has a name?

"I knew he was different by the age of three," one parent said to me. "Why couldn't other people see it? I didn't need an unpronounceable label to tell me something was wrong. I just wanted someone to tell me *what I could do to help.*"

It's a universal feeling—parents want to alleviate their child's suffering, regardless of how great or small it is, and whether or not it has a name. You don't need a label to help your child. By the time one can be matched to the behavior, often years have gone by—years of lost opportunities to correct the problem. Professionals are important for the accurate diagnosis and treatment of many learning problems. However, the use of a professional should never place you in a passive role. The decision of a professional to wait until a child is older to make a diagnosis does not mean you too should wait to become involved.

Try to Do Things Now So Differences Won't Become Problems

Many parents underestimate the difference they can make with their children. I've found with proper instruction and knowledge, no one is in a better position to positively affect their children than parents.[52] Parents see the problems before anyone else does. Parents are with their children for more hours than any professional can be. Parents understand their child's emotional states better than anyone. And no adult has a higher stake in a successful outcome than a parent. Parents of elementary school children often ask me if it's too late to make a difference with their child. The answer is *It's never too late.* Although there is ample evidence that early treatment results in quicker and more positive outcomes with fewer emotional problems, treatment in elementary school can still be effective.[53, 54] It is just harder and may take longer.

Mary's mother started early. She learned how to combine something visual with her auditory messages. Together, we explained and then demonstrated to the kindergarten teacher how she could use these simple techniques to help Mary. Mary's mother assured the teacher she would work closely with her daughter. By the end of kindergarten, Mary performed as well as the other children.

Jerome's mother didn't contact me until he received a report card of "Cs" and "Ds" in first grade. In a conference with his teacher, we devised organization strategies to use both at home and in school. It took Jerome longer to learn the strategies and use them effectively than it would have if he were three years old.

The outcome for another child I worked with was less favorable. I came in contact with Bruce and his mother when he was a junior in high school. His mother had been an advocate throughout his school experience, always trying to get better services for her son. However, she never received the support needed for challenging the public school system. The administration, continually faced with budgetary concerns, focused on the needs of the majority. The difficulties of kids like Bruce were ignored. Bruce eventually dropped out of high school, and I lost contact with him and his family.

What has become clear to me through my research and experience working with children with all types of learning differences is that the sooner help is sought, the better.. You can do three things very early to help your child: *use learning strategies, develop detours,* and *find new holes.*

Learning Strategies

A learning strategy is simply a plan to correct or minimize learning problems. For example, when I realized my son had difficulty remembering things, whenever I asked him to do something, I made sure noises and visual distractions didn't interfere with his listening abilities. Regardless of what I asked him to do—be it putting away his toys, getting ready for preschool, or any number of other things—I tried to use the same learning strategy. I knew I had to reduce visual and auditory distractions when I gave him instructions.

Similarly, as in the example of the parent who tries to read stories to her daughter, there are a number of simple strategies that can be used. For example, noise can be gradually introduced, enabling the child to develop a greater tolerance for it. The amount of uninterrupted time spent reading can be gradually increased in noisy settings. Visual strategies for focusing on the content of the story can be introduced, minimizing the effect of noise. By using rewards, the child's focus on the activity will increase. Methods for monitoring how well the child is attending can be taught. And finally, the parent can use feedback, giving the child an immediate understanding of how well she is doing. All of these simple strategies will provide the support needed to begin mastering attention. The same strategies can be used for other attending problems the child may face, such as listening to instructions or focusing on the steps needed to complete an activity. You'll learn how to use each of these strategies in Chapter 5.

By identifying the source of the problem, difficulties that children face attending in the noisy classroom may be minimized by the time they reach kindergarten. Over a three-year period, the source of the inattention can be addressed. During this time, a child will gradually learn strategies for dealing with her learning difference. We treat differences early, *before* they find outlets for expression—and what we can't prevent, we minimize.

Develop Detours

Earlier, I said learning is neurologically based—something that's part of our children's being. That doesn't mean children with learning differences can't excel. Teaching methods can be used in ways similar to highway detours—it may take a little longer to get where you're going, but you'll eventually arrive at your destination. The same is true in learning. Children with learning differences can find alternative ways of arriving at endpoints. It may not be as efficient, but the end product will be the same or sometimes even better. I remember receiving a note from Jessica's preschool teacher politely chastising me because she couldn't correctly name primary colors.

Dear Dr. Goldberg,

Jessica can't identify colors. Have her repeat the name of each primary color until she has them memorized. Thank you.

How boring, I thought. I could show her different colors in a book or on objects and, eventually, through memorization, she might learn the names of colors, but in the process view learning as something difficult and dull. But I knew "drilling" was not how my daughter learned. Instead of following the well-meaning teacher's advice, I looked for detours. I knew there were four strategies that helped her learn.

1. Use items that are concrete and visual.
2. Actively involve her in the process, rather than just telling her something.
3. Make the learning activity enjoyable.
4. Use repetition, but in a way that isn't boring.

Here's how I incorporated each of the four strategies. I bought one hundred balloons of various colors (*visual and concrete*). We sat down on the living room floor and I asked her to tell me which balloon I should blow up (*active involvement*).

"Red, Daddy," she said. I blew up a red balloon and, with a great theatrical movement, placed it under a pillow.

"But Daddy," she said with wide eyes, "It'll go bang if Mommy sits on it."

I smiled and said, "Yeah, Jessie, won't that be funny?"

She laughed and now became excited about sabotaging our house (*enjoyable*). She'd call out the color of a balloon, I'd blow it up, and then she'd place it behind plants, in the oven, in the garbage, on top of plates, inside the refrigerator, under tables, and even inside the toilet bowls. After one hour, one hundred balloons were hidden throughout the house (*repetition*), and my daughter now flawlessly knew primary colors. What was proposed as a boring activity at which I knew my daughter would fail, instead transformed into something so enjoyable and successful she still remembers it 20 years later. The task took longer to accomplish than if Jessie had a more mainstream learning style. But not only was my daughter successful, she excelled in preschool during activities requiring the identification of colors. Whenever the teacher read to the children and questioned them about the color of something in a picture, Jessie would yell out the correct answer before the teacher had even finished asking it.

Just as with the balloon activity, a number of "detours" can be developed for pre-schoolers with learning differences. They are neither difficult, nor boring. In fact, most children receive them more enthusiastically than traditional teaching approaches. Given a choice of repeating the names of colors or sabotaging their house with different colored balloons, which activity would any child choose? The earlier these detours are used, the more likely they can prevent or minimize learning problems children may encounter in kindergarten.

Find New Holes

It would be wonderful if detours always worked. Unfortunately for some children with learning differences, the frustration is not worth the goal. There's an old joke about a tourist in New York who asks someone on the street how to get to Coney Island from Queens. With a straight face he says, "You can't get there from here." And sometimes for children with certain types of learning differences, the place you want them to go is a destination they either can't get to, or the journey is so difficult, the goal isn't worth it.

I knew a family whose 5-year-old son had a great amount of difficulty with fine hand-eye coordination. The father, who had been a minor league baseball player, had visions of his son going beyond his own accomplishments and entering "the show"—the major leagues. What should have been a bonding experience became a daily disaster. The father would gently throw a baseball to his son and watch him have difficulty even placing the glove in the vicinity of the incoming ball. Batting was no more successful, not even when the ball was placed on an upright pole and the child instructed to hit it. The father was both frustrated and disappointed. The son was crushed by being unable to do something so basic, and pained by not being able to please his father. The family decided to seek the help of a counselor. At the first meeting, the father explained what he was feeling about his son's inadequacies.

"He can't hit or catch the ball. But he runs those bases like the wind. Unfortunately, if he can't hit, he can't run."

The counselor thought for a minute and then casually asked, "Why does he have to hit a ball in order to run?"

"Hitting comes before running in baseball," the father said, as if he was talking to someone who never saw the game.

"Yes," the counselor responded, "in *baseball* that's true. But why must it be baseball? Your son's problems with hand-eye coordination will make baseball an albatross around his neck and could permanently damage his feelings toward you. You're forcing him to do something he will never be good at, and worse, he'll always come across as a failure to both you and himself."

The father was devastated. He understood he was making his son the vehicle for realizing his own unfulfilled dreams.

"Let him run," the counselor continued, "but in something he can excel."

I met this family at a track meet when my son was in high school. The father told me the story and proceeded to give me the history of his son's running career. On that day, he entered three events, coming in first in all three by huge leads. By the end of the track season, he went on to become the state champion in two events and was ranked nationally in the top 10 for both. In the beginning of his senior year, he was offered full scholarships from five prestigious universities.

At times, we as parents need to choose different destinations for our children. Instead of forcing the round peg into the square hole, we may need to help our children find new holes. Identify what interests your children—what they are passionate about. Use that as a guiding light for helping them find activities in which success is likely. When something isn't clicking with your child, you may mistakenly identify it as boredom or reluctance to try something new. In fact, they may be confused about how to do the task, or the task being requested may be unsuitable for them.[55] Children who see the "big picture" but have trouble with details may be bored with a 100-piece puzzle, even if it's a picture of their favorite cartoon character. The activity is not a good match either for their capabilities or how their minds work. A better activity would involve storytelling, or a puzzle with only a few pieces. As you begin to understand how your child learns, you can select activities that not only tap into strengths, but also improve weak points. Many difficulties can be minimized or prevented if we start early.

WHY YOU SHOULD START EARLY

Parents often want to know how soon they should begin working with their child. Once a problem is noticed, start. A distinction needs to be made between behaviors a child should be developmentally ready to perform, and those he or she isn't. A list of developmental milestones is listed in Appendix 2. These are *approximations* of when children should start to use certain behaviors and understand concepts. It takes time before they are used consistently. Even developmentally normal children often have as much as a three-month difference on either side of the milestone. As you compare your children with the milestones, don't be alarmed if some skills appear to be missing. However, if a large number of behaviors are missing, you should contact the appropriate professional for a thorough assessment. The behaviors listed in Appendix 2 were compiled from The National Network for Child Care, Plainsense, the American Speech-Language-Hearing Association, and The National Institute of Child Health and Human Development.[56, 57, 58, 59] From these four lists, there was considerable overlap in the milestones, but, more importantly, they differed as to when the behaviors should appear in children. To reduce confusion, I selected the latest dates the behaviors should appear. Usually, there was only a three to six month gap.

Parents should understand most milestones are approximations. My suggestion is first identify the behavior you have a concern about, and then see when it should have been produced. No harm is caused by a parent using a learning strategy for a behavior a child is not chronologically ready to produce, unless it *becomes stressful, failures in achieving the behaviors occur,* or there are *negative consequences* for not succeeding. If any of these things happen, stop. In the 1980s and 1990s, the enrichment movement spread its philosophy that if techniques and experiences were done early, the IQs of children would improve significantly.[60] Some parents even went so far as to place a speaker playing classical music on a pregnant mother's belly to facilitate a love of music in the developing fetus. That's not what I'm promoting here. Since it's not always possible to determine if something is a learning difference or just a developmental delay corrected with age, it's best to err on the side of a potential learning difference. If the child does have a learning difference, it's addressed. If it's just a delay in development, no harm is done, provided you adhere to the three conditions mentioned above.

The early intervention approach is analogous to using a major highway, such as Interstate 5, which runs the entire length of California. Imagine Los Angeles as your child's preschool skills and San Francisco as the skills needed to enter kindergarten. From Los Angeles, you can take any number of feeder ramps to get onto the interstate. Once you're on it and head north, you'll arrive in San Francisco. However, if you don't take the interstate, your trip will be delayed. Or worse, you may take the wrong road and find yourself on the eastern side of the Sierra Nevada Mountains. Although you'll eventually get to San Francisco, you'll waste many extra hours driving on twisting mountain roads and may even encounter an occasional landslide.

By following the early intervention model, you accomplish two very important things: a bridge is created between the home and school, and emotional problems associated with learning differences are lessened or prevented.

Bridging the Gap

Early intervention acts as a bridge between the supportive environment of home and the more demanding setting of kindergarten. Take for example children whose learning differences make it necessary for them to process information slowly with few or no distractions. They can easily name the colors of objects in a book while sitting on a parent's lap in a quiet room. But what happens when they enter kindergarten? The teacher, standing in the middle of a classroom, holds up a book they can barely see, points to a child, and in the presence of 20 noisy children, gives him or her five seconds to identify the color of the house. Children, who functioned without any problems in a supportive environment, now find themselves failing at things performed perfectly at home. Something is missing in the child's learning—a bridge crossing an abyss between calm and chaos. Although parents can control conditions at home, their ability to structure what happens in school is minimal.[61]

There is an old Buddhist saying that "it is easier to wear sandals than it is to cover the entire road with leather." You can prepare your children for that enormous leap by creating a good pair of sandals. You do this by gradually introducing stressors, such as time constraints and noise. A mother I knew had a child who didn't function well with auditory distractions and time pressure. She was concerned about his eventual performance in kindergarten. During a visit to the kindergarten class one year before he would be enrolled, she saw 19 children sitting in front of the teacher as she read a story. Although they were all interested, she knew the noise level would create problems for her son. Worse, the teacher would randomly call on children to answer questions about what she'd just read. The combination of these two conditions, noise and time pressure, gave this mother nightmares. Her choices were limited. Unable to afford a private school, and living in a district with only one kindergarten, she could either wait for problems to occur or try to do something now to prevent them from happening later. She chose the latter—to create a bridge between a calm setting, in which her son thrived, to one in which, without help, he would fail. A simple strategy she used to prepare her child appears in Figure 1.5. Gradually, she began introducing background noises when she read to him. First, it was just soft music, until she felt he did as well with the music as without it. Then, the station was switched to a talk show. In order to introduce time pressure, she constructed a simple game in which he would receive a point that went toward a prize, if he answered a question before a timer's bell rang. Gradually, the amount of time allowed for a response was decreased. When her son entered kindergarten, he was able to succeed in a setting that, without his mother's help, would have been a series of endless failures. While he still had some attending problems, they were manageable. His mother had prepared him with a wonderful pair of sandals.

Figure 1.5
Answering Questions—Going From a Home Setting to Kindergarten

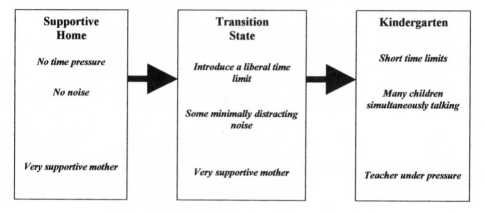

Preventing Emotional Problems

Learning differences can lead to emotional problems in children as young as two years of age.[62] Once, a parent brought a three-year-old child to me for stuttering therapy. He was the most disfluent child I had ever treated. He repeated over 50 percent of all words spoken and 80 percent of those were repeated at least three times. When trying to force out words, he blinked his eyes, raised his voice, and thrust out his little head. As painful as it was for me to watch, it was excruciating for his parents to experience daily. He began speaking when he was one and a half years old, and his vocabulary blossomed. By two, he began combining words in ways far beyond his age, and his expressed thoughts were at the level of a five-year-old. At two and a half years of age, he was on a meteoric path to everything his parents hoped for—then the stuttering began. As he experienced difficulties saying even simple words, the once talkative child became almost silent. Instead of answering in beautifully long sentences, he used single words. Instead of conversations, he only spoke when asked direct questions. On many occasions, the sounds either did not come out, or he would take up to15 seconds to complete a word. He would often burst into tears when unable to speak. I was faced with convincing this three-year-old boy success was possible. To do this, I used a learning strategy called *successive approximation* that has proven consistently effective during my 25 years of working with children. The second part of the book will discuss it further in relationship to learning problems. Successive approximation means doing a progression of things, each of which gets closer to the final goal.[63] In five days, his parents and I helped him from not being able to say more than two or three words fluently, to only having a few repetitions every three or four sentences. We did two things: His rate was gradually increased each day from very slow to normal, and we increased the length of fluency activities by one minute each day. He became completely fluent after three weeks and remains so today, ten years after therapy ended. The succession of the five steps appears in Figure 1.6. Little steps with very small increases in target behaviors enabled him to succeed.

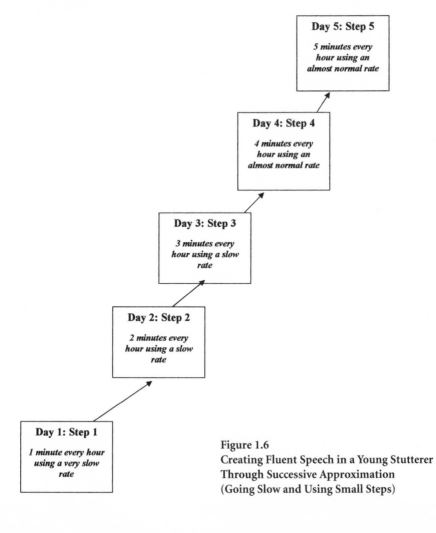

Day 5: Step 5

5 minutes every hour using an almost normal rate

Day 4: Step 4

4 minutes every hour using an almost normal rate

Day 3: Step 3

3 minutes every hour using a slow rate

Day 2: Step 2

2 minutes every hour using a slow rate

Day 1: Step 1

1 minute every hour using a very slow rate

Figure 1.6
Creating Fluent Speech in a Young Stutterer
Through Successive Approximation
(Going Slow and Using Small Steps)

Failures can be as dramatic as the experiences of the young stutterer, or as subtle as repeatedly not being able to cut out a figure traced on paper. With each failure, children begin developing a self-image of someone who can't succeed. As failures mount, their self-esteem drops. The best way of treating the emotional problems associated with failures is to prevent them from occurring. And there is no better antidote than success. Whatever it takes, make sure your child succeeds as often as possible. You can do this by reducing the amount of time spent on an activity, providing more time to respond, offering helpful cues, or reducing your performance expectations. With each success, a new brick is laid in the development of a healthy self-image. We can't always prevent our children from experiencing failure, but we can provide them with the tools to succeed. In the next chapter, you'll begin learning how to use them.

TWO

Becoming a World-Class Teaching Parent

*E*veryone kept telling her how easy it would be to teach this to her son. Relatives and friends who no longer remembered the problems they encountered teaching their own children showered "words of wisdom" upon her.

"Just show him how it's done," her mother said. "He'll be able to figure it out when he sees you do it. He's a bright child, isn't he?"

She listened to everyone's suggestions, including her mother's, and then placed each well-intentioned piece of advice into one of three imaginary baskets: *almost helpful, not helpful,* and *you've got to be kidding*! Looking at the yellowing pages of notes from her college child-development class, she wondered if her professor ever spent time with children. Lots of theories, simple situations, and clean solutions. Nothing came close to the reality she was about to face. There was still time to visit the local Barnes & Nobles. It would be two hours before her parenting abilities would again be challenged. The parenting section at the store held over five hundred books, each describing how she should deal with her child. She scoured the shelves for anything having "learning" or "teaching" in the title. Selecting ten books, she carried them to a reading table. The first one wasn't helpful. The author seemed to have as much knowledge of real children as her college professor. It was as if she was asking a gas station attendant in Detroit how to drive to Los Angeles and, while pointing west, he said, "thataway." After paging through the remaining nine books, she realized all were "thataway" books. None would provide her with the techniques she needed in one hour.

As she drove to pick up her son at preschool, she remembered how hard it had been for her as a child. She had struggled and often failed, and now was determined not to repeat her mother's mistakes. She desperately wanted to make learning easier for her son. Having failed at many things as a child, she knew how important early success would be for him.

As they walked to the car she asked, "How was school?"

"Fine Mommy," he said, his eyes focused downward.

"What did you do today?"

"Played," he said, still not looking at her.

The drive home was even more uncomfortable. For the past four days, both had tried and failed. Both knew it had to be done and dreaded it. Neither talked until they were in the house and sitting in the living room. She couldn't avoid it any longer. It was time to start.

"Now watch me," she said. "It's very easy. First you hold the laces, and then you make a loop with one hand, then the other, and then put one under the other, then pull these two outward. That's it. It's so easy. Now you do it."

He looked at her as if she were trying to explain the mysteries of the universe. That bunch of words somehow related to what she was doing with his shoelaces. And those fingers! They moved faster than his Saturday morning cartoon characters.

"Okay Mommy. Like this?" He slowly started making the loops, not having any idea even where to begin.

"No, not like that, like this," the mother said, rapidly repeating her movements.

He knew he couldn't make a completed bow. However, he tried, because it was his mother who asked. This time he managed to put a knot in his laces, smiling because he at least got past the bow part.

In frustration she said, "You're not watching. I'll do it one more time. This time watch me very carefully."

The little boy intently watched, really tried, and again failed.

"Sorry Mommy. Why can't I do it?" he said with tears in his eyes.

She too began crying. She couldn't understand why her shoe-tying lesson wasn't working. Was she so incompetent she couldn't even teach her son how to tie his shoes? Was he just being defiant? Or worse, did her son have a problem preventing him from learning even the simplest behaviors? This should have been easy. After all, parents have taught generations of children to tie their shoes. She felt like a failure and knew her son also did.

How many of us have had similar experiences? How often have you tried to teach your child something you regarded as easy to learn, yet were baffled by his or her inability to succeed? Was the learning difference so severe it prevented success? Or, although you knew *what* you wanted to teach, maybe you didn't know *how* to do it? For most parents, it's difficult to know where the truth lies. When I work with children, I always start with the assumption children can learn almost anything if I can just match the appropriate teaching strategies to their interests and abilities. You should also begin with the same assumption. Your child can learn significantly more than you think, or have been led to believe.

But how do you find the match? That mystical union of teaching skills, your child's interests, and learning style? Few parents have been taught how to do it. When your child was born I doubt anyone came into your hospital room and said, "Congratulations Ms. Jones, here's your beautiful baby girl and a set of instructions on how to teach her." Yet, a large part of being a parent involves teaching. Society expects you to teach your child a multitude of things ranging from language to societal values. While the expectation is there, the support isn't. Just like millions of other parents, you've probably been left on your own to develop teaching skills. Some of them are eventually learned through trial and error. But, like the mother and child in our example, failures tend to precede successes. And for some, there are few success stories. Most parents know *what* they should be doing. If they don't, every friend and relative will be glad to tell them. The problem I've found is 95 percent of the parents with whom I work don't know *how* to teach. In this chapter we'll explore two important areas. The first is what you need to do to become a world-class teaching parent. The second is what your child can do as a learner to make your job easier. This chapter involves the *how* of teaching. In Part II of the book, we'll look at *what* you should be teaching. You'll find successful teaching is not as difficult as you might think. Some of the *how's* you may already know. For others, you may have an intuitive feeling. And many may be new to you. You'll finally get that teaching manual they forgot to give you when your child was born.

What You Need to Do

The parent-as-teacher walks a continuum between compassionate caregiver and demanding instructor. You may find it necessary to push your child into something you believe may be difficult or painful. At other times, the emotional needs of children overshadow the learning experience you desperately want them to have. I found it necessary to walk that line first with my daughter, then my son. I wasn't always successful. Sometimes, I allowed my love to overshadow what was necessary for my children to learn. At other times, I should have been compassionate instead of demanding. Just as with most things in life, if you keep repeating something, you'll eventually get it right. Although I made mistakes, with time I learned how to be both a parent and a teacher. I've distilled my experience and the latest research on learning into 11 suggestions for teaching your children.

Start with Your Child's Needs

Always start your teaching with an understanding of your child's needs. When I work with children who have problems, I often begin by asking them what I can do to help. The answers usually amaze parents. One six-year-old girl, without any hesitation, said, "jump rope." Her parents had brought her to see me because there were sounds she either distorted or couldn't pronounce. The difficulty in pronouncing these sounds was related to problems in muscular coordination—the genesis of her articulation problems. I designed a general program that worked on muscle coordination, both for speaking and jumping rope. She became successful at both, and forced me to become more physically fit in order to match her 25 perfectly executed jumps she insisted we do each week as we worked on her articulation.

As a parent, you are in the best position for identifying these needs. You're with your child more than almost anyone else. You know how they act when they're tired, alert, emotionally taxed, and excited. No one is in a better position to identify a child's needs than you. That's the starting point. Sometimes the process is as simple as asking your child questions similar to "would you like to do _____?" or "would you like to learn _____?" Other times, you may need to be more of an investigator, observing what frustrates or angers your child. You always begin with your child's needs, not yours.

Underestimate

You risk failure if you start teaching at a level that's beyond your child's ability. It often seems reasonable to parents if their child already understands *A*, they should teach *B*. Unfortunately, this sequential logic is fuzzier than most imagine. Parents tend to overestimate their children's abilities to know one thing and then move forward. If children demonstrate a behavior once, that doesn't mean they'll be able to do it again. And if we assume they can and go on to a more advanced behavior, we may be setting them up to fail.

A mother came into the clinic with a 12-year-old child who had a severe learning problem.

"How much language does Mitch have?" I asked.

"Oh, quite a bit," she responded. "He can speak in sentences of over four words."

When I listened and analyzed his utterances, I found what the mother identified as "sentences" were really rote memorization. When he said, "I want more milk," he didn't understand that each word in the sentence was separate. He could have substituted "blah," and it would have meant the same thing. If I had taken his mother's assumption for granted, I would have begun therapy working on expanding four-word utterances to five, which would have been a disaster. I needed to go back to combining two words in a way he understood conveyed an idea. Eventually, we were able to teach him to construct sentences. After three months, "I want more milk" was used and understood by Mitch as a grammatical structure having four distinct units, placed in a specific order, and used to express a desire.

A good method to use when teaching something to your child is to start at least one level below what you think is his or her capability. Then you know there is a firm foundation for continuing forward. It also results in a number of successful experiences and a teaching model that's easily understood.

Don't Compare

Many parents look at their child's behaviors as *worse than, equal to,* or *better than* the accomplishments of other children. This can be disastrous for children with learning problems and their parents.[1] I remember a birthday party my wife threw me when our children were six and ten. We invited a woman whose children went to the same school as ours. Although not one of our favorite friends, we felt obligated to invite her. As each person came into the house, gifts were given and warm embraces exchanged. I stood at the door preparing myself to greet someone I wished had declined the invitation.

"Well, let me tell you what Martin did yesterday," she said, thrusting a package into my hand while looking around the room and talking loud enough so everyone could hear.

Not a "hello," not even a "happy birthday." She wasn't being rude; she was being who she was. It was not only important her son was achieving something, but also whatever he did had to be better, bigger, and more significant than any other child's accomplishments. She never seemed happy for her child, only for the status she believed his accomplishments gave her. It became especially annoying when she would try to compare her son's school achievements with my daughter's.

"You know, Martin got a 100 percent on Friday's spelling test. That's his eighth perfect score in a row. I just know that's got to be a school record." Then, in a louder voice she smugly asked, "And how did Jessie do?"

She reminded me of the school bully who picks on the little kid with glasses who doesn't do well at sports. You may face similar people—some may even be relatives. Don't despair. These comparisons say more about the person making them than they do about your child's abilities. In teaching, the only comparison to make is between what your child did yesterday and what your child does today. There are a number of ways we can see if children are improving. They can be doing something better, faster, or using it more often in appropriate settings. Perfection isn't a criterion you should use. When I work with parents whose children have severe learning problems, I teach them to focus on small changes in their children's behaviors. For example, I was over-joyed when a child, who would never look at people, held his glance at me for three seconds.

This emphasis on little changes is also important for children who have only mild learning problems. Take pleasure in *any* positive change and praise your child for it. Positive reinforcement is one of the most powerful tools you can use to effectively and permanently change your child's behaviors.[2] In teaching, focus on little steps—together they form a path to bigger goals. In the *Wizard of Oz*, the Munchkins tell Dorothy to "Follow the yellow brick road."[3] No matter what she asks about The Emerald City, the answer is always the same "Follow the yellow brick road." It also applies to teaching children with learning differences. Stay on the path, take one step at a time, and you and your child will make it to The Emerald City, and experience a number of wonderful things on the way. I don't know what happened to Martin after he dropped out of college in his freshman year. Jessica, however, has a successful career in the art world, in spite of spelling problems throughout school.

Teach Like You Dance
(or Would Like To)

Teaching should be like a dance—when one person leads, the other flows with the movements. There's a wonderful movie called *Shall We Dance?* in which Japanese ballroom dancers move as if each part of their body was attached to the identical part of their partner's.[4] If you watch long enough, they seem to merge into one body. With each push there is a pull. As one dips forward, the other moves back. For me, this is the ultimate image of what teaching should be. When I taught my son how to ride his first two-wheel bicycle, I held onto the back of his seat. As he started falling left, I pulled right. As he gained more balance, I held less tightly. I continually allowed his needs to dictate my movements. Together we mastered bicycle balance and were both successful. My bicycle experience became the model I use for all of my teaching. Unfortunately, some parents' preferred style of teaching is to push.

Often parents believe the only way to achieve goals is to push their children along the path, sometimes very gently, other times with considerable force. I think this is a mistake. I've found the greatest successes occur when, just as a well executed dance performance, very little *direct* pressure is applied. For example, I was working with a mother whose three-year-old child showed little interest in learning new words. For months, the mother had been drill-ing her child using a number of picture books. Although the child had a mild interest in the stories, her desire to learn new words was minimal. I suggested the mother forget the books and introduce new objects into the house without saying anything about them. I told her to have them mysteriously appear in places her daughter couldn't reach. Since it was something new, it immediately caught the child's attention.

"What's that Mommy?"

"That's a giraffe."

"Can I play?"

"Play with what dear?"

"Giraffe."

We continued the process throughout the year, placing the objects the mother would like the daughter to name in a special place. Usually, it was on top of the refrigerator. Every day when her daughter would wake up, she would run to the kitchen to see what had mysteriously sprouted out of the refrigerator. The number of words in the child's vocabulary rapidly expanded without any pushing. I don't force children to learn. Learning should be a voluntary process. The more resistance you create, the less likely something will be learned, and the more likely learning will be viewed as difficult.[5] Ideally, you should offer something so exciting and interesting that if withheld, your child will plead with you to do it. I've found the harder parents push, the more children resist. Instead of you pushing, it's best to find a way that results in children taking the initiative—have them push you.

Use Active, Not Passive Learning

Learning can be either passive or active. Passive learning is when the parent is responsible for all learning conditions. Parents direct and children comply. Passive learning is easier for parents to do than active learning, but less beneficial for children. Consider the following passive learning example when my son was four years old.

"Justin, I want you to get ready for school. Here, put on your green pants and your white shirt. I left your shoes and socks outside your room. Your lunch box is downstairs in the kitchen. I made you a peanut butter and jelly sandwich. I also put in an oatmeal cookie, an apple, and your milk. Your coat is on the stairs."

I told my son what to wear, how to put on his clothes, and what he would be eating and drinking at preschool. I decided on everything, without asking for his input. Many parents use passive learning because it's easier and quicker than involving children in designing learning activities. In the above example, my son learned only to follow a set of instructions, not how to make decisions and live with their consequences—a skill especially important for children with learning differences.[6] But if learning how to control aspects of his life was the goal of the activity, my passive example could have been made active by asking my son for input. Here's what I should have done.

"Justin, I want you to get ready for school. Do you want to wear your green or black pants today?"

"Black, Daddy."

"Why?"

"Cause I like them better."

"That's a good reason. What about your shirt? Look in the drawer with me and choose one."

"I want Mickey Mouse."

"No problem. For lunch I can make you either a peanut butter and jelly sandwich or a baloney sandwich. Which one do you want?"

"Baloney. I had peanut butter and jelly yesterday."

"And a cookie? We have either chocolate chip or oatmeal."

"Chocolate chip."

"Do you want juice or milk today?"

"Juice. Milk gets yucky."

Active learning is not only more exciting for children, but usually results in better intellectual development.[7] I was fortunate enough to observe two different preschool classes on the same day with teachers who had diametrically opposite approaches. Both loved their children and both were concerned with getting them ready for kindergarten. It was a poor neighborhood and the teachers knew these kids would start public school with many disadvantages. The first teacher used passive learning. She would give each child four different colored crayons, And then ask them to copy a picture of a color-drawn house on a large piece of paper taped to an easel. The activity was designed to teach the children fine motor coordination, color matching, and following instructions. All of these are important skills for children to have when they enter kindergarten. But could the same things be taught using an active learning method and in the process teach other things? The second teacher thought it could.

"Okay children, I want you to draw a picture of your home today. Can anyone tell me what it should look like from the outside?"

Every child's hand came up.

"A door."

"Windows."

"A Mommy."

The children's answers ranged from the usual to the bizarre. The teacher dismissed none.

"Very good children. Let's be sure to make it big." With that she drew a basic outline of a house and an apartment building on the left side of the board.

"And you can put people in front of it, in it, or even on top of it." Everyone laughed. The teacher then drew a stick figure on the bottom of the blackboard.

"It should have windows and a door." Both were placed next to the buildings.

"And you can make it any color you want! When we're done, everyone will have a turn to tell about their home."

Not only did the second teacher accomplish everything the first did, but also by making it an active learning experience, the children became involved in selecting the components of the activity and placement of objects. They were able to use creativity, formulate explanations of what they did, and begin practicing oral presentations. Not bad for a simple drawing exercise. In active learning you'll need to set rules in advance and decide on the number of choices you'll give your child.

Setting Rules

When you structure activities in which you ask for a child's input, both you and your child need to follow a separate rule. The rule you follow is not to offer choices you aren't prepared to accept. If parents neglect this rule, they're telling children that even though they have to follow the rules, adults are allowed to break them. I watched a mother offer the following choice to her son who was refusing to cooperate with my student clinician.

"Okay Jimmy, either you work with Ms. Green or you can sit there for the whole session and do nothing."

From within the observation booth I cringed, anticipating what Jimmy was about to say.

"I'll sit here Mommy," he said with a smile.

Of course the choice wasn't acceptable to the mother or the clinician. The mother was furious and my student didn't know what to do with Jimmy's choice. I remained in the observation booth and watched.

"If you don't work with her, no television tonight!" the mother retorted.

He did start cooperating with the therapist, but how could he trust his mother in the future? In the middle of the game, she changed the rules. She gave him a choice and he made a decision. Now she added a new rule. Not fair! As the maker of rules, you must be prepared to follow them, even if it means allowing your child to sit and do nothing for 45 minutes. After the session the mother, therapist, and I discussed what had occurred.

"I'm so embarrassed," the mother began.

"Why?" I asked.

"Jimmy was just terrible. He wouldn't listen or do anything right. And choosing to sit there was wrong."

"No," I said. "What Jimmy did was okay."

Both the mother and the therapist looked confused.

"You gave him a choice," I continued. "And he chose the activity that made the most sense to him. He should have been allowed to sit and do nothing for the entire session."

Never give a child an option you're not prepared to follow. You need to be prepared to allow your child to follow the rules you make. The rule your child needs is this: Once a choice is made, it's made. When my son was young, I constantly provided him with choices. For example, he could play with his toys for five minutes in the morning before we left for school, *if* he was completely prepared for the day. Initially, he would constantly want to increase the amount of allotted playtime. The first time I decided to increase it, after we had already agreed on five minutes, the wheels in his little head began to churn. I'm sure he thought, "If I can get extra time by asking now, I probably can get more time when I ask tomorrow." He was right. And each time I allowed him to expand the parameter of the rule, I reinforced the notion that rules don't have to be followed. It took a more firm conviction on my part to re-establish the limits upon which we originally agreed. However, there were a number of crying episodes before Justin realized the rule was once again in force. Nothing erodes a parent's ability to set parameters more than allowing children to break rules previously agreed upon by everyone.[8] Once done with any regularity, it becomes a pattern, not only affecting family life, but also how children interact with the world when they become teenagers and adults.[9]

How Many Choices?

Decide on the number of objects or games from which your child can choose before you begin an activity. In some cases, your child's level of understanding will dictate the number. In other cases the situation will. A good rule of thumb is the more trouble your child has with understanding or lack of structure, the fewer choices should be given. By starting out with a lower number, you can always increase it. You may create needless difficulties if you start with too many choices. When I worked with a five-year-old child whose language was minimal and who had severe cognitive problems, I gave her a choice of only two activities. She had become immobilized in the past when I offered her a choice of three different activities. While two was manageable, three was too confusing. However, the reverse occurred with a four-year-old child whose wealthy parents believed in never denying him anything. Not only did he have his own room for sleeping, but adjoining it was a "playroom," whose sole function was to house enough toys to keep an entire class of preschool children occupied for a week. Although we were working on the retrieval of information, his parents had concerns about his general behavior. They weren't accustomed to setting limits and only realized they had been responsible for his tantrums long after they began. Given this information, I was able to plan for the problem, and hopefully avoid it.

"Stu, look all around the room and choose whatever we'll play with. But it can be only one thing."

He scurried about the room, picking up one item, then discarding it. Another toy was grabbed, and halfway back to me he dropped it and looked for something else.

"I'm going to count to five. Whatever you have in your hand is what we'll play with. One, two, three, four, five!"

He was holding a wooden train set, and appeared to be thankful limits were placed on him. Children not only need to be given limits; they desire and function better with them.[10] We immediately left the playroom with his choice and began working on concepts.

Both examples are extremes of choice. What you will do with your child should fall somewhere in the middle. I like to start with a choice of three activities for younger children who have normal intelligence. It shouldn't make any difference what your child chooses—the teaching objective will be the same.

Make It Successful

Success is not something children should achieve only after repeated trials and errors. For years, parents were told success is more meaningful when children struggle. Parents of children with learning differences know how ridiculous that is as advice. Somehow, effort is supposed to make learning more meaningful and long lasting. Nonsense! Research has shown the opposite.[11] Continual failure only convinces children they can't succeed.[12] This is especially true for children with learning differences.[13] I once saw a child whose past speech-language therapist thought she had an articulation problem correctable only by surgery. The surgical procedure involved severing the skin attached between the tongue and the floor of the mouth. The therapist thought this minor surgery would give the tongue greater mobility, making it easier for the child to produce difficult sounds. In her report, she said no matter what was tried, the child just couldn't produce certain sounds. The procedure she recommended hadn't been used by competent ENT surgeons in ten years. The problem wasn't in the child's anatomy; it was in the therapist's methods. For three months, this little girl endured weekly therapy sessions during which she continually failed at producing a correct target sound. Imagine how you would feel if once every week, someone tried to teach you the same thing— and every week you failed in spite of your best efforts? I was faced with two tasks. The first was to help her correct the articulation problem. The second, and one I felt more critical, was repairing a damaged self-image. I began a five-step activity leading to the production of a sound that started as distorted and ended as perfect. The changes in difficulty between the steps were so small; they were barely perceptible to the child. I also provided visual cues to make sure she was successful. In five steps, done in five days, a child who would have undergone painful surgery was able to produce a "problem" sound with as much eloquence as a nightly news commentator. Success is infectious. When children start viewing themselves as successful learners in one area, they want to become successful in others.[14] All of the "problem" sounds were mastered in a few months, and the little girl's self-image as a failure began to change. Fifteen years after therapy, she is a forceful business executive, confident in her abilities, and has perfect speech. Think of each successful event in your child's life as a pair of amorous bunnies—each will breed a colony of new ones.

Make the Activity Fit the Child

It's easier to modify an activity than it is to change your child's learning preferences.[15] Some years ago, I supervised a new graduate student whose undergraduate training was at another university. I observed her doing articulation therapy with a 7-year-old child in a public school. The little girl substituted "w" for "r" in her speech. The student was trying to teach her to say things like "rabbit" instead of "wabbit." She would hold up a card containing a picture of something starting with the letter "r" and asked the child to name it. After watching this unsuccessful therapy for five minutes, I couldn't take it any longer and took over the session. The therapy was not only boring, but it failed to consider any of the child's learning differences documented in a two-inch thick folder following her throughout school. Because of this information, I modified the activity in five ways.

1. We repeated an enormous number of sounds to develop motor memory.
2. I attached the sound to a rhythm to develop a memory web that could aid retrieval.
3. Instead of fighting her hyperactivity, I approached it positively and used it to introduce movement into the activity.
4. Since she functioned better when she felt in control, adult control, within limits, was relinquished.
5. We moved out of the therapy room since important new behaviors are learned in the settings in which they will be used.

I rose from my seat in the corner of the room, walked to the table where she was sitting, and stood in front of her.

"Jean, I want you to stand up and face the way I'm facing and then step on the top of my shoes."

She looked as bewildered as my student, but reluctantly stood and stepped onto my shoes.

"Okay," I said. "Every time you say 'r' correctly, I'm going to take one giant step forward."

"Where to?" she asked.

"Anywhere you want me to go," I answered.

"Anywhere?" she said with a grin.

"Yes, anywhere," I said, not sure what I just agreed to.

"Then, let's walk out to the playground and into the school."

What had been a very boring activity that didn't account for this child's learning differences, now became the most exciting thing the little girl ever did at school. The activity clicked with how she learned. For fifteen minutes, with her on top of my feet, we walked from the therapy room to the playground and, with startled teachers looking out from their rooms and my student trailing far enough behind so as not to be identified with me, down the school's main hallway. It took my best diplomatic efforts to explain to a very proper principal why I was walking with a child on my shoes. But because of what I did, that little girl learned to say "r" in words in fifteen minutes, rather than spending two more months using tedious learning methods.

The way you teach will convey a lesson in life to your child. Make it arduous and your child will view learning as something that's going to be difficult—not only in one activity, but in others as well. You convey the opposite message by teaching as if your child is standing on your shoes. Together, both of you are doing foolish, but positive things. I've found if parents are light and fluid in their approach, they frolic with their children down the path of learning, rather than having to pull them along, kicking and screaming.

Make It Exciting

The heart of teaching for me is the excitement children experience when they learn something new. Think about the excitement you felt when you learned to do something that expanded your world. If you are a golfer, it could be learning how to adjust your grip so a slice became a distant memory. You may have taken a poetry class and now marvel at your ability to construct lyrical verses about life. When Richard Feynman, a noble laureate in physics, spoke about the universe when he was in his sixties, you could still hear in his words the little boy who discovered something totally new and wonderful and wanted to share it with anyone who would listen.[16] It doesn't have to be discovering the secrets of the universe—learning how to feed fish can be equally exciting. Just as it did with Richard Feynman, the excitement children experience when learning new things is something that can remain with them throughout their lives.

Unfortunately, opportunities to create excitement are often missed. Nothing turns off children more than learning activities that are too dull or difficult.[17] Introduce a little excitement and everything changes. When my son was five, I wanted to teach him about insects. I could have used any number of excellent children's books. But my son's preferred method of learning involved direct contact and manipulation—he had to touch it, taste it, hear it, smell it, or see it. And above all else, it had to be exciting. The abstractness of pictures in books couldn't hold his attention. Even if something about insects would be learned through a less direct approach, it wouldn't be retained unless a very rich memory web was created; one loaded with familiar and exciting visual stimuli. For my son, that couldn't happen with books. So I forgot about using a book, and we hiked into the woods. I stopped when I found a small clearing and drew two concentric circles in the dirt. The inner circle had a two-foot diameter, and the larger circle a six-foot diameter. I looked at them without saying anything, waiting for Justin to ask what I just did.

"What are you doing Daddy?" he asked.

"I'm making a race track."

"A race track?"

"Yes. See, here's where they start," I said, pointing to the center of the inner circle. "And there's where they finish," I continued, touching the edge of the outer circle. I then looked into the woods as if searching for something.

"Who's racing Daddy?"

"Bugs," I said.

"Where are they?" my son asked after looking in all directions.

Peering into the surrounding forest, I whispered, "We have to find them."

"But where?"

In a hushed voice I said, "They're all around us Justin. You find one, and I'll also look for one. Then we'll put them in the little circle and see who gets out of the big circle first."

His eyes opened wide and for the next ten minutes he poked under fallen twigs, looked on top of plants and dug under rocks.

"I got one Daddy! I got one to race!" he yelled just before the insect became ooze between his fingers.

First lesson, don't squeeze too hard. Although many insects perished before my son found an unwilling racer, one finally made it onto the course. The Great Insect Race was about to begin. We both stood over the inner circle, our hands imprisoning the confused racers.

"Okay bugs. Take your mark, ready, set, go!" I yelled, as we both opened our hands and dropped the insects into the inner circle.

Justin's little red ant quickly scampered out of the inner circle past my lumbering black beetle, who seemed content to stay were I dropped him. After aimlessly moving within the larger circle, the ant crossed over the outer edge.

"My ant won Daddy! I won! Can we find more and race them?"

"Sure Justin. But we need to look for different bugs."

"What kind?"

"Any kind, just not an ant or a beetle."

Not only did he expand the range of insects he would encounter, but he also began asking questions that could only be answered with new knowledge:

"Why are some faster than others?"

"Why don't they go straight?"

"What do they do when we're not here looking for them?"

"Why do they smell different when I squish them?"

"Do they pee and poop like we do?"

As we looked for the next Mario Andretti of insect racing, I attempted to answer more questions about insects than could be generated by reading ten books to Justin. We spent the next half hour racing hapless little creatures. And in the process, he learned their names, how they moved, where they lived, how easily they could be squished, and even how they went to the bathroom. We spent a wonderful afternoon together. I felt successful as a parent, and Justin joyfully learned about insects. By identifying his learning needs, I was able to construct a simple game that was exciting and educational.

Unfortunately, many children and parents may not regularly experience the excitement felt by my son and me. This is especially true when the child is thought to have a learning problem. Activities become highly structured, often involving pictures in books, and take on the appearance of an academic exercise. The excitement is purposely drained from them in order to surgically treat the "learning disorder." It becomes an activity more closely aligned with work than play. And I have never met a child who chooses work over play. But teaching, if done correctly and made compatible with a child's learning strengths, can be as enjoyable and exciting as the Great Insect Race. Children want to learn, and they can, if we don't erect walls between them and a very exciting world. Think of your child as an "emotional chameleon" who will clone the attitude you bring into the situation. If you appear uninterested or bored, don't expect your children to be enthralled by what you ask them to do. Some activity directors on cruise ships run around the decks asking passengers "are we having fun yet?" Imagine that annoying person is shadowing you when you're teaching and during every activity whispers in your ear "are you having fun yet?" Your answer should always be "absolutely!"

Use Humor

The Tibetan Lama, Chogyam Trungpa, said a genuine sense of humor involves not beating reality into the ground, but appreciating it with a light touch.[18] Although we should be serious about our children's problems, we don't need to *approach* them with a sense of gravity. While I never stopped thinking about my children's learning differences when they were young, and still have concerns, I tried to find humor in what they did and how I tried to help them. My son urinating on the sidewalk could have been embarrassing if I took it seriously, but I didn't. To this day, I still find it one of the funniest things I remember Justin doing as a child. I try to find humor everywhere. When I can't, I know I'm taking myself too seriously. There is humor in *everything*, even learning problems. I gauge how effective I am when I work with children by the amount of laughter I generate. If children are laughing at what I am doing or saying, they're listening. And if they're listening, they're probably also learning. I was once asked to substitute at our university clinic for a clinician who ran a group for children with severe learning problems. The clinician had been using a series of drawings containing a stick figure and a table. Each drawing represented one location. For example, a stick figure crouching under the table represented "under." As I began the clinician's program, there wasn't one smiling face in the entire group of six children. Worse, I was as bored as they were. I pulled out a card and asked one child to tell me what it represented.

"On," he said, but with no conviction or interest.

"You've got it!" I screamed, and proceeded to jump on top of the table.

Every child's face became riveted on me. I turned to the next child, and showed him an "under" card.

"Under! Under!" he yelled, hoping I would drop to the floor and crawl under the table.

I didn't disappoint him. All the children were hysterical. I tossed all of the cards over my shoulder onto the floor and then pointed to each child. Everyone wanted to talk. For 45 minutes, they moved me around the room. When I introduced new words, such as "jump," "fall," "roll," and "run," all the kids pleaded to be selected to make this strange adult do funny things with words. What had been an uninteresting learning activity now became something exciting because they were active, visual, involved movements, and were meaningful. I had tapped into their strengths to teach them concepts in 45 minutes that would have taken weeks or months, if I, as the regular clinician, ignored their learning styles. The following week, as I was walking down the hall with my department chairman, I heard a faint voice at the other end of the corridor saying, "fall down." Without even turning around to look, I slowly and dramatically proceeded to fall down next to the chairman. As he looked at me in shock, I winked.

"I'm alright," I whispered to him. "Just wait." Then another voice was heard. "Jump up!"

After I leaped off the floor, I heard "run," and turning around I ran with my arms flailing toward the source of my orders. The six kids, who had just gotten out of therapy, were laughing as they once again had control over my actions as if I was a marionette. Accompanying them were the shocked clinician and their astonished parents. Finding humor in what you do will give you and your child constant joy. Learn to make fun of yourself—you'll be amazed how much it will lighten your teaching and endear you to your child, and most important, help your child become successful.

Find the Right Key

Teaching, like most things in life, doesn't always go as planned. Because it's a process, it's subject to change. And with children, change is the rule rather than the exception. The need to be flexible with children who have learning differences is paramount in their progress.[19] I recently worked on visual organization with a five-year-old boy and his family. What I thought was the perfect program did not yield the results I wanted. He was able to identify five out of ten objects I had placed in one part of the room. I modified the visual images (using fewer items) and his proficiency at identifying them increased, but I still thought he could do better. I kept modifying the program. First, I increased the size of objects. I did this to make them stand out from everything around them. Since it didn't improve the outcome, I increased the number of similar objects. Still nothing. Finally, I introduced a reward. Everything immediately clicked. At no time did I ever think the lack of progress was his fault or his parents. In that case, and in all others, I always make the assumption I haven't found the right key.

Finding the right key may mean admitting you were wrong in the selection of activities or how you presented the materials. For some people, admitting they made a mistake can effect their ego. You need to put it aside for the benefit of your child. Pema Chodren said an ego is like a very fat person trying to get through a very narrow door.[20] The person can only get through that door with a great deal of effort and irritation. If you approach your teaching without a self-image to defend, you won't take setbacks personally. When I work with parents I'm never afraid to say things like, "Boy was I wrong on that one! Let's try something else." With this attitude, you'll come to feel it wasn't you or your child who failed. Rather, you didn't quite get the proper match between the methods and your child's capabilities. You'll both do better next time.

Get the Timing Right

Sometimes you may have the right key, but your timing is off. It's as if you have an idea for a new invention that will make you rich, only to learn someone patented it last week. There is a wonderful story about a person who decided to study with a famous monk. To be accepted, he agreed on two conditions: He would stay in the monastery for three years, and ask his master only one question a year.

"What is the meaning of life?" the student asked in the beginning of his first year.

The monk looked at him, and after remaining silent for several minutes, said, "You must first understand what *meaning* is."

The student returned to his room and spent the whole year in meditation trying to understand the meaning of meaning. At the end of the year it was time to ask another question.

"Master, I have spent the year meditating on the meaning of meaning. But now I think there are many meanings. Am I right?"

This time the monk sat silently for 15 minutes, then responded. "Why must there even be a meaning?"

Confused, the student went back to his room and meditated on why there must be a meaning to the meaning of life. Another year came and went, and it was time for the third and final question.

"Master, I've spent this last year as you instructed, I think I now know that there doesn't have to be a meaning to life. But I'm not sure. Please tell me the right answer."

The monk looked at him and said nothing for one hour. Then in a calm voice he said, "You must first think about nothingness before I can tell you if there is a meaning to life."

The student was outraged that the monk wouldn't answer his question. He began to ask why the answer was again changed, but the monk's attendant wagged his finger back and forth and said, "Remember the conditions, only one question a year."

He decided to extend his stay for another year, just to find why the answer kept changing. After spending the year in deep contemplation, it was finally time.

"Master, for four years you have given me three different answers to the same question. Why do you treat me so poorly?"

This time the monk smiled, leaned forward, and immediately answered the student's question with a question, "When a new baby is hungry, do you feed him meat?

"Of course not," the student said. "If you did, he would die."

The monk laughed and then said, "Each answer I gave you was the one you could understand at the time. I gave you only what you could digest. Now I'll answer your question about the meaning of life."

Supposedly, the student went on to become a great monastic teacher. Good teaching involves knowing when our children are capable of digesting certain types of information and when they can't. Just as with a great comedian's routine, timing is a critical element for teaching. You may have the right key, but your child may not be ready for it. Good timing may not always involve waiting until your child is developmentally more mature. It can be as simple as knowing when, during the day, he or she is receptive. For example, when my son was three years old, every day I had to choose between my convenience and his capabilities. When he was tired, he'd have problems with tasks requiring even a small amount of concentration. I knew I should time those requests for when he was well rested, but I couldn't always wait. When he arrived home from preschool, he would literally and figuratively be "off-the-wall." Whatever was happening there, put him into a state where his ability to attend was minimal. If I could wait until his excessive activity decreased, he would be more successful at tasks I asked him to do, and I wouldn't become frustrated. When I placed his needs ahead of my convenience, the timing was perfect and calmness reigned in our house. When I did the reverse, there was both tension and failure.

As parents, we can't always use perfect timing—the realities of family life, work, and personal needs often interfere. However, it's important to differentiate between failure caused by the inability to adjust the environment to accommodate children's learning differences, and failure that occurs even when everything possible has been done. You'll probably find many failures are caused by interference. There's no reason to feel guilty when, for very legitimate reasons, you can't create an ideal situation to prevent failure. You're doing the best you can.

WHAT YOUR CHILD NEEDS TO DO

An ancient Chinese proverb says the teacher's role is to open the door—the responsibility of the student is to enter it. Parents and some public school teachers wish they could push children through that door. Coercion has never been the best way of enticing someone to learn. The statement is true whether we are talking about an adult, teenager, or preschooler. You can't *make* your child learn—nor can anyone else. What you can do is create a physical and emotional environment in which learning is something they desire. In the previous section, I suggested 11 simple things you can do as a teaching parent. In this section, we'll look at what children need to do to complete the equation.

Make Decisions

In the clinic, we know if children are involved in determining the course of their own therapy, they do better than if we impose everything on them.[21] The same principle applies to your children. The more involved you allow them to be in their learning and acquisition of new behaviors, the more likely they'll be successful. Providing choices not only enhances learning, but also shows your children you respect their freedom.[22] When my daughter was three months old I began allowing her to make choices. My wife, our daughter's grandparents, and most of our friends thought I had gone off the deep end. Everyone believed it was the most ridiculous thing they ever heard. After all, *choice* is a value you begin teaching to toddlers, but to a three-month-old?

"The only thing three-month-olds should be taught is to laugh," one well-meaning friend said to me.

"Are you nuts?" a more direct-speaking relative asked.

Contrary to popular beliefs and the convictions of well-meaning relatives, infants can choose.[23] Let me explain how I began to teach choice to my daughter. When I went into her room in the morning, I always held up two playsuits, one in each hand.

"Jessie, which one do you want?" I asked.

I would then dress her in whatever piece of clothing her eyes had settled on. Although she had no idea what I was saying, the activity became the basis of teaching her to be responsible for her choices. She had the freedom to choose her clothes, and her selection, by eye contact, had a consequence—the playsuit she would wear. It's been twenty-five years since I first allowed my daughter to choose her own clothing. The lessons I began at three months of age bore fruit in everything she did and currently does. When people who know my daughter as an adult talk about my early teachings of responsibility, they no longer think what I did was so bizarre.

There are three areas of choice you can give children: 1) goals, 2) activities, and 3) rewards. Choice does not necessarily have to be open-ended. You shouldn't allow your child to choose among things that aren't acceptable to you. It's usually a good idea to provide a range of choices for your child. In some cases, the range can be very narrow, such as between learning how to organize either toys or clothes. Regardless of the choice, organization is learned. The range of choice can also be larger, such as allowing the child to choose any object on a specific shelf in a toy store as a reward.

Goals

If we allow children to choose goals, they will choose either the one that is of most interest to them, or given a range of uninteresting goals, the one that's least objectionable. You get the advantage in either case. They select the goal they are most likely to complete successfully. When children are given an opportunity to select goals, they learn more quickly, develop better means for achieving them, and stay focused on the activity for a longer period of time.[24]

When my daughter was seven years old she had a slight tongue thrust—her tongue came out through her teeth, producing a lisp. She was also beginning to use "you know" frequently in her language. It was a behavior she was aware of, and didn't like. Being a speech-language pathologist, I had problems with both; I knew if left unattended, they would eventually have to be dealt with later in her life and with considerably more effort. I asked her on which of the two she preferred to work. Without any hesitation, she said, "The you knows." For whatever reason, it was more important (or less objectionable) to work on that aspect of her language than on eliminating her lisp. For me, it didn't make any difference which one she chose. When one goal was completed, we would work on the second. Within a week the "you knows" disappeared. Because of the success she felt, she asked if we could work on the lisp. Although it took longer to correct, she was equally successful.

But what if your goal is even more restricted? What if it's your daughter's room that's an abomination, not the living room, not the bathroom? That's the one and only goal on which you want her to work. What do you do? Divide the room into units: doll area, books, trains, et cetera. You can point out each area and ask her which one she wants to organize. Once that's been completed, you continue on to other sections of the room. Eventually, the entire room is organized, and your child has been given an opportunity to choose the order in which it was done. You're happy because you accomplished your goal. Your daughter is happy because she was involved in the decision-making process.

Activities

Rarely is there only one way of accomplishing a goal. Multiple paths can take us to the same destination, whether we are talking about geography or learning. Allowing children to have significant input into the selection of activities has beneficial consequences. Besides allowing them to focus on what is most important and rewarding to them, it also conveys the idea they're capable of doing things that positively affect their lives. My student clinician and I were trying to teach the concepts of "smaller" and "larger" to a four-year-old child in the clinic. My student had assembled over 20 balls for the child to use. The object of his lesson was to contrast each of the balls and have the child make a judgment as to which one was "bigger" and which was "smaller." It was a well-constructed lesson and I approved of it. However, this would be *the* activity the child would do—there were no choices. Unfortunately, the confining nature of the small clinic room overshadowed the interest the activity could generate. Not only did the child show little interest, but also when she did engage, her answers were often incorrect. I wasn't sure if she didn't understand the concept or answered incorrectly because she wasn't interested.

"Do you want to stay here or go outside?" I asked as I entered the room.

"Outside!" she enthusiastically responded.

With child, student clinician, and mother in tow, I took everyone outside to a grassy area and we all sat down on the ground.

"Mary, find something that's *bigger*," I said as I pulled a small block from my shirt pocket and dropped it in front of her. When I said "bigger" I emphasized the word and even gestured with my hands in a way indicating that whatever I wanted was larger than the block. I gave her the block and again said "find something bigger." She stood up and smiled, then walked around the grassy area, picking up twigs, leaves, pieces of paper, and even insects. As she picked up each object, she put it next to the block and compared the two. Finally she stopped and grabbed an empty hamburger container. Holding both the box and the block in front of her, she let out a yell and ran back to where we were sitting.

"Bigger," she said, handing me the greasy box.

"Yes!" I screamed. Giving her a rock I found while she was looking for a bigger object, I said, "Now find something smaller." The activity lasted for about 20 minutes, until I knew she understood. We weren't sure if she learned the concepts from the activity, or if it was just the means for demonstrating an already acquired understanding. Sometimes our children act like stealth learners, acquiring knowledge without us realizing it. By allowing children to choose the learning activity, you can eliminate the "I don't want to do it" syndrome where a cloud descends over your ability to know whether children really don't know how to do something, or like some adults, just prefer to do other things.

Children should always be allowed to choose the activity through which to achieve a learning goal. Their involvement in the decision process is an important component in successful learning.[25] This will, however, impose an additional responsibility upon you. You'll need to think about, or construct at least two different activities designed to meet the same goal. Let's say your goal is to have your child share more, something he or she will need to do in kindergarten. Your initial goal shouldn't necessarily be to have your child share everything with all children. You want to just start the process. Identify two or three toys your child doesn't care too much about. With another child in your house, ask your child to decide which toy he or she is willing to share. It really doesn't make a difference what's chosen, since the goal is the same. By continually offering choices, parents provide the greatest opportunity for children to succeed and at the same time feel good about their ability to control some aspects of their lives. It's a lesson that has important consequences throughout their lives, just like my early attempt at teaching my daughter to choose.

Rewards

Choices of rewards should be limited, given children's vivid imagination and desire for almost everything. There are various ways of accomplishing this. If the reward is an object or an activity, a token economy can be established. Children receive a token for every good response or behavior. Then, they can exchange tokens for various inexpensive items or a certain number of activity minutes, such as playing a video game. You'll learn how to establish a token economy in Chapter 5. But for now, you just need to be aware of the importance in letting your child choose the reward, within the limitations you establish. I went with a mother to a large toy store so her daughter could select a prize for completing a number of learning activities. Before we went into the store, "choice" parameters weren't set.

"Sarah, you've done so well this week, I'll let you get a new doll," the mother said as we entered the store. It was too late for me to intervene.

"I want to get the new Suzie doll with all of her friends and the house," Sarah said. She selected a $75 toy she had seen on a television advertisement.

"That's too expensive dear, something under $10."

Sarah pouted. What should have been an exciting time was transformed into something disappointing. It was as if a telemarketer said you just won an all-expense-paid trip to Paris. Your initial joy evaporated when he then rattled off what you would have to buy in order to qualify for the trip. The same thing happened with Sarah. She felt her mother promised one thing (a new doll) and then qualified it (under $10). As you define the reward parameters, remember two things. First, be very clear about boundaries and, second, discuss the range of choices *before* you enter the store.

Accept Consequences

As important as it is to allow children to choose, they also need to understand their choices have consequences. Being responsible means your children are accepting the right to choose and are willing to accept the consequences of that choice. If I choose not to practice my guitar, my poor performance can only be blamed on my choice not to practice. I may use a variety of excuses, such as I needed to work on a lecture, or spend more time with my wife.

Regardless of the reason, I *chose* to do something other than practice. There may have been good reasons for the choice, but it was still a choice I made and for which I was responsible. In this example, the element of freedom exists. I'm free to practice or not to practice.

If children are taught responsibility, they must have the freedom to choose. Without freedom, responsibility can never be learned. Without responsibility, freedom is dangerous. For fifteen years, I watched two children—the same age, from different families—grow up. The child-rearing styles of both sets of parents were radically different. One set of parents was proud they minimized the use of "no" when raising their child. They believed a basis for the healthy development of a child's ego was to fully interact with the world. For them, an integral part of that process was never denying their child anything. Going to restaurants with them and their son was a nightmare. At four years of age, he was allowed to crawl under tables, disturb people, and drive the waiters crazy. His parents thought this was important for his development. The child-rearing style of the other set of parents was very different. The importance of consequences for their daughter's actions was continually stressed. She was given an enormous amount of freedom to explore her world, but always with the understanding that along with freedom comes responsibility.

"Elizabeth, gymnastics are great. But if you want to do it, practice takes place three times a week for two hours a day and that'll mean you won't be able to watch as much television because of homework."

"I understand Dad. That's Okay."

By ten years of age, Kevin, the child from the first family was uncontrollable. His freedom to explore had neither limits nor consequences. "Responsibility" was a concept he was never taught. By 13, his parents enrolled him into the strictest military school they could find. In contrast, Elizabeth was considered one of the brightest, most delightful children in her school. By 15, she was a state champion in two gymnastics events and creative in a number of artistic areas.

Freedom and responsibility are complementary concepts. Parents who don't allow their children freedom to choose run into problems when they no longer can exert control. The child now has freedom, but has never experienced responsibility. Parents who provide freedom, but don't require their children to be responsible for their actions, set their children on an early path of irresponsibility. It's never too early for children to be given the freedom to choose, learn the consequences of their actions, and accept them. I believe this is an important principle in learning. Elizabeth is an example of what happens when children are free to choose and accept the consequences of their actions. Kevin is an example of what happens when they don't. Through your teaching, you have the opportunity to create Elizabeths or Kevins—even as preschoolers.

WHY SOME TOYS AND ACTIVITIES WORK AND OTHERS DON'T

You've just spent a large amount of money on a toy the sales person assured you your child would love. It contains over a hundred pieces and can be arranged into a multitude of shapes and different activities. You lay them out in front of your child and demonstrate some of the things that can be created. She looks at them and tries to put a few pieces together. In front of her are pictures of what can be built. For five minutes she tries to make a bridge, one of the items depicted in the photograph on the side of the box. You're delighted you purchased such a neat toy. You're sure it will occupy her for hours and, in the process, she may even develop an interest in structural engineering. Then suddenly, she turns away and begins playing with her dolls.

"Honey," you say, "why aren't you playing with the new toy I bought you?"

"It's not fun, Mommy."

Figure 2.1
Critical Features of Games and Activities

Holding Children's Interests

Critical Feature	Why It Works	Examples
Mobility	Reduces mental fatigue, engages the child	Walking around the room while doing an activity
Construction	Adds the dimension of forward movement to the learning activity	Block tower, Mr. Potato Head, Legos, pasting factial parts onto a facial outline
Destruction	Gives child control doing something usually not acceptable	Knocking down a block tower
Material and Activity Movement	Engages child, adds dimension of forward	Moveable pieces on a board game, or non-board game
Completion	Sense of fulfillment or achievement	Activities having a discrete end point
Flexibility	Sustains interest in the material/activity	Bottle caps, sticks, pieces of multicolored paper, balls, blocks, paper plates, cups, etc.
Surprise	Maintains attention	Items kept in a bag, shoe boxes full of items

You're very confused. This thing cost $150, all the parent magazines touted it as one of the best new toys of the year, and your child found it boring in less than five minutes. But was it really boring or just too confusing? Often children appear to be bored with something that adults believe *should* be exciting. Sometimes the problem is not in the toy, but in the match between the child and the toy. Children constantly give clues to parents regarding what interests them. First, rule out boredom related to a poorly designed toy. There are seven critical features of toys and activities that have held children's interests for centuries.[26] They appear in Figure 2.1. If games and activities don't contain at least one of these critical features, they may be truly boring, regardless of your child's learning style. But when you see a game or activity that has many of these features and your child still appears to be bored, it may be a mismatch. These same features are also important in your design of learning activities.

Mobility

Children enjoy mobility, whether it is only one part of their body or actually physical movement around the room. Many classic children's games have this as their predominant focus and haven't changed for generations. "Hide and go seek" is one example. Children have been fascinated by this free game for generations. Every country seems to have a version of this game that has been played for centuries.[27] You can use mobility as the vehicle in which learning occurs. I worked with a family whose child was labeled "hyperactive." What I saw was a child with an enormous amount of energy. Whether he deserved the "hyperactive" label was questionable. Regardless of whether or not the label was justified, I realized we could use his energy as a way of enhancing his learning. We wanted to increase his ability to categorize items, such as toys, fruits, liquids, et cetera. I placed three boxes in front of him. We gave him a card with pictures of the type of items we wished him to find (concept). Underneath the cards were more pictures of three rooms, numbered one through three. The cards and boxes appear in Figure 2.2. We instructed him to go to each room in the order they appeared and look for three things similar to the picture on his card. When found, he was to place them inside their matching box. His parents had planted the objects earlier in each room. It was an exciting game for him; he learned the concept, worked on his organization skills, and his "hyperactivity," which could have interfered with his learning, helped facilitate it.

Figure 2.2
Finding Concepts in the House

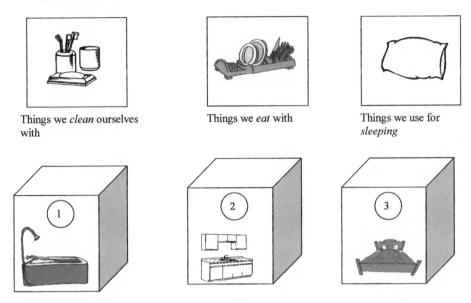

Things we *clean* ourselves with

Things we *eat* with

Things we use for *sleeping*

Construction

Children love to build and construct. It's natural to put things together to create something new, exciting, and intriguing. From one type of object, another unique one is formed. That's probably the appeal of toys such as Lego blocks whose popularity and acceptance has endured since 1949 when they were first developed.[28] Various types of construction activities can be used with children, from placing the facial features on a Mr. Potato Head to the elaborate construction of a Lego airplane. When I work with young children in their homes, I always bring a toy that can be constructed and has at least 20 parts. The child sees a picture of the finished product and becomes excited about actually constructing it.

"Lisa," I said to a three-year-old, "I'll give you a part of the dollhouse every time you use slow speech until the bell rings."

Not only was she excited about constructing the dollhouse, but she also equated the learning activity (prolonged speech) with something enjoyable. Although I wanted to limit the practice activity to ten minutes each hour, it was difficult getting her to stop. Try to find something your child is interested in doing. For Lisa, it was playing "house" with her dolls. For another child, there was nothing better than trains. Once you identify the interest area, then go to your local toy store and find an item in that category that can be constructed. Art projects tend to require more closure than other activities. I remember bringing a child to tears when I said she had to stop working with a pile of clay before completing a head of a man, an activity that had been going on for ten minutes. That was the last time I used clay during learning activities. The same suggestion should also apply with the use of paints. Art projects demand completion, regardless of the time it takes.

Destruction

The opposite of construction is destruction. The process of destroying something is not necessarily negative or a sign of frustration. Rather, it can be viewed as an attempt at control. Children may not have much control over their lives, but they can knock a block tower over, and it's acceptable. They are usually told when to eat, sleep, play, stand, walk, and talk. As they get older, parents and other adults sometimes reluctantly give up some control. Given the limitations placed on them, it's understandable why children not only would be fascinated by opportunities to express their limited power, but also seek it out. There is something exciting about the destruction of physical objects. How often do you repeatedly watch the demolition of a building on your nightly television news? When teaching children, this fascination can be harnessed by allowing them to destroy something. It can be as simple as a block tower or something more creative.

My daughter loved popping air pockets on packing sheets. It became an ideal reinforcer for working on her articulation. For every five correct productions, she was allowed to pop a pocket. And with 100 pockets on each sheet, I knew she would practice the sound 500 times without becoming bored. She never seemed to tire of this "destructive" activity. Yet, she never generalized it into anything antisocial. When you think of destruction, it doesn't necessarily have to be negative.

Movement

Activities should have an element of movement. This is the counterpart of physical mobility. It can be as minimal as moving a game piece along a path, or having a marble move through a maze of holes. Movement creates dynamism, which isn't present in things such as the use of pictures. Additionally, movement that is contingent upon a correct response can tell you and your child that progress is being made. Unfortunately, there's a tendency on the part of parents, teachers, and therapists to use board games too much.[29] They're cheap, easy to use and most of the time enjoyable. I rarely use them when working with children who have learning problems. Most have little to do with the child's everyday world. Yet, many are as popular today as they were when I was a child over 50 years ago. Surely, there is nothing terribly exciting about the *content* of games like Chutes and Ladders first published in 1943 and Monopoly, which has been sold in stores since 1935. Yet, these are two of the all-time most popular children's board games. They work because there's movement and also surprise. Children never know what card they'll choose or how far their piece can be moved. You can easily construct a game having the same principles. Just make movement and surprise the important components in the activity. Also try to integrate the activity within your child's normal environment.

I worked with a child who was fascinated by little cars. He could play with them for hours. His parents and I decided to use this activity to teach him how to follow directions. We constructed four cities in the house—in the living room, kitchen, bathroom, and dining room. The game involved players driving their cars from one city to another. The cars also had to take a specified route. He loved it and learned to follow directions. With both parents playing, I became the traffic cop and decided if drivers were following the instructions. On cue from me, the parents would occasionally go to the wrong city or go by a route I didn't specify. We used these opportunities to test his ability to correct errors. It was a wonderful game, didn't cost anything since all objects were already purchased, and because he was excited about it, he was successful.

Completion

Be sure your child has sufficient time to complete an activity that involves construction. There are few things as frustrating to a child as being allowed to begin a project and then being forced to stop before it's completed. Not being allowed to complete a project often will result in the child developing resentment. For example, a parent gave her child a sheet of paper with a figure outlined on it. The mother requested that her son, who had poor fine motor control, color within the lines. The occupational therapist had told her this activity would help her son develop fine motor skills. She also told her to limit the activity to no more than ten minutes since as the child tired, the practice wouldn't be that effective. At the ten-minute mark, the mother said, "Alright John, let's stop now." Although the activity was well thought out by the therapist and involved a reinforcing activity, it became problematic when the child wanted to finish coloring the entire sheet of paper before doing anything else.

Activities involving construction should be designed so their completion doesn't interfere with the learning goals. As I wrote earlier, the use of clay in an activity could be a disaster since the intended object never seems to be completed. The malleability of the medium lends itself to ever-changing forms. Painting also fits into this category. Although some parents attempt to place a time limit on constructive activities, problems will persist. Children are less attuned to time parameters than they are by parameters simply imposed by the activity itself. A game isn't really over when a bell rings; it's over when someone wins. A picture isn't completed until it's completed, regardless of how long it takes. A play scenario isn't done until the intended themes are fully expressed. Don't present something "big" to the child when focusing on completion as a key feature in a learning activity. Use small units. For example, as the mother who was working with her son on his fine motor skills realized, although the activity given to her by the occupational therapist could be effective, it contained a design flaw. Instead of a complete uncolored picture, she later decided to give her son a figure or object that was completed except for one small part. A picture of a man only needed his head colored. A house had everything completed except the chimney. By minimizing the extent of the creative aspects of the task, her son was able to concentrate on the development of fine motor skills. These activities still had the element of completion, but now they were manageable.

Flexibility

Flexibility should be an important feature of toys and activities. Watch the excitement of children as they open their presents on a holiday morning; they are easily amazed by complex toys that seem to do incredible things all by themselves. Two weeks later observe how often the toy is used, if you can even find it. Activities and materials that can only do one thing tend to lose their interest for children in a relatively short period of time. Consider this when selecting materials. If you will be using something whose functions and use are fixed, don't spend much time or money on its construction or purchase. Also don't expect your child to remain interested in it for very long.

The effects of disregarding this principle became painfully obvious to a new clinician I supervised who was assigned to work with a young child with learning problems. Over the weekend, she spent over 20 hours constructing what she called "a coat of many pockets." It was a magnificent jacket on which had been sewn over 50 pockets. The pockets were at various angles. They were different in size, shape, and color. There were even pockets within pockets. Some had chutes leading from one pocket to another. The clinician was sure she had developed the ultimate clinical tool for this child. She had shown brilliance in her imagination. When therapy began and the clinician began her pocket activity, the child turned away after a few minutes and started to play with a box of tissues. The tissues became parachutes, flags, and blankets to cover dolls. The coat of many pockets was only a coat of many pockets. Objects which are flexible hold children's interest for a much longer period of time since they can become something new when a current activity becomes boring. For example, a common bottle cap involves no construction or cost, yet can become a tiddlywink, flying saucer, noisemaker, or a facial imprint marker. Use your creativity and time designing in flexibility rather than "wow-ing" your child with one-dimensional toys and games.

Surprise

The unknown excites most children, whether it involves the outcome of a story or the next step in a game. Surprise can be easily incorporated into most activities. One parent I knew routinely kept everything for a learning activity in a large brown paper bag. A face was painted on the bag with a gaping hole for the mouth.

"Okay Billy, I have five things in this bag."

"Can I see Mommy?"

"Yes. But you can pick out only one of them at a time. Then we'll play with it."

The child thrust his hand through a small slit in the bag and pulled out a doll made out of rubber.

"That's perfect," the mother said as she took the doll. "Remember the game we played yesterday?"

"Yes, Mommy. You hid my car and I had to find it.

"That's right. Now I'll hide Gumby. Just like yesterday with your car, I'll give you hints where he's hiding. So you have to listen very carefully."

Although the child knew the goal of the activity, which was following directions, he never was sure what his mother would use to accomplish it. The mother would never select an item previously used. She would have her child put his hand into the bag and pull out an object. By constantly changing objects, the element of surprise was always present and the child was always eager to do the learning activity.

While surprise is a good secondary feature of a learning activity, try not to rely on it as a primary one. Surprise is momentary. Once the newness of an object or activity becomes old, it may lose its effectiveness. The mother in the above example never relied just on surprise to keep her son's interest in the activity. She used movement, construction, and flexibility in the activities. Surprise was just an extra element.

Competition

Although many would argue the competitive urge is universally found in children, cultural data suggest the opposite.[30] Some parents believe competition in young children is detrimental, while others believe it is the core of success as an adult. Competition can be negative if a child consistently loses, loses in a demeaning manner, views failures as a reflection of something missing in his or her personality, or can only succeed through a painful effort. Conversely, children who are completely noncompetitive are thought by some parents to be disadvantaged when they become adults. Regardless of one's position, competition can be incorporated into learning activities in a way that's positive, if three rules are applied.

1. Children should compete only with their past performances.
2. The activity should be designed so successes are easy.
3. If children are not successful, they shouldn't view it as a reflection on their personality.

I once worked with a child who had memory problems. His mother often asked him to do things that involved three to five steps (e.g., go up to your room, put all your toys away, and then bring down your dirty clothes). Even when the directions were given in a quiet setting and the child understood what was to be done, within ten minutes he forgot parts of the instructions. I taught the mother how to make simple requests and record her child's responses on a large poster board.

"John, I want you to look here on this board. Today is Monday and I'm going to ask you to bring down something from your room. We'll do this five times. Each time you get it right, I'll put a big star in one box."

"What are the other boxes for Mommy?"

"This one's for tomorrow," she said pointing to the second column. Tomorrow we'll see if you can get more stars than you did today."

In this activity, the child competed only with himself. An adversarial relationship was never developed. The sequence appears in Figure 2.3. For Tuesday, six boxes appeared. Each day for a week, another box was added. By the end of the week, the child successfully remembered nine individual assignments. The following week, the same sequence was repeated, but the mother gave two-part instructions.

Figure 2.3
Children Competing with Themselves

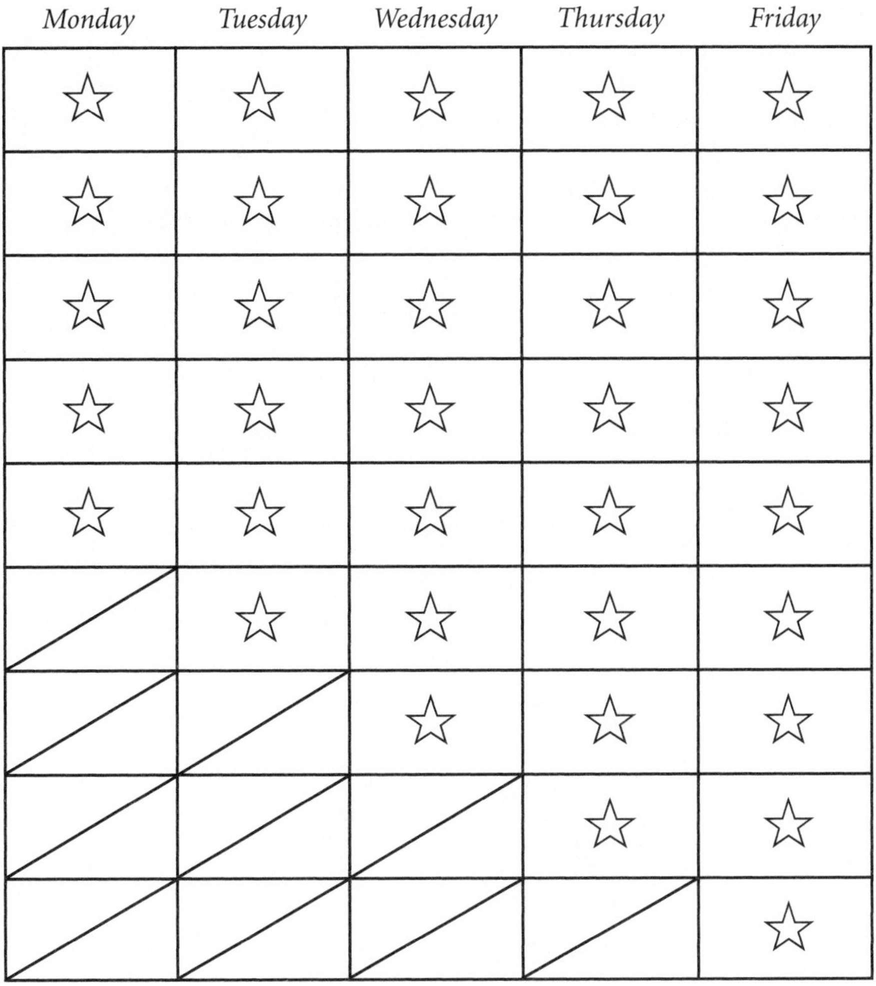

Monday	Tuesday	Wednesday	Thursday	Friday
☆	☆	☆	☆	☆
☆	☆	☆	☆	☆
☆	☆	☆	☆	☆
☆	☆	☆	☆	☆
☆	☆	☆	☆	☆
	☆	☆	☆	☆
		☆	☆	☆
			☆	☆
				☆

EFFORT AND JOY

The excitement of teaching something totally new to a child is one of the most joyous moments for parents, and given the nature of a child's world, it can be a daily occurrence. If done correctly, few things are as rewarding. You may think the effort required will leave you exhausted. Nothing can be further from the truth. Think of your life as a car battery and your child as the car's engine. The battery becomes charged when a belt attached to the engine turns an alternator. The alternator spins and creates electricity that goes into the battery and is stored for future use. If the car isn't started for months, the battery drains. If the car is driven with a loose belt, no electricity is generated and, eventually, the battery becomes discharged. However, with a properly tightened belt and a regularly driven car, electricity is generated and the battery remains fully charged. The journey your child takes will either deplete your energy or enhance it. Keep that belt property tightened and a trip from New York to California becomes a joy. Allow the belt to loosen, and you may get stuck on a back road in Nevada at midnight with smiling coyotes looking down on you from a bluff.

THREE

Understanding Your Child's Feelings

*J*oyce fluctuated between shy and aggressive. Around other children, she refused to play, even when they approached her first. She never initiated play or conversation. At three years of age, Joyce had a number of behaviors that caused her parents concern. They consulted a noted child psychologist who specialized in learning differences. His observations were identical to those reported by the parents. However, his assessment of why the behaviors occurred was different. While the parents looked inward for reasons about how they may have caused their child to have behavioral and psychological problems, the psychologist saw the problems as originating from Joyce's learning differences. She had problems with storing information. Together with her parents, he developed a simple intervention program, in which first Joyce's learning differences were addressed, and then she was reintroduced to play activities with other children. The shyness that hid her embarrassment at not being able to do certain activities gradually diminished. She finally understood how to play with children and enjoyed their company. Her aggressiveness, which was a reaction to continued failure, abruptly stopped since she was continually succeeding at the activities designed by the psychologist.

Children with learning differences often hide their problem through behaviors that can be misunderstood.[1] That's not to say all inappropriate behaviors are rooted in learning differences. I worked with a child whose anger was pervasive. No matter what her mother would do, her daughter's inappropriate anger would erupt in ways embarrassing the mother and making language therapy impossible.

"I know her anger is related to problems with language," the mother said to me right after an outburst.

"Are there certain types of situations in which you tend to see her anger arise?" I asked.

The mother thought for a moment, then said, "No. She has these outbursts at least four times a day, sometimes they're mild, at other times she's out of control."

I asked the mother to keep a simple notebook for describing the outbursts—no evaluations, just observations of what was occurring before, during, and after the event. After looking at the notebook the following week and observing the child for two sessions, I came to the conclusion the anger wasn't related to problems with language. I referred her to a child psychologist who was more qualified than I to deal with the problem. Her assessment, and the one that proved correct, was the child was having a great deal of difficulty sharing her parent's love with a new baby brother. The psychologist gave the parents suggestions with specific courses of action that could be used to modify family interactions. The anger dissipated, and we were able to resume language therapy in two months.

At times you may be able to differentiate emotional reactions related to a learning problem from ones that are not. Look at the activities occurring just before the behavior, during it and immediately afterward. With Joyce, there were no obvious patterns relating to her learning problems. The reliance on good observation is important, not only when looking at anger, but for any emotion that appears inappropriate. If, after reading this chapter, you can't tell if the reactions are related to learning differences, contact a professional.

WHEN YOUR CHILD KNOWS SOMETHING IS WRONG

We either don't give young children enough credit to know they're different, or we hope they won't see it. When they realize they're failing, either through the inability to accomplish something, or by the reactions of others, an emotional pall can overcome them that not only affects their current feelings, but also how they may view themselves throughout life.[2] What may seem inconsequential to others may stay a focal point throughout adulthood. One of my best graduate students always appeared to be tentative when explaining something to me or presenting a therapy program. I knew it was more than being humble. Something else was going on.

"I have a question for you Janice," I said.

She looked as if the weight of the world was about to be dropped on her.

"Yes Dr. Goldberg?" she said, her eyes avoiding mine.

"You're one of my best clinicians. Your work is impeccable, you interact beautifully with children, parents are pleased, and your skill level is far beyond that of other students. Yet, you always seem so tentative. Why are you so unsure of yourself?"

After a pause, she looked at me and said, "I have a learning disability. Throughout school I was made to feel I couldn't succeed. And I did fail a lot.

But eventually I learned how to grasp things as well as everyone else. I just did it a little differently."

"But that was the past." I said. "You're a very successful young lady now."

Tears started to form as she said, "When I was very young I hid my feelings from everyone, even my parents. No matter how successful I am, my past is always in my present."

"I don't understand. How can something that happened when you were a child still affect you now?"

She took a deep breath and proceeded to teach me something I didn't realize about the persistence of a feeling many adults still have about their differences.

"When I'm working with a child, I'm always wondering if I'll to be quick enough to figure out what I should do next. When I was young, it took me more time to process things than other kids. I did fine when I had enough time. But I'd crumble when the pressure was on. I still get that feeling whenever I have to change something quickly with a child."

"But whenever I've observed you, I never noticed any delay in your reactions. I couldn't see any processing problems. Not only that, but you always shift therapy in the right direction."

"I know," she said quietly. "It doesn't make any difference that I do everything right—the feeling never leaves."

I found this phenomenon in many adults, ranging from a successful vice president of a major corporation to someone working for minimum wages at a fast-food restaurant. For many people, *feelings persist even though behaviors change*. I don't know if my student ever got over her fear of not being able to react quickly enough. However, she opened my eyes to the importance of minimizing failures children experience. The ability to understand and express these feelings may be beyond the linguistic and cognitive ability of very young children.[3] They may hide them because they are too painful to face, they don't want to disappoint you, or they may not fully understand them.[4] I've found in my practice if the feeling of failure can be eliminated or prevented early in a child's life, they tend not to be present when they become adults. Unfortunately, the reverse is also true. Failure messages can persist for years or even a lifetime.

The Messages

Feedback alerts children they didn't do the task correctly. When your child fails, use feedback as an opportunity to correct the problem. When my son would have trouble with short-term memory, I would make the failure message into one that was positive.

Figure 3.1
Graphic Cues for Storytelling Comprehension

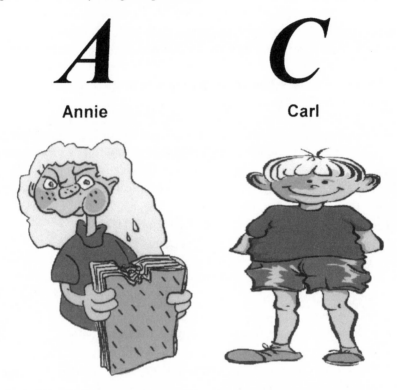

"Justin, you didn't remember the names of the little boy and girl in the story."

"I know Daddy."

"Let's see if there is something we can do to make it easier. I'll draw a picture of the girl and the boy. I'll put the first letter of the girl's name on this side of the paper over her picture and the letter for the boy over his picture. A for Annie and C for Carl." Pictures similar to the one I originally used appear in Figure 3.1.

"Can we read some more, Daddy, about Annie and Carl?"

"Of course we can Justin."

As I read, I pointed to the picture of the child mentioned in the story. Instead of allowing Justin to feel he couldn't succeed, we used the failure message as a springboard for success. The strategy I used is known as *multiple cueing*. It's nothing more than providing a series of cues that help children learn. Gradually you fade the cues out. It was important for my son to feel he was accomplishing something without needing me to provide the complete answer. That's also a principle in all learning activities. *Never give the complete answer unless all else fails.* Think of this as mental gymnastics. By requiring children to choose between two things rather than giving them the correct answer, their little brains are required to do a few push-ups. It's not a big deal, but even something as simple as choosing between two things in order to find the right answer helps their intelligence develop.[5] Whenever we read together, I would provide Justin with pictures of the people, objects, or places in the story. His short-term memory dramatically improved. Recently, researchers have found mental exercises even help slow down the cognitive deterioration of Alzheimer's patients.[6]

Sometimes as children struggle to solve a problem, you can witness how they attempt to solve it. When this happens, you can gain a unique insight into the type of error your child is making. For example, a child is given a wooden block puzzle; she has to correctly orientate each piece to make it fit. As pieces are placed within the cutout form, the child receives a message: It's right or it's wrong. The correct or incorrect message given to the child is related to the process of putting a puzzle together. Parents may wish to walk their children through the failed activity with hints of how they could have done it *differently*. Let's look at the example of a child who puts a puzzle piece upside down in a puzzle frame and doesn't understand why it won't fit.

"Deborah, let's look at this piece."

"Alright Mommy."

"Does it look right?"

"Yes Mommy."

At this point, the mother has a choice of making this a passive or an active correction. A passive correction would involve the mother saying something like, "No, it's not right." Then the mother places the piece in correctly and says, "This is how it should go." While taking a minimal amount of time, it's not as helpful as following more active learning approaches.[7] In active learning, the following would occur.

"Deborah, look at this piece," the mother says as she points to another piece that was placed in the form correctly (Figure 3.2). Pointing to both pieces she says, "Is this one like that one?"

"No Mommy, they look different."

"How do they look different?"

"This one's down and that sticks up."

"That's right Deborah. What can we do to make this one look like that one?"

"I don't know."

"Let's try turning it."

Deborah kept moving the piece randomly, often getting close to placing the

Figure 3.2
Puzzle Piece Example

piece in correctly, but never quite doing it right. If the mother could introduce a more structured approach, the problem would be solved.

"Deborah watch me," the mother said as she pulls out a correctly placed puzzle piece and puts it incorrectly into its hole. "I'm going to move it like this," she said as she slowly moved the piece clockwise until it fit into the hole. "Now you do it with your piece."

"Okay Mommy," she said mirroring her mother's movement. As she turned it clockwise the piece dropped into the form.

"I did it Mommy! I did it!"

In this example, the mother did a number of very simple things that helped her daughter not only understand that an error occurred, but also what could be done to correct it.

1. Gave feedback
2. Provided an example of a correct placement
3. Gave her daughter an opportunity to solve the problem using a strategy (unsuccessful)
4. Modeled the correct behavior
5. Again allowed her daughter to solve the problem (successful)

The mother reacted to her daughter's failure by continually providing cues that enabled her to solve the puzzle. As you watch your children attempt to do things that result in failure messages, take the time to walk them through a strategy that will result in success. Don't provide the correct answer until you've exhausted all learning strategies. Requiring them to choose between answers when the correct one isn't known strengthens children's learning ability. Even just asking your child to answer "yes" or "no" or choosing between two easy answers provides an opportunity for strengthening the learning process. For example, a mother was working on having her son remember two-part instructions, something that eluded him. He usually would get the second part of the instruction correct (*then, bring your toy train to me*), but would often forget the first part (*Sam, put your shirt into the dresser and…*). She began the correction when he brought a doll instead of the train.

"Sam, I didn't ask for a doll. Do you remember the toy I asked for?"

"Not a doll Mommy?"

"No Sam, Was it a train or your pillow?"

"My train!"

By not telling him directly what the toy was, Sam was forced to go through a cognitive process of matching the past direction and the current cue. The choices posed in the mother's question were very distinctive. The purpose was to make it easy for Sam. However, later in his training, she required him to make finer distinctions, such as choosing between the train and the bus. Always try to give your child choices when an error is made. Your feedback can turn an unsuccessful experience into one that's successful. There are two types of instructive feedback: *simple* and *explanatory*.

Simple feedback is passive. It can be used for children who you don't think can independently correct the problem even with very direct cues. For example, a child is having a great deal of difficulty understanding why a puzzle piece doesn't fit. The picture of the completed puzzle is placed in front of him and then the instruction begins.

"Your pieces are upside down. Look at this picture. See how it's done? Now you put them in just like this one."

This simple feedback strategy uses *modeling*. It merely requires the child to match what he or she is doing to what is seen. You've used this strategy everyday of your child's life. As you talked to your child, you present a language model your child tries to emulate. Initially, he or she doesn't do it perfectly. Sounds or words may be missing. You may have said, "This is milk," to which your child responded, "milk." Modeling is a widely used learning strategy that is very effective.[8] However, it presupposes the child understands the model and while not capable of imitating the whole, can pick out the relevant parts. For example, a father says, "Oh my, look at how fast that airplane is flying." His three-year-old son tries to imitate the father's linguistic structure, but can only focus on a few parts. He says, "Fast airplane." Although modeling is effective, it's not as important as explanatory feedback in developing a child's cognitive ability.

With explanatory feedback you provide strategies that help your child independently solve problems. For example, a child is trying to match a Mr. Potato Head he's constructing with the one that appears on the box. He can tell the two are different, but doesn't know where to begin to change his version. Your role is to get him on the right track, then step back. First, you place the box with its picture next to his figure, and then begin your explanatory feedback.

"Let's look at the picture on the box," you say. "First, look at the ears. Are they where you put them on the head?"

"No," your child says after comparing his object with the one on the box.

"Where can we place this one so it looks like that one?" you say, pointing to the right ear of both the picture and his Mr. Potato Head.

Without any hesitation, he moves the ear to the correct position.

"Now, how can we make this ear look like that ear?" you say, pointing to the left ear.

Again, without any hesitation the left ear is correctly positioned. With explanatory feedback, you allow children to connect the dots, a process that helps develop cognitive ability. Although explanatory feedback has more benefits than simple feedback, you may not always be able to use it. At times your child may be too impatient to go through the entire process. Or because of other activities, you just may not have the time. Using either form of feedback is significantly more beneficial than just giving the correct answer.

Parents as Messengers

We have all heard the often-quoted line "don't kill the messenger," as if the messenger is a neutral figure just delivering a message. The quote assumes the two are separate. Nothing can be further from the truth with children. When looking at error messages given to children, the message and the messenger are equally important. In fact, at times the messenger may overshadow the message. When children fail, they may receive feedback from adults and other children. As parents, we are constantly giving our children feedback. It can be as direct as telling them they did something wrong, or indirect as when you show disapproval by your posture.

Parents are giant billboards constantly broadcasting messages to their children. We tend to only think about the verbal messages. Yet that's only one of five ways in which messages are sent.[9] Parents can send messages through their choice of words (*you did that wrong*), tone of voice (*negative or disappointed tone*), nonverbal behaviors (*a frown or nonengaging posture*), and consequences they impose (*you didn't do that right, so no ice cream tonight*). From early infancy, children have shown the ability to attach certain types of emotions to a parent's tone of voice and nonverbal behaviors.[10] This ability predates a child's understanding of words. As language is learned, there is less reliance on intonation and nonverbal behaviors, yet both remain important. We're so focused on the use of language we're not aware of a significant amount of information sent through intonation and nonverbal behaviors—unfortunately, children are.

Words

We often aren't aware of the words we choose when talking to our children, nor their impact. Think of all words as having one of three qualities: negative, neutral, or positive. We're not going to bother with neutral words, only ones that give positive or negative messages. While researchers and child psychologists could spend endless pages discussing gradations of these words and a range of emotions they could trigger, as a parent, your needs are different. You need something more practical and useful. A small list of words I believe carry either a positive or negative impact appears in Figure 3.3. Some words, such as *bad* are almost always negative. However, others, such as *shouldn't*, can

Figure 3.3
Positive and Negative Words

Positive	Negative
yes	no
terrific	bad
wonderful	not good
great	poor
perfect	miserable
good	wrong
correct	incorrect
right	ugly
beautiful	disappointing
happy	sad
thank you	stop*
sorry	don't*
do	can't*
can	shouldn't*
should	naughty
OK	
nice	

*May not be negative, depending upon the context

often be either positive or negative depending upon the context. It's not that neutral words aren't important, they are. Think of them as a communication highway on which everything else flows. What draws a child's attention are the speed bumps appearing on the highway, the positive and negative words. When my graduate students or I treat children, I insist parents become co-therapists. Part of the preparation is analyzing verbal interactions with their child. I was working with a mother whose relationship with her son was very negative. She loved him, and if anything was overly protective. In spite of her efforts to gain his love, he seemed to remain aloof. She had no idea why. I audiotaped the entire one-hour session of the mother and child working with my graduate student. Before the next weekly session, I asked her to come in for a conference.

"I know you are very concerned about the relationship with your son."

"Yes," she said.

"I also know you love him very much." She nodded in agreement. "Do you have any idea where the problem lies?"

She sighed deeply and then said, "No. I've thought about it over and over again, and I don't understand."

I pulled out the tape recorder and the transcription I made of last week's session. I've found parents often can't hear or remember what they say to their children. Often what they think they said isn't even close. Worse is their interpretation of the message's meaning. A tape recorder acts as a mirror of truth.

"I tape recorded the interaction with your son last week. On balance, do you think it was more positive than negative?"

"I thought is was very positive. I kept trying to help him."

"I've edited the tape so the only things we'll hear are the words you said to him."

As we listened to the tape, she finally understood why she was having problems with her son. For the 50-minute session, 50 percent of her utterances had at least one negative word in them. Some of these appear in the left column of Figure 3.4. Usually, there was also a negative tone. We looked at the transcript and I explained what she thought of as "helpful" were really critical statements.

Figure 3.4
Transforming Negative into Instructive Statements

Negative	Instructive
Didn't I tell you that you couldn't do that? Can't you listen?	I know you would like to play with that toy, but right now we are working on your speech.
We went over that last week after therapy. Why can't you remember it?	I know that it may be hard to remember the things you did last week. Let's see if we can make it easier.
You're acting like a bad boy.	I don't like it when you run around the room.
How could you have done that?	I don't understand why you did that. Can you tell me?
When I say no, I mean no!	Remember, we agreed at the beginning that we wouldn't play with the ball until all the work was finished.
Well, you finally got it right.	That was great! You continued trying until you got it right.
You didn't misbehave as much this week as you did last week.	Your behavior was so much better this week.

The ears of children act as fine-tuned receptors. They don't hear subtle innuendoes, minor qualifications, or abstract ideas. What are pulled out of parents' statements are words that are concrete and simple. Words like "no," "bad," "wrong," and "terrible" so overshadow everything else, nothing else may be heard. Choose your words wisely. That doesn't mean if children do something wrong, they shouldn't face negative consequences, just that parents have options in the way they can express concerns. A child knocks a carton of milk off the table and a parent decides to admonish him. Which of the following two statements would you find more acceptable? Less demeaning?

What's wrong with you? How could you have done that?

or

You know, when you put the milk on the edge of the table it's easy for it to drop on the floor.

Both statements refer to the same event. The first statement is an attack on the child's very being. Behaviors can be easily corrected, core personalities can't. It says he or she isn't all right. And framed in the words chosen, there's little the child can do to correct it. There's nothing instructive in the first statement. It's just damaging. The second statement is instructive; it contains the essence of teaching. It says nothing about the child's cognitive ability or personality—it focuses on a behavior. The statement not only says the behavior was wrong, but also gives instructions for how to correct it next time. The mother and I, using this comparison, looked at the transcript and I showed her how each of her negative statements could be transformed into something instructive. The transformation appears in the right column of Figure 3.4.

We don't want to do anything that will hurt our children. Unfortunately, without ever realizing it, we often do. In the heat of the moment, or when our minds are occupied by something else, we may not be aware of what we say. Words may be spoken that your child was never meant to hear. But, it's just like the unattended barn door; once it's open, the horses leave. Many parents are unaware of the language patterns they use. To become more aware, I've developed an easy and informative exercise that many parents find helpful. Audiotape your interaction with your child for 30 minutes. Disregard the first 10 minutes. During that time you'll be too conscious of what you're saying to be natural. But listen to the remaining 20 minutes. Use this tape not only to analyze the words you are using, but also your tone of voice, which is covered in the next section. For this first exercise, write down each sentence you said and your child's verbal reaction. A blank form is provided in Figure 3.5 (see next page). Compare the positive and negative words you use with those listed in Figure 3.3. If there is a positive word in your sentence, color it with a blue marker. If it contains a negative word, use a red marker. Do the same for your child's reactions. You might begin to see a pattern in how your child reacts to the words you use. Try to increase the number of positive words and decrease the number of negative ones. As the balance shifts from negative to positive, I think you will see the same shift in your relationship with your child. Additionally, his or her self-image will become more positive.

Tone

How often have you said to someone, "It's not what you say, but how you say it?" Children pick up on the intonation patterns of parents before they do the meaning of words.[11] It's not surprising they can detect joy, love, appreciation, disappointment, and anger, regardless of the words you choose. During a time in my life when I was overwhelmed with work, I still tried to spend as much time as I could with my children. My daughter was seven years old and my son three. I thought I was doing a reasonably good job of hiding my frustrations with the internal politics of the university. That is, until I heard my daughter talking to my wife.

"Mommy, why is Daddy always angry?

"I don't understand Jessie. Has he been saying angry things to you?"

"No Mommy, he never says angry words."

Figure 3.5
Analyzing Your Audiotape

Write in yours and your child's statements for 20 minutes. Color every positive word or statement with a blue marker. Use a red marker for negative words or statements. Look for patterns and compare the number of negative to positive statements.

	Your Statements	Your Child's Responses
1		
2		
3		
4		
5		
6		
7		
8		
9		
10		
11		
12		
13		
14		
15		

Positive	
Negative	

Positive	
Negative	

"Then why do you think he's angry."

"He *sounds* angry."

Although I always chose my words carefully, I couldn't hide the frustration I was feeling with events not related to my family. Unfortunately, my daughter couldn't tell my anger had nothing to do with her. All she heard was a negative intonation pattern—the words were secondary. Just like my daughter, your children may have difficulty knowing your negative intonation pattern has nothing to do with them. Even more problematic is when you are having some negative feelings about your child and believe because the words are positive, so also will be the message. You may be fooling yourself. Children learn to recognize their parents' intonation patterns. No parent's pattern is identical. However, we are amazingly consistent when it comes to our intonations.[12] It's almost as if they've been given a shot of truth serum that takes its effects when we aren't consciously trying to use this communication medium to deliver a specific message. Children learn to associate these patterns with specific behaviors and feelings.[13]

When your child does something particularly endearing to you, think about the intonation pattern you use. Then think about something that made you angry. How did the pattern change? As the patterns are continually associated with specific events, children learn quickly what their parents are feeling, and react accordingly. Although there are many different types of intonation patterns, try to identify on the audiotape you made for the prior section, those you use to convey seven different emotions. There's no one intonation pattern that's the same for everyone in spite of what some popular books profess. A Supreme Court Justice, Oliver Wendell Holmes, said he couldn't define pornography, but he knew it when he saw it. The same is true for intonation patterns. I've found parents can easily identify their own ways of expressing these emotions even though they might not be able to explain or define them. Don't be concerned it isn't the "right one." In Figure 3.6, place one letter to identify each emotion in the right column of the form. There will be many statements you'll identify as neutral. These could involve descriptions, answers to questions, or asking your child to do something. Don't be concerned about these. It's not that they aren't important, but in this section we're concerned about those intonation patterns that may have either a negative or positive effect on your child's learning. You're going to identify two things in this exercise. The first is to look at the balance of intonation patterns. Ideally, there should be more love, joy, humor, and encouragement statements than ones identified as containing either disappointment or anger. When a concern statement is identified, there should be something that indicates the concern is about a behavior, not something related to your child's personality. I worked with a father who took genuine joy in his three-year-old daughter,

Figure 3.6
Identifying Your Emotions

Once again look at your statements in Figure 3.5. Label each one using the code below.

L = Love   C = Concern
J = Joy   D = Disappointment
H = Humor   A = Anger
E = Encouragement   N = Neutral

Statement Number	Emotion
1	
2	
3	
4	
5	
6	
7	
8	
9	
10	
11	
12	
13	
14	
15	

Total Number of Emotion Statements

	Emotion	Number of Statements
L	Love	
J	Joy	
H	Humor	
E	Encouragement	
C	Concern	
D	Disappointment	
A	Anger	
N	Neutral	

whether it be in the way she asked for something or even in something with which she was having difficulty. His intonation pattern was consistently positive with a corresponding effect upon his daughter.

The second exercise involves examining whether or not there is consistency between your intonation and your words. As long as there is consistency, you're sending a unified message to your children—they hear that you love them, not only in the words you chose, but also in how you said it. Problems occur when the tone and words aren't in agreement.

"Mommy, I love you," a three-year-old says to his mother, after breaking an expensive antique.

"Yes, I love you too," the mother responds using an angry tone after seeing the broken object.

When children are faced with conflicting messages, they rely on their most competent communication channels—intonation and certain nonverbal behaviors.[14] A child, who hears the words "I love you," carried on an undeniable tone of anger, either becomes confused, or relies on the intonation pattern. Children use intonation patterns to know how their parents are feeling. Once you are aware of their importance, you'll also notice the message being sent to your child—regardless of the words being used. In many cases, it's as important as your words. In other cases, it's even more so.

Nonverbal Behaviors

Every part of your body has the ability to send messages to your child: face, arms, hands, legs, and posture. We monitor some of them, such as our face and posture, and so do our children. From a very early age, they associate certain facial displays with parental feelings.[15] The same is true of postures, though postures convey more general emotions such as engagement or disengagement.[16] They watch these nonverbal behaviors, which can serve as a more accurate message of your feelings than the actual words you use. Although other parts of the body, like arms, hands, and feet also send messages, children usually give them less attention. Your face and posture are what is most important. When I work with children, I generally move closer to them and angle my body in their direction. If possible, I adjust my eye level to theirs. It says, "I'm here for you, I'm not a threat, and I'm interested." Whatever expression I wish to convey with my face is exaggerated, so there can be no question of what I want them to believe. When I smile, it's big. When they do something I approve of, the look of joy on my face is unmistakable.

If you have access to a video camera, you might wish to record your nonverbal interactions with your child. Nonverbal behavioral analysis can get quite complex, and there are wide disagreements about their interpretation amongst

Figure 3.7
Nonverbal Behaviors

Make a videotape of your interaction with your child.

Use a 1 to 5 rating scale, with 1 being little presence of the nonverbal behavior and 5, extensive presence.

Nonverbal Emotion	Rating
Facial expression indicating happiness	
Posture leaning into the child during shared activities	
Closeness to your child during shared activities	
Frequent affectionate touching	

experts.[17] Therefore, if you decide to analyze your behaviors, keep it very simple. A form you can use appears in Figure 3.7. As you can see, you'll only look at a limited number of these behaviors: your facial expression, posture, closeness to your child, and the extent of your touching. It doesn't make too much sense for our purposes to be very analytical, since nonverbal behaviors can change very rapidly and are often measured in microseconds. It's best to use a rating scale from 1 to 5. One is the least and five the most. In Figure 3.7, rate the strength of the four behaviors. Look for behaviors your child can read as positive—the presence of the listed nonverbal emotions.

Nonverbal behaviors are devious creatures. They can reveal true feelings when we don't monitor them. When they're monitored, they can be used to send messages that are less than honest. Children can rarely tell the difference between their uses. When you want to emphasize a verbal message, the use of nonverbal behaviors can heighten their intensity. For example, if you are very pleased with something your child did, a fully animated smiling face goes a long way. Conversely, if you are upset about something having nothing to do with your child, that feeling may be conveyed along with a verbal message of pleasure. The incongruity may be disconcerting to your child as it was to my daughter. Watch those nonverbal behaviors; they tend to have a mind of their own.

Consequences

Consequences should be related to specific behaviors. They can be *positive*, like receiving a hug for putting dishes into the sink, or *negative* as when a mother yells at her child for breaking an expensive lamp he wasn't supposed to touch. They can be *proportional*, as when a child is told if he doesn't clean his room there won't be any television that night, or *disproportional* as when a child is sent to his room for the entire day because he was disrespectful to his grandmother. Consequences can be *material,* like receiving an ice cream cone for listening, or *immaterial* such as a parent yelling angrily at a child. Regardless of the type of consequences used, they send messages. Child-rearing methods vary with culture and personal style, and no attempt is made here to suggest one approach for all children. However, regardless of your parenting style, there are three guidelines that cut across all approaches.

1. The consequences should be spelled out before the activity is started.
2. The administration of consequences should be consistent.
3. The consequence should fit the behavior.

It's important to let the consequences of behaviors be known to your child, before you ask him or her to do something. When they aren't, children begin questioning the fairness of rules.

"If Mommy says them after we start, that's not fair."

Even when the consequences are known before an activity begins, their administration should be consistent. I watched a young teacher who was having difficulty controlling his class repeatedly say to the same child, "If you don't get back into your seat, you'll receive a demerit." After the teacher said the same thing four times, the child had no reason to expect a demerit would ever be given. Children are pragmatists. They learn from what we do and say. If you are consistent with the consequences, you'll find children will resist less. Needless to say, even if you are consistent, the consequences should be appropriate. I was working with a wealthy family whose idea of a positive consequence for a minor correct response was a $20 toy car. It was difficult to explain while it was terrific their child was able to comprehend a paragraph in the program we were working on, a more appropriate reinforcer would have been a tiny fifty-cent plastic toy. Consequences are a part of life and send clear messages to children. Use them appropriately and you not only enhance the learning process, but also prepare them for the future.

Children

Feedback between children tends to be very direct. Subtlety is not a strong suit for three-year-olds. Since it's direct, it can be brutal. I often brought my children into my graduate classes. They loved it, and so did the students since they were able to watch me do demonstration therapy. I would also run little experiments to see how my children, who had normal language and intelligence, would interact with children having various degrees of language problems and cognitive difficulties. When my son was four years old, I brought him into the clinic to individually play with two different children who were receiving language therapy. The first child had a rare and severe cognitive problem making it difficult for him to use language in a social context. When asked a direct question, he would sometimes respond with an answer—rarely was it appropriate. He would never initiate any conversation. If you asked him a direct question, such as "what is this," he would say, "truck." Sometimes it was a truck, sometimes it wasn't. Rarely would he play with anyone in a group. The second child had Down's syndrome, which is a genetic disorder that can lead to a variety of cognitive, language, and motor problems.[18] Although very sociable, the only words the little boy could use were "yes," "no," "Mommy," and his name. Both children were the same age as Justin. Without explaining anything to my son, I asked him if he would like to meet two new kids and play with a lot of toys he never saw before.

"Sure Daddy, that's fun." With the video camera running, he went into the room with the first child.

"Justin this is Jerry. You guys can play with anything in the room." The room was filled with every great toy I found in the clinic. From behind the glass observation mirror, I would do a running commentary for my class.

"Can we play with anything Daddy?"

"Yes Justin, and you don't even have to put things away when you're done. I'll be right out here and I'll come back in a few minutes. Okay?"

"Sure Daddy."

Justin was excited about the toys and meeting a new child. He never had problems interacting with new children. He always initiated contact and knew the rules of play so well children sought him out on playgrounds and at pre-school. Jerry was playing with a cash register, repeatedly pressing the keys and waiting for the cash drawer to open. With each sequence he would say, "That costs $4." Justin sat next to him and watched for a few minutes, clearly confused as to what Jerry was doing. Finally he spoke.

"Jerry, do you want to play store?"

Jerry didn't respond. He just kept repeating the sequence.

"Jerry, why don't I get some toys and you can sell them to me?"

Justin went around the room and gathered 15 toys and laid them in front of Jerry. Then, pretending to be a customer, he faced him.

"I want to buy this airplane. How much?"

Jerry didn't respond. He continued hitting a key and repeating, "That costs $4," over and over again. Justin was clearly getting frustrated. He looked around the room and found a box of Legos and brought them to Jerry.

"Jerry, let's build something." He started building a tower and placed some pieces in front of Jerry.

"It's your turn, put the Lego here," he said, tapping on the top of the highest piece.

Jerry stopped playing with the cash register and picked up the piece Justin had given him.

"Lego on top," he said as he placed the piece on top of the tower.

Justin became excited. Finally, this kid was going to play with him. Pushing a pile in front of Jerry, Justin said, "Here's some more."

"Lego on top again," Jerry said, and then went back to the cash register.

It was the last interaction Justin had with him. No matter what toys Justin would place in front of Jerry, he wouldn't play. Justin would continually modify the activity, often taking a subservient role, so Jerry would become interested. Jerry would acknowledge the object, saying things like "airplane," but refused to do anything about it. Eventually, Justin went to the far end of the room and found something to play with—by himself. Five minutes later, I entered the room.

"Justin, Jerry has to go now," I said. He looked relieved. "But I have someone else for you to play with." The look of concern returned. "His name is Billy."

"Do I have to play Daddy?"

"Just for a little while Justin, then we'll go and get something to eat."

As Jerry left, Billy entered the room and immediately picked up the airplane and gave it to Justin.

"Let's play airplane," Justin said, clearly relieved that this would not be another child like Jerry.

For 15 minutes they played with many toys in the room. Not once did Billy say one word to Justin—he had few words to use. But his play interaction was perfect. He shared, took turns, and reacted appropriately to whatever Justin did. They developed an immediate friendship. After 15 minutes, I entered the room.

"Justin, it's time to go."

"Can't we play a little longer Daddy?" Billy nodded his head in agreement.

"I'm sorry Justin, Billy has to go now." Both children were clearly disappointed I stopped their play.

After Billy left, Justin and I went into my class to discuss his reactions to both children. Before I began the experiment, I assumed language was determining variable in how most children played with each other. I thought a child with normal intelligence would feel more comfortable with a disabled child if he or she had a similar amount of language. I was dead wrong.

"Justin, would you like to play with Jerry again?"

"No Daddy. Never!

"Why not?"

"He wouldn't play with me. He didn't even talk to me."

"And what about Billy?"

"Can he come over to our house to play? I like him."

"Why Justin?"

"He played. We talked about everything."

Billy never said one word during the 15-minute interaction. "Talk" for Justin involved something other than words. It could have been the intonation pattern or even the nonverbal behaviors Billy used. It was clear if children don't know the rules of play, other kids would eventually shun them regardless of language ability. Justin was an exceptionally tolerant child when it came to playing with other children. He gave Jerry abundant opportunities to interact before he abandoned him. Most children aren't as patient. The inability to use social rules of play often leads to very direct messages from children: *I don't like you, go away.* The messages can be devastating for children who clearly want to make friends, but don't know how. You may have a child who has this problem. Children don't have to have a severe language or learning problem to not understand the rules of play. The solution to this problem is teaching the rules children use and expect others to follow. It's done in two ways. The first is to teach the rules as if they were strategies, and second is to script dialogues between your child and other children during simulations you conduct. You'll learn more about these techniques in Chapter 8.

THE REACTIONS: THE OBVIOUS AND NOT SO OBVIOUS

When children fail, they often feel there's something wrong with them.[19] This type of reaction not only shapes who they are, but also the adult they may become. It's important to recognize the subtle and the more obvious reactions to failure. These include failure masquerading as *boredom, humor, reluctance, illness,* and *anger*. Think about the last time your child expressed one of these emotions, and ask yourself three questions.

1. Was the emotion appropriate or inappropriate?
2. Was it in proportion with the activity or totally out of proportion?
3. Does this behavior seem to have regularity in occurrence (e.g., when you ask your child to do something he or she is not very good)?

In this section, you'll learn how to identify failure masquerading as these misleading emotions; how to discuss them with their child; how to explain the failure as the result of a changeable behavior, and not something inherently wrong with your child; and finally, how to enable your child to deal with difficult learning situations rather than rely on these emotions.

Boredom

How often have you seen your child become bored with something you were sure he or she would be excited about? Sometimes, for very legitimate reasons, it's a toy or game that's truly boring. However, at other times, the boredom may be deceptive. Your child may want to do it, but chooses not to because it's too difficult. A mother became concerned when her son refused to play any games involving balls and running. He pretended to be bored with baseball, soccer, and even kickball. At five years of age, he was removing himself from activities that would integrate him into social playgroups. Physically, he was coordinated, and when by himself, he would repeatedly kick a soccer ball farther than any of his peers. Yet, when asked by his father if he wanted to join the soccer team, his response was always, "No, it's boring." His boredom with the game was a way of avoiding an activity that taxed his ability to attend to a multitude of things occurring simultaneously. There was too much going on in both practice and games. Children were running, parents were shouting, instructors were yelling, and he was expected to perform in the midst of it. He wasn't bored with soccer; it was just too confusing.

Parents can do two things when children use boredom as a way of avoiding a situation that's too difficult. The first is to find alternative activities in which the learning difference doesn't interfere. This child gravitated toward music. When his mother asked him if he'd like to play an instrument, he immediately responded with a big smile, "The piano!" It was an activity that was linear and allowed him to function extremely well in a nonchaotic arena. However, some parents may believe it's important for their children to do activities that initially may be difficult. For those children, the activity needs to be broken into small units and each disruptive part systematically and slowly added. If those techniques were applied to our example, the father could have instructed the child in how to kick various shots for a few days. Later a friend could be invited to join them for some casual play. Then possibly another friend could be introduced into the activity with parents standing on the sidelines, pretending to ignore the kids. The next step might be to begin a little game for a short period of time. Eventually, the child who said he didn't want to play soccer would end up begging his father to enroll him in the league. And that's exactly what happened with this real example. The child not only excelled at soccer because of the way his difficulties were systematically desensitized, but he also did very well as a young pianist in an activity that was more conducive to the way he processed information. These parents provided their son with both a detour and a new hole to fill.

Humor

Humor is a very disarming way for children to deal with a fear of failing. While rare in very young children, I've found it in children approaching five years of age. Sometimes the humor occurs before an activity is even started. Children learn it's more likely parents will back off if a joke is made rather than an outright "no" or an honest answer given. It doesn't happen often, but parents can identify it by looking at patterns of usage. Does the child have a genuine sense of humor that should be encouraged? Or, does the humor occur when an activity is too difficult to do? When my son was in kindergarten, I received reports from his teacher that said he was becoming the class clown, something that delighted the other children, but frustrated the teacher. I asked her if I could come to the class and see what was happening. She quickly agreed. I'm sure she felt my presence would thwart Justin's disruptive behaviors, if not forever, at least for that day. Justin wasn't pleased when I told him about my visit. Just like his teacher, he falsely assumed the purpose was disciplinary. Sitting in the back of the room, I began observing not only Justin, but also the teacher. Within the first ten minutes of class I realized what the problem was, and it wasn't Justin. The teacher would rattle off three or four things and expect the children to follow the instructions.

"Children, I want you to select four crayons for the tub in the left corner. Not the one in the right corner. Then go to the back of the room and take one of the medium-size pieces of paper, sit with your partner, and draw a picture of the house I told you about in the story."

Justin, who needed to see instructions in a concrete form, was lost, as were many other children in the class. There was no clowning with me there. He wanted to do his best to please me. He would try to remember what she said and appeared frustrated when he couldn't. I noticed similar expressions on the faces of at least five other children. They, just as Justin, also needed to see not only *what* they were to do, but also the *order* in which it was to occur. Unlike Justin, they didn't have the gift of humor to hide their frustration.

Following the end of the class, I had a difficult conversation with the teacher. It isn't easy to explain to anyone they are the source of a problem. Explaining this to an older, experienced teacher was extremely difficult—especially when she saw me as the father of the problem. After I explained alternative ways of providing instructions to the five children I observed having problems with auditory instructions, she agreed to provide the children with visuals on the board they could follow. For example, if the children were expected to do three things, she would place three graphics on the board depicting the activities. They were placed in the order they were to be done, with the appropriate number below. After each child did one of the activities, he or she would go to the board and place a checkmark by their name. After implementing simple suggestions like these, Justin's misleading use of humor stopped the following week, and I made a convert to a different style of teaching.

Reluctance

There can be many reasons children are reluctant to engage in an activity. It may be related to a fear that was conditioned by a past event.[20] It could be parents have told them about the scary nature of something, like, "Don't talk to strangers; they can be very bad people." Or maybe there is a frightening aspect about the physical configuration of something. Most of the time, parents can easily identify these situations. But what about something that doesn't fall into any obvious categories, such as the reluctance to do something most children would assume to be fun? I've found most children are like giant sponges wanting to absorb everything a new and exciting world has to offer. When I see a child who doesn't fit that mold, I look for causes. I worked with a three-year-old child who was reluctant to play with other children. She was bright and after a few sessions during which she would barely look at me, we were finally able to play. Her language was at the five- to six-year-old level and her artwork, for a three-year-old, was beautiful. But she refused to play with other children in her house, the park, or the preschool. She also had a very severe stutter. Sometime in the past year, when she was at a park playing with some children, she began to speak, repeating initial sounds, whole words, and sentences. The other children thought something was wrong with her. The way they dealt with something unexplainable was rejection. Her reluctance to play was based on her rejection by other children. It took several months to teach her to speak fluently. Eventually, she was able to play with children. Nobody likes to fail, not even children. If they continually fail at an activity, they may be reluctant not only to participate in it, but also unfamiliar activities that contain elements similar to the one at which they failed. They don't want to fail, so they don't try.

Illness

How often have your children feigned illness when you were absolutely sure nothing was wrong with them? The first reaction parents have, after they have ruled out real illness, is to try cajoling or insisting the child engage in whatever would be prevented by the feigned illness.

There can be a variety of reasons for pretending to be ill. But parents should look for patterns. What is it about being ill prevents your child from doing?

"I'm not feeling well Mommy."

"I just took your temperature and you ate everything at breakfast. I don't think you're sick. We're going to the Gymorama. So get dressed *now*."

"But I don't feel well Mommy."

"We're going and I don't want to hear anything else."

Sounds familiar? I'm not sure that's the best approach. Children are just as rational as adults; though we rarely make the equivalency. Many of our fears are similar: loss of love, fear of rejection, and failures, to name just a few. Children express their needs and desires in ways different from us. As adults, we often choose to run away from those things causing us anxiety. So do children. However, children have fewer "run away" options. Being "sick" is a great one, since they have learned parents will allow them to do nothing other than lay around and play with their toys. Forcing a child to do something that causes anxiety is as reasonable as your mother dragging you into your boss's office to confront him. Neither makes sense, nor is appropriate. When you start seeing patterns of "illness," do four things:

1. Rule out the possibility of a real illness.
2. Try to determine if there are any similarities between the events or activities when your child feigns illness.
3. Construct a play activity in the home simulating the feared activity.
4. Finally, turn it into game in which children can slowly encounter those things that may be creating anxiety.

Instead of confronting your child with your knowledge nothing is wrong, take a kinder and more fruitful approach. Use the occurrence to gain a better understanding about what causes anxiety in your child. Then, deal with it by systematically reducing the threatening nature of the activity.

Anger

Anger is not the healthiest emotion for children or adults. It's probably the most debilitating masquerade for a fear of failure.[21] You can see it when the response of children is all out of proportion to what they are asked to do, or the result of something they are doing. It can also be frightening to parents since they either don't know how to respond or become concerned there's something psychologically wrong with their child. Repetitive inappropriate anger may be an expression of something requiring the services of a professional counselor. But before going that route, parents should look at what immediately precedes the outburst. Don't think in terms of "this is a reasonable request" when you look at what the child is being asked to do. That's not the most helpful thought, nor one that will give you insight into your child's behaviors. Rarely do parents ask their children to do something unreasonable. If you use these markers to determine if the response was appropriate, you'll always believe the anger wasn't justified. A better approach is to look at what tasks or behaviors your child will need to perform in order for the activity to be successful. Therein may lie the reason for the anger. Children may not be angry about your request. Rather, anger becomes a way of avoiding something at which they are afraid they'll fail. A father came to see me about his four-year-old son who would become quite angry whenever the father asked him to identify letters in a storybook. He knew his son would need to read in kindergarten and wished to give him a headstart. I asked the father to keep a diary of when the anger occurred. After one week, we realized his son only became angry when asked to do anything involving reading. I suspected a reading problem. An evaluation by a reading expert revealed that his son had dyslexia, a problem in which the brain has difficulty matching sounds with written letters. After working with the reading specialist for two months, not only did the anger vanish, but also the little boy would plead with his father to read together.

The Effects of the Present on the Future

As much as we hope painful feelings our children have won't affect them the rest of their lives, we often find they do. I spoke with a woman in her mid-thirties who learned differently. Throughout public school, she was told she couldn't do certain things because she had a "learning disability." This advice, though always well meaning, created a self-image still affecting her, years after it was first said. Though a successful executive in a large corporation, she still reacted instinctively when someone, familiar with her strengths and weakness, suggested that "maybe someone else should do that." She felt she not only had to take on the assignment, but also do it better than anyone else could. Usually she was successful, but at a great emotional and physical expense. The time and effort she needed to put into the activity was exhausting. And when unsuccessful, all the gremlins of her youth would reappear. For her, the negative feelings she had as an adolescent were just as fresh 25 years later.

How we react to our children as preschoolers can affect them later in life. Instead of telling your children what they can't do because of their learning differences, try to find new ways for them to accomplish tasks or activities.

For example, soccer was gradually introduced for the little boy in the previous section. If you can't develop detours, try to gently steer them on to other pursuits, like substituting a musical instrument for a physical activity. Try not to make them feel certain avenues of interest are out-of-bounds. You do this by making the activity easier. The more successful parents are with their preschoolers, the less likely well-meaning but uninformed people can create scenarios that are destined to repeat themselves endlessly like bad nightmares.

FOUR

Kindergarten,
A Whole New World

Kindergarten can be a scary place both for children and parents. It's filled with strange little people and an adult who doesn't know your child. It's not just a physical place, but also a stage in a child's life when a parent's ability to protect is limited. For three to four hours a day, your child won't have you there to intercede and explain. A stranger is given the responsibility for his or her physical, emotional, and intellectual well-being. While parents can wait for the child to do things, the teacher can't. What only needed gentle cajoling by parents may, of necessity, now require a quick admonition by a teacher. It's a new world for both children and parents, and one your child might not be prepared for, even if he or she attended preschool. Having a learning problem can aggravate the anxiety you and your child may feel. You can reduce the anxiety by not waiting until kindergarten begins before you act. In this chapter, we'll approach kindergarten as if it's a whole new world. You'll learn how to prepare for it, learn the value of readiness lists, what the law says about your rights, and finally how your role as an advocate can prevent many problems from occurring.

KINDERGARTEN READINESS LISTS

There are many surprises in life. Some are quite harmless and often result in unexpected joy. But there are others that are similar to storm clouds that, without warning, can cause devastation. For some parents of children with learning problems, kindergarten readiness lists can be as destructive as a violent thunderhead. It's a document often not given to parents until a few weeks or months before their child enters kindergarten. These educational funnels act as hoppers into which children are expected to drop, eventually coming out the other end, indistinguishable from all other educational products. Unfortunately, many children with learning problems can't fit into the funnel.

The Lists, What Do They Really Mean?

Almost every school has something they call a "kindergarten readiness list." It's a compilation of intellectual, social, and motor skills all children who enter kindergarten are expected to have. The rationale is these are the skills necessary for children to be successful in kindergarten. For most public schools, they're suggestions. For many private schools, they serve as mandatory checklists for selection and admission. Many of these lists are undifferentiated—all desired behaviors, sometimes up to 50, are listed. Other lists are divided into categories, in which related individual behaviors are grouped together. While the category lists have some similarities, they often reflect the school's orientation and philosophy. Figure 4.1 shows three commonly used categories, with slight variations, that appear in the readiness lists of many schools. Behaviors are listed within each category. Most are specific enough so parents can compare what their children are capable of doing with what they are expected to do. The earlier you can acquire your child's school readiness list, the earlier you can prepare.

Public School Readiness Lists

If you are intending to send your child to a public kindergarten, your local school district office should be able to supply you with a kindergarten readiness list. They tend to be uniform for all kindergartens in the district. As you review it, look for indications of which behaviors the district believes are most important and if any are *required* behaviors rather than *suggested* ones.

There are limited courses of action public schools have when it comes to accepting children into kindergarten. First, they may say these are only suggested prerequisites. Even though children may not have some or even many of the behaviors, they still will be allowed into kindergarten. However, with

Figure 4.1
Typical Categories of Readiness Lists

Group 1	Group 2	Group 3
Care for Personal Needs	Social Behaviors	Concept Development
Intellectual	Classroom Conduct	Physical Development
Social	Communication Behaviors	Health and Safety
Health	Task-Related Behavior	Number Concept Development
	Self-Help Skills	Language
		Writing
		Reading
		Social & Emotional Development

many missing behaviors, they may suggest your child stay in preschool for an additional year. However, for children with learning differences, an additional year of preschool without emphasis on developing learning strategies often doesn't prevent the problems from occurring. It just delays them.[1] Second, the public school administrators may indicate that while your child may not qualify for mainstream kindergarten, he or she is eligible for a special education program. Depending on the number of required behaviors your child doesn't have, you have a choice of accepting the placement into a special education program, having your child remain in preschool until the behaviors are acquired, or contesting the school's decision.

Private School Readiness Lists

If you intend to enroll your child in a private school, your options are limited. Most private schools use the readiness lists as entrance prerequisites. Some have formal tests that are used to evaluate your child. These can range from simple to sophisticated, and few to many. They may require you to pay for testing by an educational psychologist or they may have a special day scheduled for an interview and testing. Knowing what tests are used will not give you as much information as knowing what behaviors they're looking for. These schools often wish to select children who they believe will become outstanding educational performers.

Many of these schools are not open to children who learn differently, either in their admission requirements or classroom accommodations. A few private schools do focus on children who learn differently. These schools tend to accept children with a wide range of abilities.

The simplest approach to finding these places is to contact the private schools listed in the classified section of your telephone book. A better approach is to search the Internet for "Private Schools" in your area. For most listings, there should be a subheading for "special education." Rarely will a heading of "learning disabilities" appear. Never "learning differences." Once you have identified a private school offering special services, inquire if they have programs for children who have "learning disabilities" and if they use a readiness list. Use the term "learning disabilities" rather than "learning differences" since some school administrators may find the term confusing. Others may equate "learning differences" or "learning disability" with reading problems. Be patient and explain what behaviors you're concerned about. In San Francisco, out of 96 private schools listed, only 12 offered any special services. At least half of these weren't appropriate for children with normal intelligence who had learning problems. I found similar ratios in New York City

Figure 4.2
Get-Along Behaviors

Listens to stories without
    interrupting
Sits appropriately for up to 15
    minutes
Attends to teacher in large group
Answers questions when asked by
    adult
Recognizes authority
Avoids dangers and responds to
    warning words
Follows simple rules
Role as part of group
Stays in own space
Does not disrupt peers
Monitors own behavior
Expresses emotions and affections
    appropriately
Takes turns
Uses words like "please," "thank you,"
    and "excuse me."
Works/plays cooperatively with
    adults and children
Shares and takes turns
Respects others
Takes care of personal belongings
Respects belongings of others
Interacts and defends without
    aggression
Feeds self
Cares for own toileting needs
Asks for assistance when needed
Communicates needs
Complies quickly with teacher
    instructions
Separates from parents without being
    upset
Puts away toys when asked

They're like the grease allowing the gears of a machine to work. None may be a part of learning, but without them, the learning process in kindergarten may be severely hindered. In Figure 4.2, 27 "get-along" behaviors are listed that often appear on readiness lists. There's nothing absolute about any of these behaviors. I'm sure some would argue many are really more than "get-along" behaviors; they're precursors to learning. That may be true. However, what's important is these are the types of behaviors that make a kindergarten teacher's life easier in a class of 20 children. The less time he or she spends dealing with a child's disruptive behavioral problems, the more time can be spent on those more directly involved in learning.

I was working with a four-year-old child who had a great deal of difficulty not interrupting. Although not the focus of therapy, both the mother and I were concerned. Few things are more annoying to a teacher than a child who continually interrupts. James was curious about everything. It was a quality I didn't want to quash. However, he didn't understand the rules for when questions were appropriate. That became the new focus of my therapy—learning what verbal and nonverbal signals need to be present for a question to be asked. It took the mother and me over three months to teach James the rules. When he entered kindergarten, he was able to apply them. Not perfectly, but at least well enough not to appear any more disruptive than the other kids.

Some parents have trouble appreciating the importance of "get-along" behaviors. I had an interesting conversation with the mother of a four-year-old who was a colleague of mine at the university. She was appalled at what the school had on its readiness list.

"Can you explain to me why 'neatly gluing' is something that will be important for Jean to academically succeed in kindergarten?"

3. Ask her to look at the list and indicate which of the behaviors she believes are important for your child to be successful in *her* class, and are there others not listed she would like your child to have. If she's willing, ask her to rate them in terms of importance with
   1=very important
   2=important
   3=not that important.
4. If your child can already do all of the behaviors, terrific, he or she is ready.
5. If there are behaviors that are marginal, nonexistent, or likely not to be performed within the chaos of a classroom, start working on them in order of their importance.

Your short interaction with the teacher accomplishes two very important things. First, you now have a template for what the kindergarten teacher will be using when interacting with your child. The behaviors she identified may not be ones you think are important, either in your approach to child rearing, or in your child's learning. Think of these behaviors as ways of reducing things that may interfere with learning. While some may in fact be important, you may view others as fluff.

The second thing you accomplished by meeting with the teacher is you showed her a respect many parents often neglect. Your actions said you believed she was so important in the development of your child you were willing to defer to her judgment regarding your child's education. That's heady stuff for any teacher to experience. Not only does she feel important, but also she's now able to identify you as a parent who really cares about your child. Although other parents probably care as much as you do, you're 1 of 20 who made your concerns known. Your child becomes someone special because of the interest you showed and the respect you gave her. When you call with a concern, you're not just another message that has to be responded to after a very hectic day of work. You're the parent who made her feel important, respected, and wanted. You go to the top of the callback list. You become special—and so does your child.

One way of grouping behaviors on readiness lists is to divide them into three types of functional behaviors: get-along, academic, and motor. Although each will be examined separately, they're interconnected. For example, most "get-along" behaviors require learning. Most motor behaviors involve things that have been learned, stored, and now appropriately retrieved.

Get along Behaviors. There are some behaviors that help different learners be accepted by the teacher and other children. These are the "get-along" behaviors, such as sitting in a seat, not interrupting, and saying "please" and "thank you." They can be the most important behaviors for some teachers.[2]

Figure 4.2
Get-Along Behaviors

Listens to stories without
  interrupting
Sits appropriately for up to 15
  minutes
Attends to teacher in large group
Answers questions when asked by
  adult
Recognizes authority
Avoids dangers and responds to
  warning words
Follows simple rules
Role as part of group
Stays in own space
Does not disrupt peers
Monitors own behavior
Expresses emotions and affections
  appropriately
Takes turns
Uses words like "please," "thank you,"
  and "excuse me."
Works/plays cooperatively with
  adults and children
Shares and takes turns
Respects others
Takes care of personal belongings
Respects belongings of others
Interacts and defends without
  aggression
Feeds self
Cares for own toileting needs
Asks for assistance when needed
Communicates needs
Complies quickly with teacher
  instructions
Separates from parents without being
  upset
Puts away toys when asked

They're like the grease allowing the gears of a machine to work. None may be a part of learning, but without them, the learning process in kindergarten may be severely hindered. In Figure 4.2, 27 "get-along" behaviors are listed that often appear on readiness lists. There's nothing absolute about any of these behaviors. I'm sure some would argue many are really more than "get-along" behaviors; they're precursors to learning. That may be true. However, what's important is these are the types of behaviors that make a kindergarten teacher's life easier in a class of 20 children. The less time he or she spends dealing with a child's disruptive behavioral problems, the more time can be spent on those more directly involved in learning.

I was working with a four-year-old child who had a great deal of difficulty not interrupting. Although not the focus of therapy, both the mother and I were concerned. Few things are more annoying to a teacher than a child who continually interrupts. James was curious about everything. It was a quality I didn't want to quash. However, he didn't understand the rules for when questions were appropriate. That became the new focus of my therapy—learning what verbal and nonverbal signals need to be present for a question to be asked. It took the mother and me over three months to teach James the rules. When he entered kindergarten, he was able to apply them. Not perfectly, but at least well enough not to appear any more disruptive than the other kids.

Some parents have trouble appreciating the importance of "get-along" behaviors. I had an interesting conversation with the mother of a four-year-old who was a colleague of mine at the university. She was appalled at what the school had on its readiness list.

"Can you explain to me why 'neatly gluing' is something that will be important for Jean to academically succeed in kindergarten?"

"No, not directly," I responded. "But for her kindergarten teacher it may be an important 'get along' behavior."

She looked confused by my response.

"For whatever reason, Jean's teacher believes neatly gluing things is an important skill for the children to have in *her* class. Maybe it has to do with not wanting to spend much time at the end of the day cleaning tables. Regardless of the reason, *it doesn't matter*. This will be a behavior that will affect many other things."

"But what does it have to do with learning?"

"Directly? Probably nothing," I responded. "But think of it as a billiard ball ricocheting against balls it wasn't intended to hit. That glue smear on the table may affect how this teacher views Jean in many other ways."

As much as we would like to think adults can compartmentalize children's behaviors, few can do it systematically or cleanly. Children who brilliantly complete a task in kindergarten won't receive the praise they deserve if the teacher views them as disruptive. Whereas compliant children who never interrupt may receive accolades from the same teacher for doing something mediocre. Think of your own life. You probably do the same thing daily with friends, acquaintances, and work colleagues. Equanimity, the ability to treat everyone the same, is a lofty goal, and one not often reached. When was the last time you praised the heroic efforts of an individual you disliked? When you look at "get-along" behaviors, don't make any judgements on their value. These are simply things that will make it easier for your child to be successful in a specific setting. Think of the teacher's list of "get-along" behaviors as something similar to the skills you needed *before* doing something very important. You may not have thought of them as important, but unless you adhered to them, nothing followed. Getting to work on time may not be something that interferes with the brilliant work you are accomplishing, but without doing it, your job may be in jeopardy.

Learning Behaviors. The second set of behaviors are those directly related to learning, such as being able to follow instructions within noisy settings, remembering simple instructions, and being able to comprehend the meaning of a short simple story. Behaviors like these, and the ones that appear in Figure 4.3 are involved in intellectual development.[3] Some may have more importance than others for the teacher. Sixty-two behaviors related to learning are on this list. It's an overwhelming list of cognitive skills children are expected to be able to do by kindergarten. Many lists are divided into categories, such as concept development, language, and reading. While these categories are appropriate, we aren't going to use them. Rather, I'd like you to think about what type of processing skills each behavior requires. Many of the behaviors on the readiness lists can be categorized into ones requiring attention, understanding, storage,

Figure 4.3
Learning Behaviors

Listens and follows short directions	Makes choices
Stays with an activity until it's completed	Recognizes colors
Holds book upright, turns pages front to back	Knows body parts
Curious, persistent and exploratory	Expresses ideas with drawings
Knows first and last name	Uses descriptive language ("That's a *tall* building.")
Knows names of family members	Uses simple conversational sentences
Recognizes name in print	Uses sentences that include two or more separate ideas
Reads along with you when listening to favorite story	Pretends, creates and makes up songs and stories
Puts together a simple puzzle	Talks about everyday experiences
Understands basic concepts (e.g., clothes, vegetables, up, down, under, etc.)	Asks questions about how things work
Tells left from right	Expresses ideas so others can understand
Tells the meaning of simple words (e.g., bicycle, apple, gun, shoes, hammer, water, etc.)	Tells or retells stories
	Writes name
	Identifies rhyming words
Recognizes groups of one, two, three, four, and five objects	Identifies the beginning sound of some words
Counts to 10	Identifies some alphabet letters
Recognizes some common sight words like "stop"	Tells stories after they are read
	Looks at pictures then tells stories
Recognizes a problem exists	Repeats a series of four numbers without practice, such as "Say after me 7-2-6-3"
Understands actions have both causes and effects	Repeats an eight to 10 word sentence
Understands general times of day	Speaks in complete sentences of five to six words
Uses strategies to solve problems	
Recognizes print in surroundings	Sings songs
Picks up book and tries to read	Recites simple poems, nursery rhymes
Identifies basic shapes	Produces writing-like scribbles or letter-like forms
Sorts objects into groups of different color, size, and shape	Expresses emotions and affections appropriately
Recognizes and creates new patterns and designs	Recalls and follows directions for tasks previously described
Works with blocks, sand, and art materials to create something new	Completes work appropriately
Completes simple puzzles	Uses a variety of material
Follows two to three part directions	Interacts and defends without aggression
Finds material needed for tasks	Open to new things
Generalizes skills across tasks and situations	Asks for assistance when needed
Monitors own behavior	Communicates needs

Figure 4.4
Behaviors Categorized by Processing Skills

Attending Behaviors
Listens to stories without interrupting
Listens and follows short directions
Sits appropriately for up to 15 minutes
Attends to teacher in large group
Stays with an activity until it's completed

Understanding
Holds book upright, turns pages fron to back
Curious, persistent, and exploratory
Knows first and last name
Knows names of family members
Answers questions when asked by adult
Recognizes name in print
Reads along with you when listening to favorite story
Puts together a simple puzzle
Understands basic concepts (e.g., clothes, vegetables, up, down, under, etc.)
Tells left from right
Tells the meaning of simple words (e.g., bicycle, apple, gun, shoes, hammer, water, etc.)
Recognizes authority
Recognizes groups of one, two, three, four, and five objects
Counts to 10
Recognizes some common sight words like "stop"
Recognizes a problem exists
Understands actions have both causes and effects
Understands general times of day
Avoids dangers and responds to warning words
Uses strategies to solve problems
Recognizes print in surroundings
Picks up book and tries to read
Identifies basic shapes
Sorts objects into groups of different colors, sizes, and shapes
Recognizes and creates new patterns and designs
Works with blocks, sand, and art materials to create something new
Completes simple puzzles
Follows simple rules
Role as part of group

Stays in own space
Follows two to three part directions
Answers questions
Finds material needed for tasks
Does not disrupt peers
Generalizes skills across tasks and situations
Monitors own behavior
Makes choices
Recognizes colors
Knows body parts

Storing Information

Retrieval of Information
Expresses ideas with drawings
Uses descriptive language ("That's a *tall* building.")
Uses simple conversational sentences
Uses sentences that include two or more separate ideas
Pretneds, creates and makes up songs and stories
Talks about everyday experiences
Asks questions about how things work
Expresses ideas so others can understand
Tells or retells stories
Writes name
Identifies rhyming words
Identifies the beginning sound of some words
Identifies some alphabet letters
Tells stories after they are read
Looks at pictures then tells stories
Repeats a series of four numbers without practice, such as "Say after me 7-2-6-3"
Repeats an eight to 10 word sentence
Speaks in complete sentences of five to six words
Sings songs
Recites simple poems, nursery rhymes
Produces writing-like scribbles or letter-like forms
Expresses emotions and affections appropriately
Takes turns
Recalls and follows directions for tasks previously described
Completes work appropriately

and retrieval. A few behaviors may involve combinations. All the behaviors I found on the lists appear in Figure 4.4 in the processing area to which it's most closely related. Compare the list of behaviors the teacher provided you with those that appear in Figure 4.4. Most likely, you'll find problem behaviors will cluster in categories, like those requiring attention or appropriate usage. For example, your child may only be able to listen for five minutes to a story you're reading to her. During that time, she's constantly interrupting you, often with questions that have nothing to do with the story. Occasionally, she may even forget your request that she turn the page when you've finished reading it. All are related to difficulties with attention, although each is a separate problem.

I'm sure you've noticed no behaviors were listed under "storage." That's not because there aren't any. Rather, we only know about storage problems when children attempt to retrieve information.[4] A child who doesn't remember the teacher's instruction given 10 minutes ago may have been intensively listening, but was unable to store it for future use. Problems with storage are only known and corrected indirectly. We know there is a problem in storage if the child was attending and fully understood the directions, yet was unable to retrieve them. We treat the problem by working on how information is presented and requested. None of these listings is set in concrete. They should be used as general guidelines for determining the type of problems your child may have. The strategies you'll learn in Part II are ones designed to have a positive effect on all of the behaviors in each category. For example, a child may have problems listening to stories without interrupting, has problems following short directions, or is unable to follow a teacher's words in a large group. Although all are separate problems, they may improve if children can learn how to focus in the presence of noise.

Motor Skills. There is a significant amount of time devoted to play in kindergarten. Some of it is used just to release energy, while at other times it becomes the vehicle on which fundamental academics are learned. For example, kickball on the playground is not only an activity for strengthening legs and dispelling pent up energy; but it also involves understanding rules. Cutting out dolls not only teaches fine motor coordination, but depending on what the teacher said, it could also involve the development of memory. There are 14 motor skills cited in readiness lists. These appear in Figure 4.5.

Figure 4.5
Motor Skills

Cuts with scissors

Ties shoes

Traces basic shapes

Buttons shirts, pants, coats, and zip-up zippers

Bounces ball

Draws and colors a picture, beyond scribbling

Ties a knot

Walks backward for five or six feet

Able to stand on one foot for five or 10 seconds

Able to walk in a straight line

Holds a crayon

Rides a tricycle

Uses chalk or magnetic letters

Draws a self-portrait

Motor skills seem to be the end products of prior information processing. For example, if children are to execute (retrieve) a specific motor behavior such as holding a crayon, in the past they would have needed to watch a teacher or parent demonstrate the behavior (attention), then store the information (memory), and finally correctly execute it (retrieval). A problem at any stage prior to the child's use of a crayon could cause problems. How is a parent to know which of the information-processing areas is at fault? Most likely, by looking at clusters of behaviors falling within an information-processing area. For example, if there are many behaviors that are problematic in the attention area, a child's inability to correctly hold the crayon may be related to not attending to the teacher when she or he demonstrated how to hold it.

Lists, even those developed by experts, should serve as general reference points, not as imposing documents designed to scare. These lists are not the gatekeepers for success. A child who learns differently may have problems within one or more of the information-processing areas. The absence of some behaviors will become pointers you can use to locate *general* areas of problems. You can do two different things to prepare your child. The first is work on each and every missing behavior, and in the process drive yourself crazy and make your child feel inadequate. The second is work on improving the information-processing area in which the behaviors are found. The second makes more sense than the first.

What's Legal and What's Real

I received a phone call from a distressed mother who didn't understand why the school wasn't providing the special attention her son needed. Diagnosed with an auditory processing disorder when he was four, she was assured by a public school administer in her district that Jim's problem would be "adequately treated." He assured her the classroom teacher would be informed, as would the classroom aide. If a determination was made that her son qualified for special services from the learning disabilities specialist, an Individualized Educational Plan (IEP) would be developed, and special services provided. The mother felt at ease. Competent, trained professionals would address the needs of her child. But it never happened. The kindergarten teacher had never been trained to address the needs of children whose listening problems interfered with learning. And even if she had, 22 children in a room whose walls echoed and amplified even the slightest sound would make her efforts challenging at best. The aide was actually a parent of one of the children in the class. Though she did carry out all of the basic tasks the teacher asked her to do, they were mostly menial, such as passing out materials, cleaning up spills, and making sure the children were following the "Simon says" activities. While she tried to give all of the children equal attention, her focus was clearly on her own child. Additionally, she never received any training from the district about how to facilitate learning . The school, whose staff had been reduced by budget cuts, welcomed anyone who came through the doors to help. In the middle of September, Jim's mother called the principal to arrange an IEP meeting. The principal told her he was on the list for an evaluation.

"But he's been evaluated by a private specialist already, with a doctorate in learning disorders" the mother said. "Jim's been diagnosed with an auditory processing disorder."

"Yes, I know he has," the principal calmly responded. Daily, she had conversations such as this one with parents. "You see, the law requires us to independently assess the problem before we can provide special services."

The mother wasn't sure if the information was accurate or just self-serving. "When will he be tested?" she demanded.

"That's hard to say. You see, we've had a massive cut in our budget. We now have only one person in the district who can diagnose learning disorders. We'll let you know as soon as he can be scheduled."

What the administrator didn't tell the parent was there is a specific amount of time between when a child is identified and when services are to be provided. If services start beyond that period of time, the school district is in violation of federal laws. However, if the child is not identified, the clock doesn't begin to run. With limited personnel, there is an advantage to delaying identification. Testing for Jim didn't begin until mid-November. A meeting was scheduled with the mother, kindergarten teacher, learning specialist, and the principal's delegate, who was the vice principal, right after the Thanksgiving recess. The results of the testing were presented at the meeting. The recommendation was for two weekly 20-minute group sessions with the learning specialist. The IEP document was placed in front of the mother and explained. Then with the three imposing figures looking at her, she was asked to sign it, thereby agreeing with the recommendations.

"Please sign here," the assistant principal directed as he repeatedly tapped the signature line.

"No," the mother said.

"No? I don't understand," the administrator said, not expecting any opposition. "Is there a problem with our recommendations?"

"Yes, there is. Do you really think my son's problem can be corrected with only 40 minutes a week? And then with other children? Do you *really* think that?"

The vice principal looked at the learning specialist for help. She sighed and gave a response she knew would make everyone angry.

"Unfortunately, I can only provide 40 minutes a week. I have a caseload of 45 children I'm expected to work with, and I'm on call for every teacher in this school. We're understaffed and can't provide the services we would like. If I see your child more often, someone else's child will be denied services. I'd like to see him more, but I can't."

This was not the response the vice principal wanted to hear. He was even more furious with her next comment.

"You know, by law you don't have to approve the IEP, you can appeal it."

"Yes, you can," the vice principal quickly said, "But that may take three months. During that time, we can't provide even the 40 minutes of special time a week to your child—that's not our decision, it's the law you know."

The mother also questioned the veracity of this administrator. Now she was faced with a terrible dilemma. Two months had already gone by, and an additional three would be required before the case would even be heard. And she wondered if the process would be as intimidating as this meeting. Her child came home almost every day in tears because of problems understanding the teacher's instructions. There was no guarantee anything other than the 40 minutes would be given after the appeal. Behind glistening eyes, she signed the IEP.

While this mother's experience may not be typical of interactions between parents and public school administrators, it's one I hear often from distraught parents. The staffing and training of many public school personnel may not be adequate to meet the needs of children who learn differently. Although some organizations such as Mel Levine's All Kinds of Minds Institute, are doing a terrific job of training teachers to address the needs of different learners, they have a long way to go before a significant number of teachers learn how to modify classroom activities.[5] And even with knowledge, the physical and economic restrictions many school districts face may prevent dedicated teachers from doing what they know should be done.

Often services mandated by law fall short of children's needs. As enrollment increases and personnel numbers decline, what qualified for services five years ago, may not tomorrow. A hierarchy of severity has already been informally developed in many schools that dance around federal law. Children with some types of learning differences no longer qualify. It's as if public schools have been transformed into battlefield MASH units, where a triage procedure is required. Children, whose condition is viewed as severe, are treated first. Those with moderate problems receive services next. And children whose problems appear to be minor *in comparison to other children* usually must fend for themselves. Unfortunately, many children with learning differences fall into this neglected category. In many schools, the learning specialist treats children who learn differently *only if* they qualify under a learning disorder category. The learning specialist is responsible for addressing specific needs and informing the classroom teacher what should be done with your child. With increasing caseloads and reduced public school funding, it's unlikely the services your child will need can be adequately provided, even with an IEP mandating minimum services.[6]

It's not that public school personnel don't care. They do, so much so that many have retired rather than work under conditions they find unacceptable. They've been mandated to provide services that are impossible to deliver given too little money and not enough trained staff. The approach taken by parents to get the services their children need is often adversarial. They and their advocates start with the assumption that the only way of getting what is due is to fight for it. In some situations where the school administration is uncompromising, this might be necessary. However, that shouldn't be where you begin. I recently was asked to be present at an IEP meeting in a local school district that in the past only provided necessary services after a lawsuit was filed. I had expected the worst. However, there was a new director of Special Services and the proceedings were remarkable. Instead of the hostility I expected to find, there was a spirit of cooperation. Given a restricted budget, the session became a problem solving event where the needs of the child were paramount to all. By starting with the belief everyone wanted the best for this child, we were successful. However, if we assumed it would be an "I win, you lose" interaction, our meeting would have been very different. Always start with the assumption that public school personnel want to do the right thing, given the limitations under which they operate.

SEPARATE AND NOT SO EQUAL

We are all familiar with private clubs that, trying to convey an image of nonexclusivity, accept a few individuals who are very different from all other members. While the new member is assured he is "one of us," he may never feel completely accepted. The same is true for many children with learning differences when they enter school. Since 1975, the federal government guaranteed services for children with disabilities. If the problem could be diagnosed and was on the approved list, services were provided. "Learning disabled" was, and still is, on the list. Many professionals and educators did not realize then, and still don't realize, what the label may do to children and parents. When an identifying label, such as "learning disabled," is used, something very ugly can happen—what began as a difference now becomes something negative that may define and limit a child's life. It's an example of how a word can

shape reality. If enough people continually call a horse a "duck," everyone may eventually believe it's a duck—even the horse.

While the original intent was without malice, the results of labeling may be negative. The only way children who need extra help can receive it is if the child is labeled. Without the label, some school districts believe they can't legally provide extra help. One of my best graduate students had a learning problem. In order for her to understand my lectures, which typically run for three hours, she needed to audiotape everything, transcribe it, outline the material, and then discuss the material with me during my office hours. These time-intensive strategies, learned in elementary school, enabled her to be successful in college. She became one of the most outstanding speech-language pathologists I ever trained. She explained to me that, even in elementary school, she knew she was different. Not only because of the difficulty she encountered in the classroom, but also because a learning disabilities teacher pulled her out of class two times a week for "special" treatment. She appreciated the help she was receiving from the specialist, in spite of the pullout treatment and her classmates' realization that she really wasn't equal. Without being labeled, she never would have received the services she needed, since at that time few classroom teachers knew how to help children with learning difficulties. She never would have gone to college without being labeled. Labeling may be a necessary evil we will need to live with for some time.

In most public schools, the thrust of providing services to children with learning problems is not through classroom teachers, but rather specialists who work with children on a pullout basis. Although children with learning differences are accepted in the public schools, they are often treated as more separate than equal—they're "one of us," but not really. Often, parents dread the day when their preschooler, who clearly has a learning difference, is labeled, begins receiving "disorder" services, and starts developing the self-image of someone who can't learn. That's not a necessary condition. Just as with my graduate student, the negative effects of labeling can be prevented. Parents can work with their child's teacher from the first day of kindergarten to prevent it. Ways of working with teachers are explained in Chapter 9. Many teachers are becoming more receptive to rethinking individual learning differences and are realizing labeling and pullout may not be the most productive techniques for helping some children.

The Law—What It Was Intended to Do

In 1975, federal legislation was passed entitling all children with specific disabilities to a free quality education. It was called the Individuals with Disabilities Education Act (IDEA). On paper, it guaranteed that appropriate services

would be provided to over six million children who qualified. Qualification required testing by school personnel to determine if a child fit into any of the following disability categories:

1. mental retardation
2. hearing impairment, including deafness
3. speech or language impairment
4. visual impairment, including blindness
5. serious emotional disturbance
6. orthopedic impairment
7. autism
8. traumatic brain injury
9. other health impairment
10. specific learning disability
11. deaf/blindness
12. multiple disabilities

There is a very precise definition of specific learning disability and an addendum of what is not a learning disability. No other category of disability has this exclusion clause.

> The term means a disorder in one or more of the basic psychological processes involved in understanding or in using language, spoken or written, that may manifest itself in an imperfect ability to listen, think, speak, read, write, spell, or to do mathematical calculations, including conditions such as perceptual disabilities, brain injury, minimal brain dysfunction, dyslexia, and developmental aphasia.
>
> The term does not include learning problems that are primarily the result of visual, hearing, or motor disabilities, of mental retardation, of emotional disturbance, or of environmental, cultural, or economic disadvantage.

There is an interesting qualification for children between the ages of three and nine. If children in this age group are thought to just be developmentally delayed, then state and local school authorities have the discretion whether or not to qualify the child.[7] When money and staff are abundant, this clause allows some school districts to be more lenient in qualifying children who didn't meet the strict standards of the learning disabilities requirements. However, during times of economic hardship, this backdoor method of providing needed services is closed by many school districts.

Qualifying for Services

There are no national standards used to qualify children. Each state, and sometimes even each district, can determine which testing procedures they will use.[8] They only have to have on file their policies and procedures with the appropriate state of federal agencies. What this means is throughout the country, different tests are being used to qualify children. Some of these tests may have lower or higher thresholds than others for what is identified as a "qualifying disorder." I recently worked with a nine-year-old child whose family just moved to an affluent school district. They had lived in a large city with a shambled school budget that operated under a court-mandated order to provide special education services. One of the first things the new school district did was language testing, since the classroom teacher suspected a problem. The test results were unequivocal. This child had serious expressive and receptive language disorders. For reasons that remained unexplained, the large city school district did not find anything abnormal about this child's language for four years, in spite of her scoring in the lower 25 percent of language ability nationally.

Once a school district has identified a child as needing services, they have up to 65 days to begin treatment. With a lack of funds and personnel, there isn't an incentive for many districts to provide speedy services. A number of years ago, I was involved in a case where a large school district attempted to manage their fiscal problems by using a "politically correct" argument. It was the special education administrator's position that labeling children as needing special services was demeaning to the child and racist for minority children, since some minorities were overrepresented in the special education population. In order to prevent this from occurring, his approach was to establish teams of school personnel to treat the problem in the classroom—prior to any testing being done. Parents of children who desperately needed services were furious. A child, even with limited language, couldn't be seen by a speech-language clinician. Rather, the child's problems would be addressed in class with a regular teacher, a classroom aide, and occasional visits by the speech-language clinician. Only the clinician had any training in delivering special services. When I spoke to her, she was in tears.

"I don't care what they're saying about labeling children. What they're doing is unethical. It's wrong. How can I help Delores if I need to work through the teacher and aide? They won't even let me do any testing."

The approach the district was taking was clearly financial, with calls to racism as a matter of convenience. The position lost its legitimacy when a parent's group was formed, in which 65 percent were minority parents. They demanded children be identified and services provided to qualified children. It took a

very public debate, meetings of outraged parents, front-page newspaper stories, and the support of professionals both in and outside of the school before the federal courts held the school district in violation of the children's civil rights.

Getting Services

Once a child qualifies for services, a plan is developed for providing them. You'll either get a call from someone in the school or receive a written notification asking you to attend a meeting with the classroom teacher, a specialist, and an administrator to discuss an intervention program for your child. Sometimes, even the child is invited to attend. At this meeting, the specialist will recommend an intervention program and ask you for input. The program, usually written in very general terms with short-term objectives (one year), is in the form of a prepared document that only requires the entry of agreed upon terms. This document is called an Individual Education Program (IEP). Even though it's a requirement of the federal government, each state and sometimes local districts can structure its outline. Once the parent signs it, the document goes into force. The parent has agreed that whatever is on the IEP is appropriate for his or her child. The IEP is not set in stone. At anytime the parent can request that it be modified. Every year the document is reviewed.

You don't have to sign the document if you can't convince the school team that what they are proposing isn't appropriate. You have the right to appeal. Many parents I have spoken to didn't reject the IEP in spite of serious concerns. Facing three to four professionals who are united in their recommendations can be very threatening. If you believe you'll feel uncomfortable, bring an expert or advocate to the meeting. This can be someone within the area the child needs services or it can be a member of a child advocacy group. In either case, if the school district is proposing something you think is inadequate, your expert is there to dispute it. On one occasion when a mother asked me to be present during an IEP meeting, she and I were able to radically change what was being offered for her child—not through threats, but rather by showing the administrators that what we were proposing made sense. The presence of an expert not only gives you increased leverage with administrators, but also clearly sends the message you are prepared to appeal the school's recommendation if you believe it's inappropriate.

TAKE A BREATH

It's important to be aware of everything that can occur in the beginning school experience, both the positives and negatives. Parents with children who have

learning problems often try to avoid looking at what may happen. It's like seeing a wild animal approaching and believing if you just close your eyes, it will go away. You'll probably feel good right up until the time you become dinner. Public school personnel aren't the enemy. Most want to do the right thing. Often they are prevented from doing it because of financial and personnel shortages. By your actions and support, you can help them help your child. Your child will shortly enter a new world that without preparation can be difficult. As a parent, you can create a bridge between the home and school that not only will prevent many problems from occurring, but also create the conditions for a wonderful experience. Starting with the next chapter, you'll learn how to do it.

Part II

Learning Differences, Problems, and Solutions

You've learned many things in the past four chapters. Why it's important to think in terms of your child's behaviors and not labels. How to become an outstanding parent-teacher. How children's learning problems may affect their feelings. And finally, you've gained an understanding of the new world of kindergarten. It's now time to work with your child. We'll look at the problems through their eyes in each of these chapters. We'll first look at seven learning strategies you'll be repeatedly using. I've found these to be most useful for children with learning differences. You'll find them easy to understand and, even more important, immediately effective. We'll use these simple methods repeatedly in Chapters 6 to 8. Each of those chapters is devoted to one type of information-processing problem. For example, Chapter 6 is about attention problems. For each problem, we'll apply the strategies in a way that'll make your teaching effective. As your child reduces, avoids, or overcomes the effects of a learning problem, you'll understand why.

FIVE

Strategies to Help Learning

S he tried to learn how to print her name for three weeks. A simple task for most children, but for Sarah, a daily reminder she was different. The seeds of failure were being planted at four years of age, not by adult ogres, but by a compassionate preschool teacher and a parent who only wanted the best for her child. Kindergarten was only a month away, and her mother wondered if she would be ready. While bright, Sarah had problems with fine-motor behaviors like writing and coordinating arm and leg movements. An examination by a pediatrician didn't reveal anything abnormal when she was three years old.

"Don't worry," the pediatrician said, "I'm sure it's just developmental. By six, she'll be functioning like other kids her age. I've seen this thousands of times in my practice."

Instead of calming the mother, the pediatrician increased her anxiety. She left wondering how she couldn't worry. The pediatrician only looked at the physical development of her child. The mother was also concerned about her emotional well-being. Two years may not seem like much time to an adult, but for children it's a large percentage of their lives. Having a billboard shoved in your face everyday saying "you're different" means by six, one-third of this child's life would be intimately involved in failure. I don't find that acceptable, and neither do most parents. In working with this mother I ignored the fact that, eventually, Sarah probably would have motor skills within a normal range—she had a specific problem *now*. One that not only was of concern to the parent, but also to Sarah. The differences became obvious to her when she compared how she printed her name on drawings with her preschool class-mates. Her mother and I used seven fundamental change strategies:

1. A good design
2. Advance instructions
3. Making learning positive
4. Doing it often
5. Using little steps
6. Monitoring
7. Providing feedback.

First, we designed an activity accounting for Sarah's unique style of learning (*using a good design*). Then we set the framework for the activity. We explained what we would be doing, how it would be done, and why we were doing it (*advance instructions*). Not only did we design an enjoyable activity but also, when it was over, there was a reward for Sarah (*making it positive*). We had Sarah practice writing her name on everything, from her juice bottle to some of her toys (*doing it often*). We didn't start by having her write her entire name, just the first letter, using a dotted outline surrounded by boarders her mother placed on each object, similar to the one in Figure 5.1 (*using little steps*). She could immediately see if she was on target as she wrote her name if her "s" remained between the unbroken lines (*monitoring*). Her mother then told her not only if what she did was right or wrong, but also why (*feedback*). Gradually, the boldness of the outline was reduced, leaving only the faintest hint of an "S," as shown in Figure 5.2.

The outer borders were also narrowed. The same procedure was done with "sa," then "sar," "sara," and finally "sarah." Within two weeks, Sarah was joyfully printing her name on everything. Seven simple strategies—one very happy, successful child. We identified a specific problem, ignored labeling, and provided strategies to correct it. That's the exact procedure you'll learn how to do in the next three chapters. But first, I'll explain each of these very important strategies.

Figure 5.1
Writing Between Bold Lines

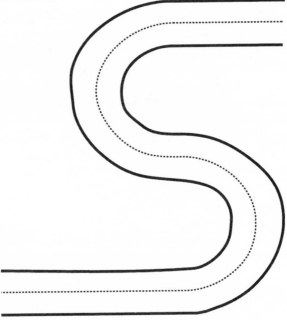

Figure 5.2
Writing Between Faint Lines

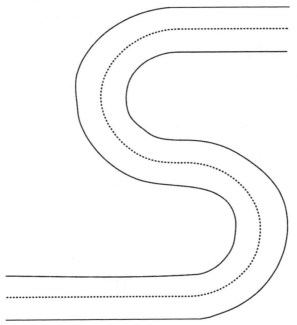

Think of these strategies as if they were principles of cooking. You just entered a gourmet cooking school where you're first taught how to make sauces, prepare vegetables, cut meats, sauté and bake. Not once during the first week of training did your instructors talk about specific dishes or recipes, in spite of your repeated requests for how to make duck á l'orange, creamed potato soup, or French country bread. The focus was on *technique*. You only began using recipes after two weeks of mastering each technique. Once starting the preparation of specific dishes, you realized how easy it was to modify them. Knowing how to prepare a yeast mix and kneading enabled you to easily switch from French country bread to an Italian ciabatta, to a Jewish hallah. You'll find the same process when teaching your child. All children learn in a unique way. However, the same principles of learning apply to all. It's just a matter of knowing how to adjust the ingredients. This chapter will help you become a chef and not just a cook.

USING A GOOD DESIGN

You probably want to just rush in and start helping your child. Although sometimes this works, a better approach is to first understand how your child learns.

Then build that knowledge into your activity. It won't take that much time. In the example of Sarah, the mother and I spent about 15 minutes designing the activity. Good designs have more to do with the *presentation* of materials than anything else. The presentation can significantly help children learn if eight things are done:

1. Keep it simple.
2. Present it slowly.
3. Reduce time between saying and doing.
4. Keep instructions and explanations short.
5. Make it visual and concrete.
6. Show it in different ways.
7. Make it stand out.
8. Use context in teaching.

Keep It Simple

We all have a tendency to make things much more complicated than they need to be. Children learn more quickly if you strip things down to the basics.[1] They also prefer simple rather than more complex learning activities.[2] In the movie *City Slickers,* the cowboy eventually shares his secret of life with the main character.[3] He holds up one finger and says, "One thing, that's the secret of life." Throughout the movie, the main character ponders the cowboy's philosophy until he comes to realize the focus of life should be on one thing. This philosophy applies directly to the design of your learning activity. Identify the *core* thing you want to teach your child. That should be the overwhelming emphasis of the activity.

For example, I was working with a mother who was trying to teach her four-year-old son how to get himself ready in the morning for preschool. There was much she wanted him to do: select his clothes, button his shirt, zip up his pants, go to the bathroom, gather the pictures he would take to school, put on his coat, and remember his lunch box. This is an enormous number of things for a four-year-old to remember. We had to simplify the process. I had her establish "stations" that were numbered and everything associated with the station was located there. For example, at Station 1, which was the bathroom, his toothbrush and a wash cloth for his face were placed together where he could reach them. At Station 2, which was his bedroom, he found his underwear, a shirt, socks, shoes, and a pair of pants. The same type of groupings occurred for each type of thing his mother wanted him to do. Within a very short period of time, he was able to prepare himself for preschool. We simplified the process, focusing on the sequence of things necessary for preparation. Never forget the purpose of your activity. First identify, and then magnify its most important element. In this example it was sequencing.

Present It Slowly

There's an old Tibetan saying to "Make haste slowly." In our fast-paced society, we've been conditioned to do everything fast, from driving to eating our meals to explaining things to our children. For *all* children, slower is better.[4] For children who learn differently, this is an even more important principle. Unfortunately, there aren't any research studies or charts giving us the ideal rate of presentation. However, there are two rules of thumb I use:

1. Slower is *always* better than faster.
2. If a child is having any problems with the material, slow down the presentation.

You can do two things to slow your presentations. The first is to speak more slowly. The second is to use pauses. Of the two, speaking more slowly is easier. The best way of determining your rate is to take a five-minute sample on a tape recorder. You'll arrive at your rate of speech per minute by dividing the total number of words by five. Your rate should not exceed 150 words per minute when teaching children. This is a benchmark I try to use. Although there is no solid research showing this is the best rate, I've found it's one generally below the threshold for confusing most children.

We assume it's just as easy for children as adults to focus on our speech, regardless of its rate. Generally, there can be problems for both adults and children when the rate of speech is fast.[5] As speed increases, certain parts of the message can be lost or distorted. I was working with a mother of a four-year-old who seemed to have problems comprehending what his mother said. Although she was very careful about the structure of her speech, the child still had problems.

"I'm very aware of the words I choose to use. Also, I don't use grammar that's beyond what Scott understands. I think he has an attention-deficit disorder."

"What type of problems does he have?" I asked.

"When I ask him to do certain things, sometimes he misses part of what I say."

I had a good idea where the problem would be found just by listening to her speech. I analyzed her rate first speaking to me, then to her son. They were virtually identical—almost 250 words per minute. A very fast rate for comprehension, for both adults and children. Although at that rate, a child without any learning problems could probably have a cursory understanding of what was being said, it was too fast for anything complex or unfamiliar. We practiced slowing down her rate to fewer than 150 words per minute when speaking to her son. It took two weeks of intense work before she was able to consistently and almost unconsciously uses the new rate. Very quickly, she saw a difference in his ability to comprehend. Using a slower rate improves comprehension for all children. It's even more critical for children who have auditory-processing problems.[6] Your rate of speech shouldn't be faster than your child's ability to understand. There are many things that can affect understanding, and we'll address each of these in Chapter 7. But there is one thing that cuts across all information-processing problems, and that's how familiar your child is with what you are saying.[7] Generally, the less familiar he or she is with the context and content of what's said, the slower you should make your speech. For example, you're introducing your child to a game that contains a series of unfamiliar rules or a social situation that your child hasn't encountered. Consciously make a decision to slow down.

The second thing you can do to adjust your rate is pause between different parts of a request, instruction, or description. For example, "Jean, I want you to go upstairs...(pause), put on your red dress...(pause), then come downstairs."

It's a very simple procedure, yet one that's effective. By briefly pausing between different parts of an instruction, the child has time to process one unit of the message before continuing on to the next. Gradually as your child becomes more proficient, your pauses can be reduced. I worked with a child whose ability to process information was severely impaired. We would start with keeping each instruction, request, or description to a short sentence. We would only continue after he indicated either by his speech or actions that he understood what we said. Often, we had to wait up to ten seconds before proceeding. But instead of being continually confused by the words thrown to him, he was successful. It was a marvelous transformation to watch, almost as if you were listening to a foreign language you couldn't understand. Then, without warning the words were spoken in English. The same type of transformation occurs when children who have continually failed begin experiencing success.

Reduce Time Between Saying and Doing

When you are instructing your child, try to keep the amount of time between the instruction and what your child is asked to do as short as possible. Children's accuracy suffers as the length of time increases between the end of an instruction and the beginning of the task.[8] This seems to be related to limitations in short-term or working memory. At times I would ask Justin to do something when he was in the middle of another task. The following conversation occurred when he was eating dinner.

"Justin, I'd like you to put your bike back in the garage. It's blocking the sidewalk."

"Sure Daddy, as soon as I finish my ice cream."

It was a large bowl, and it took him ten minutes to finish. Since his face and hands were covered with chocolate ice cream, my wife needed to do a thorough cleaning. As he got off his chair, droplets of melted ice cream became visible on his pants, the chair, and the floor.

"Justin, here are some paper towels," my wife said. "Please wipe up the mess."

Twenty minutes had passed between the time I asked Justin to put away his bike and the first opportunity he had to do it. During this time, he was responsible for finishing his food, being cleaned, and cleaning. I saw him playing with his trains when I came back into the house.

"Justin, I asked you to put your bike in the garage. You haven't done it yet."

"Are you sure you asked me, Daddy?" he replied.

This lapse between giving and the execution of an instruction is problematic for all children.[9] It becomes even harder if other things occur during the intervening time. In some children with certain types of memory problems, even a shorter lapse has results similar to the one with Justin. A few minutes delay in very severe cases can even cause problems. For some children, their ability to hold things in short-term memory is limited.[10] There is no way of determining at what point a "problem" exists. Also, what is problematic in one setting may not be in another. To avoid problems, it's just better to keep the time between requesting and doing short. For Justin, just waiting until he finished his ice cream would have produced better results.

Keep Instructions and Explanations Short

Keep your instructions and explanations short when explaining something to your child. Think of yourself as an editor who is given the assignment of taking a rambling 1,000-word article and reducing it to 500 words without changing the main theme. We often provide more information than needed when we instruct our children. I was working with a mother whose child had language problems. Part of this mother's training was to have her develop more precise ways of providing instructions and giving information to her daughter. Below is an example of how she described an event her daughter was witnessing and didn't understand.

"Suzy, over there by the drugstore is a policeman. He's the one wearing the blue uniform with the gun on his belt. You remember, we talked to someone just like him at your Uncle George's house last year at Christmas. His name was Tom. I don't know the name of this policeman. Anyway, he's giving that man a speeding ticket for doing 45 miles per hour in a 25-mile-per-hour zone. That was reckless on the part of the driver, what with so many children around. He'll have to pay a hefty fine for his lack of consideration."

Can you identify what this mother was trying to explain? Who are policemen? Something about last Christmas? Rules of driving? This 100-word explanation, while an interesting conversation to have with a 5-year-old, is filled with unnecessary information. The lesson the mother wanted to teach her daughter was why people shouldn't speed. But nonpertinent words and thoughts hid that message. The mother gave her daughter too much information. While it served as the connective tissue holding together some ideas, the intended message got lost within it. If this were to be an explanation rather than a conversation, it could be as short as the following.

"Suzie, cars shouldn't go fast here. There are too many children on the street. That man in the blue car was going too fast, so the policeman is giving him a ticket. A ticket is a piece of paper that says the man did something wrong."

Not as conversational, but a lot more instructive, and less than half the number of words.

Make It Visual and Concrete

Many of the instructions given to children are only spoken. At times, just words are enough for learning to occur. However, with some children who have listening problems, or when the instructions are complicated, using visuals or graphics makes a big difference.[11] A visual or graphic takes what you say and makes it concrete and lasting. When you say, "Joyce, go into the backyard and bring back your toys," as soon as the words stop, so do the thoughts for some children. But if a picture of the yard appears on one card and toys on the other, the concepts remain long after the words stop. Auditory attention is improved when children can look at what you are saying. They can quickly identify what's important by focusing on something concrete. When they know what should be done, their confidence increases and learning becomes more satisfying.[12]

Making something visual and concrete not only enhances attention, but storage and retrieval become easier.[13] Accuracy and speed also improves.[14] I once worked with a child who had a great deal of difficulty with time concepts, such as *before, now,* and *later.* He was having problems with time because it's abstract. Where is *now?* Can I see *later?* Where did *before* go? These abstractions had to be made concrete for him to understand time. What my student and I did appears in Figure 5.3. *Before* was denoted by a blue-colored square with an arrow pointing to the left. *Now* was a red triangle with a circle in the middle. *Later* was a green rectangle with an arrow pointing to the right. As my student read, the appropriate time card was touched when it appeared in the story. For example, when she read "Now the horse is galloping," she

Figure 5.3
Making Time Concrete

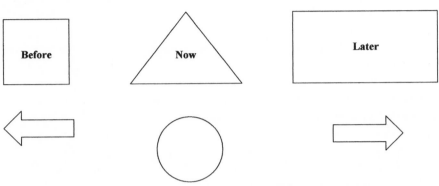

would increase the volume of her voice when saying *now*, pretend to gallop, tap loudly and repeatedly on the red triangle card, briefly pause, and smile at him. Not only did time become concrete, but she provided a series of visual and auditory cues that focused his attention on the critical element of the activity—the concept of time. Then, she asked him to tell the story, in his own words, using *before*, *now* and *later*. As she requested, he pointed to the cards at appropriate places throughout his version of the story. In one 45-minute session, he finally understood time—a problem with which he had always struggled. At our next session, his mother excitedly told me what occurred during the week.

"I couldn't believe it," she said. "We were in the restaurant and Dean wanted to order pancakes. He had them last month and he really liked them. As he talked about those pancakes, he used his left hand and pointed left. Then, when he wanted to order pancakes, he brought his left hand into the center of his body, and said 'And *now* I want pancakes.' Then, moving his right hand to the right, he said, 'And I think I want them *tomorrow* too.'"

Dean was not only able to learn something in the clinic, but was able to apply it without help in a different setting. Although we hadn't worked on "tomorrow," he knew it was later than "now." Learning the order of the days in the week became a snap for Dean.

All children learn better when you couple spoken instructions with something visual.[15] This is even more important for children who learn differently.[16] Eventually, you want children to follow just spoken instructions. But initially, successes will be greater if you couple something visual and concrete with your words. It can be something as simple as showing the number of things needed to be done by writing numbers on a piece of paper, then checking them off as each activity is completed.

Show It in Different Ways

Often what we want to teach our children is something that needs to be applied in various settings. For example, if children were confused about something, we would like them to ask for clarification, whether from a parent, teacher, or friend. Yet, we tend to show only one example of what we want children to learn and assume they'll be able to apply it in other situations. A parent instructs a child, "When you don't understand, say so." With some children, even the words are supplied, such as "I don't understand." Some parents assume once a child demonstrates the ability to tell them "I don't understand," he or she will use it with other people. Unfortunately, this often isn't true. Concepts are learned quicker and applied in more settings if many different versions of them are presented.[17] In our example, the mother simulated various people and different settings with her child. After starting with the example of themselves in the living room, she simulated a school setting. The mother pretended to be a teacher and instructed her imagined class of children. There were directions, stories to read, and suggestions for doing things.

Figure 5.4
Levels of Understanding

The child was supposed to say, "I don't understand," if she was confused. In front of the child was a card with three squares, similar to the one in Figure 5.4. The top square is a smiling face, indicating the child understood what was said. The next square contained a face with straight lips indicating that the child may be slightly confused. Below that was a sad face, meaning she was totally confused. The child was given a chip and asked to place it on the most appropriate square either during or immediately after the mother's presentation. After this simulation was completed, the next one began, which was a play situation with children. The final simulation involved adults in various settings. With the mother by her child's side, she could monitor if the child understood how to ask for clarification, regardless of who was making confusing statements. Although the activity didn't improve the child's ability to understand some things, it gave her a valuable tool to use enabling others to compensate for her problems.

Make It Stand Out

In teaching, whatever is important should stand out, while everything else fades into the background.[18] For example, in advertising, usually one feature of a picture in a magazine is highlighted to get the reader's attention. If it's an advertisement for a vacation resort in an outdoor magazine, the resort's magnificent trout-filled stream might appear in the foreground, with other activities appearing smaller in the background. The same resort advertising in a golf magazine would feature their golf course in the forefront of the advertisement, with a distant shot of the stream in the background. By highlighting or making one part of a presentation stand out from everything else, not only is the viewer's attention manipulated, but changes also occur in thinking. Highlighting gives things an added sense of importance. We can use the same advertising technique to enhance learning in children.[19] Take, for example, teaching the use of articles, such as "a" and "the" to a child who frequently omits them. Normally, when asked to say "the boy runs," the child responds with "boy runs." To teach her to use articles, the parent might decide to use a three-card system in which each card represents one unit of the utterance. On each card, for children who don't read, a symbol is used to represent a word. The cards might look like those appearing in Figure 5.5. Although each word in the utterance is noted, there is nothing to indicate the article is the focus of the activity. By minimally changing the presentation (Figure 5.6), it becomes very obvious to the child where to direct her attention. The same activity is presented, but with modified cards, the child's attention is focused more on the first unit because it is larger and has a different color. In presenting almost any kind of material, similar modifications can be made. It could involve objects that can be highlighted through colors, shapes, textures, or other characteristics.

Figure 5.5
Equal Emphasis

Figure 5.6
Emphasis on First Card

Making distinctions between the most important feature and everything else also strengthens recall.[20] In speech, for example, you can increase the volume of the words you want your child to focus on, or even use a different pitch to make it stand out. In the above example of the child with the article problem, the parent might want to vocally accent the article in her speech as she touches the article card. The distinctions both in speech and in your graphics should be huge, since over a period of time, the distinguishing features of what is thought to be most important diminishes.[21] Everyone has driven down a street and encountered an incredibly gaudily painted house. The first time you saw it in contrast with the other houses on the street, you probably went into shock—the difference was too great. Your shock diminishes each time you drive down this street to work. By the end of the month, you probably don't give it any notice. If the house were only mildly gaudy, you probably would ignore it after one or two days. The same type of selective attention occurs when you highlight what you want your child to learn. The power of the distinction fades over time. Therefore, the greater the initial difference, the less likely it will fade.

Use Context in Teaching

Children learn significantly better if you teach something in the context in which it's usually found.[22] However, there's a caveat—the context has to be familiar. If it isn't, a child's ability to learn something new is decreased.[23] The less familiar children are with the context, the more problems they'll have with learning. For example, a father wished to teach the words *bear*, *tiger*, and *elephant* to his son. In order to do this, he constructed an elaborate activity involving the creation of a zoo game. The child had never been to a zoo and didn't know what one was. The game, while being very creative, contained confusing elements, like cages, feeding times, and controlled open spaces. Instead of facilitating an understanding of these animals, the zoo game made it more difficult for the child to learn. Realizing the problem, the father stopped the game and took his son to the zoo. Now, he had a familiar context for the game. And the child's ability to learn not only the three words, but also other concepts related to captive animals, increased. Context doesn't always require a visit. Simply elaborating on a situation is enough.[24] For example, a mother wants to teach her daughter how to cross the street. After explaining she should only walk when the light facing her is green, the mother proceeds to describe everything related to the crosswalk.

"Marie, you will be seeing three different lights on top of a pole."

"Where's the pole Mommy?"

"If you look on the other side of the street, you'll see it."

"What kind of lights are they?"

"On the very top will be a green light. If you see that you can cross the street."

"Okay Mommy."

"Under the green light, there will be a yellow light. If that comes on, that means the green will go off and the red light will be coming on soon."

"Red means I don't go right?"

"That's right, Marie."

"But what do I do if the yellow comes on when I'm walking?

"If you've already started to cross, hurry across the street. If you're just beginning to cross, come back. Even though you're watching the light, always see if cars are coming. And when you cross, always stay between the two white lines."

In this example, the mother provided the context within which she wanted her daughter to act. It's contexts like these that provide the "hooks," making retrieval easier.

ADVANCE ORGANIZING STATEMENTS

Imagine entering a movie 20 minutes after it began. Unfortunately, you knew nothing about the theme or plot before coming to see it, so you can't just jump right into the action. Gradually, over 20 to 30 minutes, you begin to understand what must have happened in the beginning of the movie. Even though you caught up with the current action, you still don't feel comfortable. You have to guess what happened before you arrived. And the movie rolled on all during the time you were retroactively recreating plots, scenes, and motivations. That's similar to what happens when children aren't told

Figure 5.7
Model Advance Organizer Statements

Advance Organizer	Example
What	We are going to throw this ball into that basket
How	I want you to stand behind this line and throw it when I ask you to
Why	This game will make it easier for you to play with your friends in the park

what, *how*, and *why* they'll be doing something. These are called advance organizing statements. By stating these three things before an activity begins, children develop a sense of focus and purpose that greatly helps learning.[25] It focuses their efforts. Many parents and even therapists think they're only important to use the first time an activity is done. That's a mistake. You should use them before beginning every activity, regardless of the number of times your child has done it. Model statements appear in Figure 5.7.

What We Are Doing

By explaining to children what they will be doing, they're able to focus on the task and two important consequences result. Success rates increase, and what was learned is retained better and longer. I was supervising a student who was working with a child who had comprehension problems. Not once during the four activities I watched did the clinician directly tell the child what they were doing. When I came into the room during the fourth game, I decided to see if the child had even the vaguest idea what he was doing.

"Bobby, this looks like fun," I said pointing to the game. "What are you doing?"

"Playing a game."

Bobby's focus was on the game, rather than the learning goal.

"Yes Bobby," I said. "You're playing a game, but the game will make it easier for you to understand things. Like when your teacher says something in front of the class and you don't know what she means."

His eyes lit up as if he just had an epiphany. Yes, he was playing an enjoyable game, but he now understood it would help him in his class. Once he understood that the *what* was improving comprehension and not pure play, his responses quickly improved in both speed and accuracy. Even simple focusing statements before an activity begins diminishes the time it takes to respond and also increases the success rate for tasks, both easy and more difficult.[26,27] One mother I knew wanted to teach her child basic self-care skills, such as folding her shirts rather than throwing them into the drawer. She could have just said, "Watch me," or "Do what I'm doing." However, she began with the simple statement, "June, I'm going to show you how to fold your shirts." By not just showing what should be done, the mother's statement directed June's attention to something very specific.

Focusing statements increase the retention of general information and specific items.[28, 29] For example, a father is trying to explain to his son what's happening during a baseball game. Just by explaining the basic rules, his son will be better able to remember what's going on during the game. In our baseball example, the father could also have explained how batters set up for different types of pitches. The specificity of these statements would take his son to another level of understanding. Advance organizing statements are very powerful. They can focus a child's attention with the intensity of a laser. To enhance the already powerful effects of advance organizing statements, you can also use visual cues.[30] In our shirt-folding example, the mother became very creative.

"June, look here at this drawer," she said pulling out a drawer in which the shirts were neatly folded. Then another one where the shirts were just thrown in.

"Should we make this drawer look like that one Mommy?" June asked, pointing to the drawer of folded shirts.

"Yes dear, that's exactly what we are going to do."

Although the mother could have used a picture of folded shirts, the real model was better. Whenever possible, use real items.

How We're Doing It

Children often have concerns regarding the activities they'll be asked to do. The anxiety might be sufficient to interfere with learning if they have experienced many failures.[31] Simply describing how the activity will be done before it starts can eliminate some of the fear. You can describe activities in various ways. The simplest is to just describe its sequence. I was working with a mother whose daughter had problems with turn taking. In the past, her inability to understand how to take turns made it difficult to interact with other children. To reduce any anxiety she might feel, the mother spent time explaining how we would do the activity.

"Vicki, we're going to play store."

"I don't know how to play it Mommy."

"It's very easy. First, I'll be the storekeeper and ask you questions. You know I'm the storekeeper because I'll be behind this counter.

"What will I be Mommy?"

"You'll be the customer, because customers stay on this side of the counter. Then we'll switch and you'll be the storekeeper and I'll be the customer and you'll ask me questions. Whoever is the storekeeper asks questions. Whoever is the customer answers them."

We were under no delusions this simple game would immediately enable Vicki to become a better playmate. It was only the first of many steps needed to help her understand the rules of turn taking. By explaining turn taking through a simple and fun game, we avoided creating the anxiety she often felt facing interactions governed by rules she couldn't understand. For most children, descriptions such as these are fine. However, for other children, you may need to go into more detail. This is especially true when activities are complicated or the fear of something new is great. I was working with a young child whose ability to learn was impaired by some severe emotional problems. When faced with anything new, he refused to interact. The only way I could get him to do a new activity was to explain it in detail. What before felt threatening was now familiar.

"Jeremy, we're going to play the car game today so you can learn how to follow directions."

"I don't know how to play it."

"I'll show it to you. You and Daddy will each have a car."

"What color will mine be?"

"Red"

"What will I be doing with my car?"

"I'm going to tell you which room to drive the car to and then you'll do it."

"Do I drive it slow or fast?"

"Any way you want Jeremy."

The questions just kept coming, until he knew every aspect of the game. Often when children keep asking questions, they're sending a message—I need to know more about this before I feel comfortable. As laborious as it was, until I answered every one of Jeremy's questions, he wouldn't participate. It was too threatening without information. A good rule of thumb to use is the more unusual, threatening, or different the activity, the more explanations and details should be provided, even if your child's problems don't approach those of Jeremy's. Knowing what will occur often significantly relieves children's anxiety of what to expect. The use of a graphic representation, such as the one in Figure 5.8, can also be very effective in explaining what will be done. A chip can indicate where the child is in the sequence. Instead of a sequence, time can be substituted, with each card indicating the amount of time that will be necessary for each activity. The representation can have various levels of abstraction. Blank cards can be used merely to indicate where the activity is in a sequence. Or it can be more literal, using graphic representations or words. For example, if three sequential behaviors are required, parents can move their finger from one card to the next as the behavior is being produced. For children who have difficulty

Figure 5.8
How We're Doing It

Reading	Kicking Game	Talking with Mom and Dad

either doing an activity for a certain amount of time or wish to do it beyond the allowed time, beginning, middle, and end cards could be used. This can also be done for the entire activity, separating it into parts.

Sometimes, words don't work. The activity may be too complicated, it may have too many parts, or your child's ability to understand may not be up to the words you are using. When any of these situations occur, either forget about the words, or couple them with a demonstration. I watched a father try to teach his daughter how to kick a soccer ball. They were standing off to the side of a group of kids practicing. The father hoped his daughter would see how much fun this was and would ask to join the team.

"Sweetie, I'm going to show you how to kick the ball. What I want you to do is to bring your right foot all the way back as you plant your left foot on the side. Then, when it's completely back, bring it as fast as you can forward, but bend your ankle just a little, then contact the ball straight and follow it through so your foot is in front of you."

This four-year-old child looked like her father was trying to explain Washington politics. The coach of the practicing team was close enough to watch the father's attempt. After his eyes stopped rolling, he approached the father.

"Would you mind if I showed your daughter how to kick the ball?"

"No, not at all," the father gratefully said.

"Now watch me," the coach said as he placed the ball in front of his foot and then gently kicked it. Then placing another ball in front of the little girl, he said, "Now you kick it."

Without any hesitation, she kicked the ball ten yards. The father was amazed, the coach smiled knowingly, and the little girl was thrilled.

"Daddy, can I join the team?" she said.

Sometimes, there just aren't enough words to explain some things, even those that are simple. Since we often don't know when those times will occur, it's best to demonstrate whenever possible.

Why We Are Doing the Activity

Mysteries are appropriate for novels, but not for teaching children with learning differences. Children need to know why they're doing an activity. If your child's ability to understand allows for it, always explain the reason the activity is being done. Children tend to be less resistant and become more actively involved when they know why they're doing an activity. Often what is obvious to us is vague to them. They may not understand why they're asked to do a specific activity, or its positive consequences. For example, remembering everything they need for preschool is not something children dwell on or even think about. But for the parent of a child with memory problems, it becomes an example of much broader issues. You probably wouldn't get very far with the following explanation to a four-year-old: "George, the reason we are doing this is to improve your memory. You won't forget as easily after we play this game."

Too sophisticated and abstract for most four-year-olds, the explanation needs to be made more concrete and meaningful. Such as, "George, we're doing this to help you remember to bring your lunch to school. If you forget it this week, I won't be able to bring you any food and you'll have to wait until I pick you up." Now that's direct, concrete, and meaningful!

MAKE IT POSITIVE

How often have you thought your child should do something just because it was the "right thing" to do? You believed your child should want to do it without the promise of a reward. If children can't find anything positive about the learning activity, the likelihood they will be successful just because they *should* do it is remote. Some parents even believe by "offering bribes" children will start to expect rewards for doing everything. This fear of providing rewards began in the 1960s, when researchers equated rewards with M&Ms, Fruit Loops, and a variety of other foods.[32] The unfortunate message conveyed to parents was, if you want your child to do something, offer money, food, or other treats. Many parents were appalled by what they saw as an immoral value, and researchers, by simplifying the role of rewards, did little to correct the misconception. Believe it or not, our children are just like we are when it comes to receiving rewards. If you dislike almost everything about your job, why do you stay? The paycheck of course! Welcome to the world of M&Ms and Fruit Loops. Unfortunately, parents think about only one type of reward or "reinforcement," as clinical researchers refer to it. But there are two other forms of reinforcement that are significantly more powerful and important for learning. I'll describe all three, explain how you can use them when teaching your child, and if possible, why you should avoid using punishment. Wanting to do things that are rewarding is a value found in all people. It's not something that has to be learned; it's part of who we are. We all move toward things that give us joy and away from those that don't. In this regard, our children are just like us.

Doing

Ursula Le Guin said, "it's good to have an end to journey toward; but it is the journey that matters, in the end."[33] Her poignant statement emphasized the importance of finding pleasure in the *doing* of something, not just in an end product. Finding pleasure in doing an act is known as intrinsic reinforcement, and is the most powerful type of reward for both children and adults. I love playing four-wall handball. The act of moving, making shots and doing things I never thought possible, creates a wonderful feeling in me. I'm never concerned how long the game takes or who wins. Intrinsic reinforcement is very powerful since it's not dependent on anything external. It's an internal feeling so rewarding, both adults and children wish to experience it again and again. I can still remember seeing the expression on my son's face when he started to roll on his first pair of in-line skates. After going two feet, he fell and scraped the only part of his body we hadn't protected—his nose. He wanted to continue even though his nose was bleeding and he was crying. No matter how painful his injury, the joy he experienced gliding on the sidewalk outweighed the pain of a scraped nose. Fifteen years later, it's still one of his favorite activities. If you have a choice of behaviors to work on with your child, try to find one that's intrinsically reinforcing. The reinforcement can come from either the new behavior or the activity used to master it. An example of a rewarding behavior would be the joy a child feels when being able to describe things with new words. A rewarding activity could involve moving an adult around the room using new words that in and of themselves, the child didn't find rewarding. This would be similar to the children in the clinic who dictated my movements through words.

Completing

Not all activities and behaviors can be intrinsically reinforcing. In those situations, look for something that involves a rewarding completion. When I was living by myself in graduate school, I had a great aversion towards cleaning. I hated everything associated with it. After all, I had much better things to do, like discussing the great issues of the world with friends and watching movies with esoteric themes. After a few weeks, my basement apartment looked like a hovel, with green things growing on my dishes. Eventually, I cleaned everything, even those dishes. I still hated the task, but I wanted a desirable end product, which was a clean apartment. The clean apartment was my reward for doing something I didn't want to do. It was the completion of the cleaning process, not the cleaning, that was rewarding.

The same dynamics work with our children. One day, Justin was invited to go skating with a friend. He had to be ready at noon when his friend's parents would be coming to the house to get him. They were going to a new skate park all the kids were talking about. In order to skate there, you had to have full protection: kneepads, wrist guards, elbow pads, and a helmet. I knew these items were spread throughout the garage with everything piled in a jumble of unrelated things. Justin, just like me, would place objects wherever it was convenient. Tools were with toys, automobile parts with baseballs, and garden tools everywhere. I explained we had two hours to find everything or he wouldn't be allowed to skate at the park. It wasn't my decision, it was park policy. He surveyed the garage and then expressed a look of panic accurately reflecting the chaos he saw.

"Justin, the only way of finding all your skating equipment is to put everything in special places."

"Why don't we just look for my skating stuff?" he asked.

"Because it'll take longer."

He wasn't buying my logic. So I had to up the ante.

"Justin, you'll have a whole shelf with special boxes just for your skating equipment. And we'll have a shelf for Mom's gardening equipment, a shelf for the car supplies, and one for my tools. The only rule we'll use is if you touch something, it has to go on the right shelf."

He still wasn't pleased, but started to pick through the piles of objects. I knew his helmet was in an area that would be attacked last. In less than 30 minutes, not only did we find all of the skating equipment, but we had also organized the garage. My son received no enjoyment from the activity, but its completion was rewarding. It allowed him to find everything he needed to skate. When you can't find an act that's reinforcing for your child, look for a reinforcing completion. Although less powerful than a reinforcing act, a completion can still be an effective tool for teaching.[34]

A Payoff

At times however, your child may not find anything reinforcing either with the act or its completion. Then, a payoff is necessary—a familiar form of reinforcement. A payoff is a reward having nothing to do *directly* with the act or its completion. A salary is the best example of a payoff. A salary is not attached to any one activity. You can get a salary for teaching, driving a bus, or thousands of other jobs. The automobile plant worker may not get any pleasure from pressing the buttons that create an endless supply of shiny bumpers [*doing*], nor receive pleasure from seeing the finished product [*the completion*], but he enjoys the paycheck received every two weeks for his work [*the payoff*].

I remember using a guide when fly fishing in Florida. Although he was amiable and helpful, it became apparent he took little pleasure in fishing. The joy of fishing left years ago. Now, the only reason he guided was for the money. He confided in me that on other days he doesn't guide, he never touches a fishing rod or even thinks about fishing. Although a payoff is the least powerful of the three reinforcements for increasing motivation, it still can be very effective.[35] Ten years after my guide lost interest in fishing, he still was on the water three days every week.

One of my most successful clients was an individual who was motivated to change only because of a payoff. He was promised the vice presidency of a major corporation with a seven figure salary if he eliminated his stuttering. The increased status and salary were positive enough to get him to do activities he didn't find pleasurable. Conversely, a professional baseball player I treated couldn't find anything reinforcing in the act of speaking fluently, its completion, or a payoff. With a salary in excess of $5,000,000 a year and absolutely no negative consequences because of his stuttering, he couldn't find anything reinforcing about fluent speech and quit therapy after two sessions.

There are things children must learn to do in which neither the doing nor completion is rewarding. For many children, things such as getting ready and organized for preschool fall into this category. Although we may see the relationship between skills such as these and those needed in kindergarten and beyond, children may find the relationship, at best, tenuous. Regardless of how often we try to explain, something gets lost in the translation from adult thoughts to kid actions. Why should they do something whose act and completion aren't rewarding? They shouldn't. You may need to provide a payoff to urge them along in learning the importance of some behaviors, such as self-help skills. For example, I worked with a mother whose 5-year-old child continually resisted doing common hygienic activities such as brushing his teeth. He would eventually do everything, but it became a nightly battle. The mother would always win, but the struggle taxed her emotional well-being. We constructed a

Figure 5.9
Points

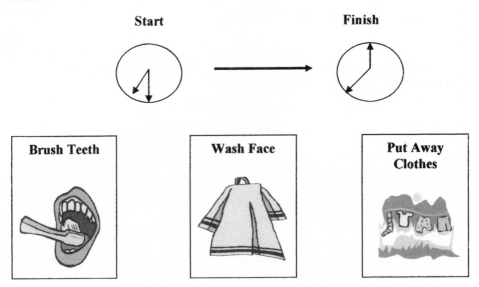

game and depicted it using a card similar to the one in Figure 5.9. He was required to complete each bathroom activity before 8:00 P.M. By then, he had to brush his teeth, wash his face, and put all of the dirty clothes into the hamper. The first alarm went off at 7:30 P.M.. This was the signal he could begin taking care of the bathroom needs. At 8:00 P.M. the second alarm would go off. If the three activities were completed by then, he received a point. If even one thing wasn't done, no point. He was able to trade seven points for a toy car. The use of points or rewards may not fit in with the idea of what you believe children *should* be. However, it's what they *are*.

Using All Three

I always try to develop activities having all three rewards. The stronger and more extensive the reinforcement, the more likely learning will occur, and the behavior remain. Here are four simple principles you can use to make learning activities positive.

1. There should be *at least* one form of reinforcement present.
2. The most powerful form of reinforcement is in doing the activity, followed by its completion, then the payoff.
4. The presence of two reinforcers is better than one.
5. The presence of three is best.

When my son was 5 years old, I began teaching him how to ride a two-wheel bike without training wheels. I designed a learning activity involving all three reinforcers. He loved pedaling [*doing*], so I knew it had to be successful. If he just started to pedal without any assistance, he would fall down, and pedaling would become less than enjoyable.

"Justin, I'm going to let you ride your bike without the training wheels."

He had been riding with them for the past three months. A frightened look came over his face.

"But Daddy, I'll fall down."

"No you won't Justin. I'll hold on to the back of the seat. Don't worry, as long as I'm holding the seat it's just like having wheels. What do you think?"

"Okay Daddy, but don't let go!"

The first reinforcer was in place. Pedaling would remain an enjoyable activity. Now it was time to make the completion of the act of pedaling reinforcing. I placed four rubber cones in a row on the sidewalk. The first was about 10 feet from where we would start. The second 15, the third 25, and the fourth 50.

"Justin we're only going to go to the first cone. Does that sound alright?"

"Will you hold my seat?"

"Of course."

"Then it's okay."

He started pedaling with me running behind him and reached the first cone without any difficulty.

"I did it Daddy, I did it!" he shouted. Not only was the act of pedaling rewarding, but so was reaching the cone (*completion*). He rode back to the starting line with me holding on to his seat. Two of the three reinforcers were in place. Now it was time to introduce the payoff.

"Justin, that was great. You know how you wanted to get some things for your bike like streamers and a bell?"

"Yes Daddy."

"Well, each time we get to another cone, and go back to the starting line, you'll get one of those things" (*payoff*).

His eyes widened. "Let's go again!" he screamed.

"Now Justin, we don't have to go right away to the next cone. Why don't we do five little trips back and forth to each cone before we go to the next?"

He thought for a minute weighing the fear of rapidly increasing his distance against the immediacy of getting the bell and streamers. I needed to tip the balance in the favor of more practice at each step.

"We have the whole day to ride. Even if you do everything very quickly, we won't be able to buy those things until tomorrow."

"Okay. I'll do each one five times then. This is fun."

I'm sure Justin would have continued with the activity even if I hadn't included a payoff. But the promise of the streamers and bell did two important things. The first was it became an insurance policy if the practice necessary for developing his new skill became boring. Second, it would serve as a marker for the continued improvement of his riding skills.

As we continued to practice and I sensed Justin was balanced, I gently began to remove my hand without him realizing it. After doing this repeatedly, it was time to tell him.

"Justin that ride was your best. And you did most of it *all by yourself.*"

A look of concern quickly replaced a smiling face. "What do you mean, by myself, Daddy?"

"Sometimes my hand held the seat, but other times it was just off it." Then I quickly added, "but I was ready to grab hold if you lost your balance."

"Was this the first time you did that Daddy?" he asked as if he was a detective.

"No Justin, that was the fifth time you rode most of the way without me holding on."

The smile returned. "I rode by *myself?*"

"Yes you did."

"Let's do it again, but this time don't hold at all."

I did hold on, but now I let Justin know when my hand was raised. By the end of the day, he was riding by himself. The next day would be spent on turns. The following day I would start worrying about the jumping tricks he thought he was ready to try.

Tracking Points and Payoffs

I was once asked to observe a therapy session of six children with varying degrees of intellectual and emotional problems. The therapist was trying to teach them self-awareness. He did this by placing a full-length mirror in front of the each child and talking about what the child was seeing. If the child looked at his reflection for at least ten seconds, the therapist felt his goal was accomplished. The children sat in a semi-circle and, one by one, the mirror was thrust in front of each child. It took all of the control I could muster not to say anything about this very bizarre therapy method. Worse, after finishing with the last child, the therapist gave a piece of candy as a reward to the children who looked at their reflection for at least ten seconds. From the time he started the "self-image" activity until he finished, ten minutes had transpired. None of the children had the slightest idea why they did or didn't receive their piece of candy.

When rewards are provided, they should be given as close as possible to the behavior and should be part of a larger reinforcement schedule. I was working with a mother whose five-year-old daughter had memory problems. We choose to work on a number of behaviors using the strategies contained in this chapter. The first behavior was simple—remembering to put her dirty clothes into the hamper at night. Since there was nothing reinforcing either about the doing or the completion of the activity, we had to introduce a payoff. Actually, three different payoffs. The first was a little doll costing only a

Figure 5.10
Multiple Reinforcement Schedule

| Column 1 | Column 2 | Column 3 |

Place one token here for each correct response. When all circles are covered give a reward and place a. token in Column 2. Repeat the process until all circles are covered

For each covered circle, give a larger doll. When all circles are covered give the doll house in Column3 few cents. The second was a larger doll costing a few dollars. And finally, a wonderful dollhouse costing about $25. We used these in what is called a *multiple reinforcement schedule*. This simply means the more correct behaviors the child accomplished, the greater the rewards. It's a very effective method for moving children forward in learning.[36] The tracking system we used appears in Figure 5.10. Each day she remembered to put her clothes in the hamper without being prompted, she received a sticker (column 1). After five days of successes, she was given a small doll. For every five days of successes, she also received another sticker that was placed in column 2. When column 2 was completed, she received a larger doll. The process was continued until three large dolls were received. After receiving three large dolls, she received a dollhouse in which all the dolls could be placed. The mother was concerned that once there would be no rewards, the behavior would vanish. It's been one year since the child received any rewards for putting her dirty clothes into the hamper. Rarely does she have to be reminded to use the hamper. It became a part of her behavioral repertoire. That's the goal of almost everything we will be doing—to make behaviors automatic.

This multiple reinforcement schedule and its tracking devise did three important things. First, it provided immediate reinforcement for the child. This child loved stickers, and just seeing the stickers covering the happy faces was reinforcing. For some children, stickers only serve as markers, indicating they did something correctly. Something additional needs to be provided for them. In our example, if our child didn't find anything reinforcing about the stickers, tiny inexpensive pieces of doll furniture could have been used. The second importance of multiple reinforcement schedules is it stresses forward movement. That is, the more a behavior is correctly done, the more things will be provided. The third consequence of this system is it allows children to see how close they're getting toward a goal.

Don't Use Punishment to Learn

There are only two types of punishment. One involves giving something negative and the other takes away something positive. A child is repeatedly told not to touch an expensive vase. One day, he not only touches it, but knocks it over causing it to break. His father, angry because he didn't listen, spanks him (*giving something negative*). Spanking is a very obvious form of administering punishment. But there are subtler, yet more devastating ones. For many children, the love of their parents is the most important thing in their lives. A parent who uses a negative voice or even says, "You've disappointed me," may have a greater impact on a child than one who spanks.[37] The second form of punishment involves removing something that's positive.[38] For example, a child refuses to put her toys away in spite of continued requests from her mother. Out of frustration, the mother comes into her daughter's room and says, "Because I've asked you four times to put your toys away and you didn't, I'm taking away your video game for a week."

The video game, which was positive, is taken away as a form of punishment. However, neither form of punishment should be used in teaching a child new behaviors—they just aren't effective.[39] If a behavior is developed because a child fears punishment, the new behavior quickly diminishes or vanishes as soon as the fear is eliminated.[40] A good analogy is a four-way stop sign. Even though there is nobody other than you at the intersection, you still come to a complete stop. Not because you think it makes any sense, or you feel good about it, but rather because you fear a police officer may be hiding around the corner, just waiting for you to coast through the intersection. You stopped because you don't want to be punished by receiving a ticket. Imagine if police officers in your town could no longer give traffic citations for coasting through intersections with four-way stop signs, even though it is still the law. How often would you come to a complete stop? Overnight, this practice you've abided by since you began driving vanishes. Remove what is punishing and whatever it created disappears. Whether it's something in your driving or in your child's behavior. If children are to learn, they should be motivated because the change will result in something positive occurring, not because they fear something negative will happen if they don't.

You're probably wondering if I think there is any useful purpose for punishment. For learning *new* behaviors, absolutely none. However, it can be effectively used for reducing or eliminating some things that *interfere* with learning.[41] These are called "maladaptive behaviors." For example, if sitting in a chair is necessary for a child to learn something, like the words in a book, then some parents might feel it's appropriate to punish the child if he or she gets out of the chair. For many parents, decisions on whether or not to use punishment involve basic child-rearing issues. Some strongly believe there's no place for it in raising children. Others, with as firm convictions, believe it's unrealistic not to use it. They believe at times only the threat of punishment, or its use, will control a child's behavior. Regardless of one's philosophy, I think everyone would agree punishment should be the last resort in getting children to do what we would like them to do. Just like many other parents, I too have used punishment when my children were young. However, whenever I resorted to it, I understood the failure was mine, and not my child's. For whatever reason, I wasn't able to construct an environment in which it was more positive to do something I desired them to do, than what they preferred to do. *If* you believe in using punishment to stop maladaptive behaviors, go through the following three steps:

1. Determine if you can create a learning activity that is so enjoyable, your child won't want to misbehave. If you can't, go to step 2.
2. Create a situation in which the maladaptive behaviors can't occur. For example, if you know your child is easily distracted when you are trying to teach him or her something, eliminate those things that are distracting, like too many toys in the learning area or the presence of noise coming from a television or radio. If this doesn't work, you may wish to move on to step 3.
3. Eliminate something positive or administer something negative, *only* if repeated attempts at steps 1 and 2 don't work.

I always prefer to use the first two ways of eliminating maladaptive behaviors. I was working with a child who had difficulty controlling his hands during learning activities. He would grab hold of whatever was on the table and begin playing with it. This was related to his problem with attending. His mother, witnessing the same problem at home, would often give him ultimatums such as "if you don't keep your hands on your lap while I'm reading to you, we won't go for our daily visit to the park." This use of punishment had limited effectiveness. Usually within a few minutes, first one hand then the other would emerge from under the table and pick up and grab whatever was in sight. My student clinician thought physically restraining his hands by moving the table up against the wall would help. The troublesome hands now began fussing with his pants. I entered the room and modified the game.

"George, we're going to play a new game," I said, as I pulled the table back to the middle of the room.

"I want you to hold his bunny." I placed it in his left hand. "Hold it very tight so it can't run away."

He held the puppet with a look of delight while the right hand kept moving on the table.

"Now, here's a snake. Hold it with your other hand. But remember he wants to leave the room, and you can't let him do that or the game ends. So you have to hold him as tight as the bunny." He nodded excitedly.

Instead of setting up any punishing situations, what I did was to make it impossible for the disruptive behaviors to occur—if George wanted to continue playing the game. As long as he held the toys, his hands were controlled.

"Okay. Now, I'm going to say a sound. The one sound the bunny is afraid to hear is 's.' Remember that's the sound you're trying to learn. If he hears it, he jumps into his hole," I said, pointing to an open box. He smiled broadly.

"Now the snake isn't afraid of the 's' sound. He's afraid of all other sounds. When he hears any sound other than 's,' he jumps into this can."

He was delighted with the new game intended to teach him sound discrimination. For 15 minutes, we played the game. And for the full 15 minutes, his hands held onto the toys. I created a situation in which the maladaptive behaviors couldn't occur. They would be incompatible with something he really wanted to do. Try something like this the next time you see your child doing anything that interferes with learning. Instead of using punishment to eliminate it, incorporate the behavior within the learning activity.

GETTING USED TO IT

Almost one thousand years ago, a wise Indian philosopher said that everything is easy once you get used to it. He was describing the processes of *desensitization* (doing it a lot) and *conditioning* (becoming familiar). Neither of these techniques is new. While used for thousands of years in everything from learning simple to complex behaviors, they began to be rigorously examined in the late 1950s.[42] Throughout the 1960s, they were applied to a large variety of behaviors.[43] Clinical scientists known as operant conditioners, or behaviorists, used them. They believed all human behaviors could be reduced to actions based on rewards and punishment. People did things because they were rewarded. People didn't do other things because they were either neutral or punishing.[44] By the 1970s, their work was being questioned.[45] Not because they did sloppy research, but rather because in their efforts to reduce all human behaviors to their simplest forms, they ignored what made people human. The negative reactions against these individuals and their techniques were all encompassing. It was a classic case of "throwing out the baby with the bath water." Good techniques along with questionable ones were ignored. For the next 30 years, many therapists, including me, used two of their techniques: desensitization and conditioning. Why? Because they allow children to become successful and feel good about themselves.

Desensitization

Imagine being very afraid of something. Something that you *rationally* know can't harm you. Just thinking about it creates anxiety. This is called a phobia.[46] There are three ways most people try to deal with it. The first is avoiding the threatening thing at all costs. A fear of flying is one example. I friend of mine was so distressed about the flying, even a drive past the San Francisco International Airport was avoided. She took an alternative route that was 15 miles longer than the one she needed to drive. Also, at 35, she had never flown on an airplane—nor intended to.

The second approach is to confront the threat head on. It's a radical approach that's rarely successful. The person usually suffers a great amount of trauma in their efforts and becomes even more anxious. A good friend of mine had a fear of heights. It was something that had been with her as long as she could remember. Although not severely debilitating, there were occasions when it did interfere with what she wanted to do. On a rafting trip down the Grand Canyon, a short hike was planned. My friend decided to come along in spite of a warning the ledge would occasionally become narrow. She thought if there was ever a time to confront her fear, this was it. The first part of the hike went well. However, gradually the ledge began to taper as we ascended. She continued on, successfully confronting her fear, until she had to jump over a 12-inch break in the ledge with nothing but 500 feet of air beneath it. She froze, unable to take even one step forward or backward. It took three people to coach, cajole, and eventually carry her back to a wider part of the ledge. Not being able to get over her fear of heights even in protected areas, made the possibility of conquering it in the middle of the Grand Canyon at best, infinitesimal.

The third approach, and the one most successful, involves desensitization.[47] Think of desensitization as first introducing a very mild form of what's causing you to be anxious. As the person becomes comfortable with the mild representation, a new one with a slightly greater threat value is introduced. Gradually the process continues until what was causing the problem is finally presented in its complete entirety. The whole procedure from beginning to end may be rapid or require years of therapy. Take for example, the fear of dogs. A dog bit the father of a child I was treating when he was young. Throughout his life, whenever he was even within 20 feet of one, regardless of size, he visualized the animal attacking him. It would have been comical watching him cowering in front of a toy poodle if you didn't know what was behind his reaction. His muscles would automatically tighten, and he sweated profusely. If he didn't retreat, his anxiety would cause him great distress. With a new family and a child who desperately wanted a puppy, he decided to address his fear after 25 years of avoidance. He visited a behavior therapist who used a modified version of a common desensitization approach.[48] Over a three month period, he was first shown a picture of a small puppy and asked to do a series of relaxation exercises until he felt comfortable looking at it. Then a picture of a full-grown dog was introduced while doing the relaxation exercises. Next, a cute stuffed animal dog was placed on the table and the exercises repeated. This was followed by a real life representation of a dog in toy form. Following this, a real dog was led into the opposite end of the room on a leash. Next, he began petting the dog when doing the relaxation exercises. After three months of therapy, he got over his fear of dogs and bought his daughter a St. Bernard puppy, who when fully grown became his constant companion. Desensitization is also effective for reducing behaviors such as test anxiety,[49] separation problems,[50] hostility,[51] abuse,[52] and a multitude of other learned behaviors.

Desensitization can be used in two ways with children. The first is with *learned behaviors*, with steps similar to those taken in our dog example. Children who learn differently may have had failing experiences making them reluctant to try something again.[53] For example, a child who repeatedly failed at a game requiring hand-eye coordination may be reluctant to try it again because she fears the internal or external consequences of not succeeding. Although not as traumatic as the adult who feared dogs, it can interfere with the child's development. The desensitization procedures for children whose problems involve learned behaviors are not as complicated as those the therapist used with the father of my client.

The second way desensitization can be used is to make it easier for children with *neurological* problems to learn. For example, a child who has trouble following directions in a noisy environment can be gradually desensitized to noise. Similarly, a child who visually becomes confused when too many things are occurring can be desensitized to the presence of many stimuli. While desensitization for both learned and neurologically based behaviors are effective, desensitizing for the latter may not be as successful. Often, the problems can be diminished, but not necessarily eliminated. For example, the child who has trouble following auditory directions with 25 children simultaneously talking may not follow the directions as accurately as other children in the same noisy classroom, but with the use of listening strategies, can do quite well.

Desensitizing Learned Behaviors

I worked with a five-year-old child who feared interacting with other children his age. One of Bruce's problems was not knowing the rules of play. Although initially wanting to play with other children at the age of three, they reacted negatively to him. Without knowing how to play, his genuine attempts were viewed as odd by other children. The kinder ones just went to another part of the playground. But others started making comments about his strangeness. It was so traumatic for him, he not only refused to go back to the playground, but also didn't want to interact. When his parents enrolled him at preschool following the event, he never played with anyone. Neither the mother nor the preschool teacher was successful in getting him to play with other children. I suggested a desensitization procedure for learned behaviors.

In consultation with a psychologist, we developed a program in which play situations were first simulated with his parents. They took the role of children and began using appropriate rules of play, often explaining them as they were performed. When their son, who loved playing with his parents, would imitate the rule, they would compliment him. He was corrected when a rule, such as "no hitting," was violated. After a few weeks of very successful activities, it was time to introduce a real child. A younger cousin, with whom Bruce was comfortable, came to the house. Bruce, his cousin, and his parents did an activity with simple rules for a very short period of time. Eventually, a second child who lived in the neighborhood came to the house, and the two children, along with one of the parents, played. Finally, the children played by themselves. Within a short period of time, the child felt comfortable and confident enough to play with other children at preschool.

In the above example, we shifted the balance from unsuccessful to successful experiences. It's similar to a child's seesaw. Think of an unsuccessful child weighing only 40 pounds. Sitting on the opposite end is a 60-pound brute holding down the board. The lighter-weight child can never get back to the ground unless one of two things happens. Either the intimidator gets off the seesaw or extra weight is placed on the opposite side. Being a bully, we know the 60-pound child has no intention of leaving. We're left with only one option—to put more weight on the smaller child. This is analogous to the balance children feel between successful and unsuccessful experiences. Whatever has more weight dominates. Bruce's fear of failure was rational. He had a long history of failures. Why should he believe that future encounters would be any more successful? By gradually creating little successful experiences, his weight grew sufficiently to move his side of the seesaw back to the ground. Create these successful experiences gradually for your child. Whatever you initially decide as being an appropriate time line—double it. I've found the pain parents feel for their children often leads them to rush the learning process, whether that involves desensitization or other learning strategies. No one ever failed because they learned something slowly. The same can't be said for rapid learning.

Neurologically Based Behaviors

Many of your child's problems aren't learned. They have a neurological base. That doesn't mean the same procedures can't be used. They can, with slight modifications. In Bruce's case we not only were concerned with a learned fear, but also one that had a neurological base—his inability to understand the rules of play. In desensitizing the neurological aspects of a learning problem, we aren't trying to change the brain's wiring, although some argue that it does occur in some children.[54] Rather, we're trying to minimize the effects of something interfering with learning. Imagine a pile driver operating one block from your office. The intensity of the noise drives you crazy when you arrive at 9:00

A.M. You couldn't hear what other people were saying, and probably couldn't concentrate. By 11:00 A.M., you were getting used to it. Not only were you able to understand what people were saying, but your work productivity improved. By 4:00 P.M., you were almost oblivious to the noise. Its volume never changed, you *adapted* to it. That's what we're looking for when we desensitize children's neurological learning problems.

Your child is not choosing not to learn. Rather, because of the brain's circuitry, factors may be impeding it. In conditioning, we will be reducing the effects of these factors. In each of the following three chapters, we'll use the desensitization strategy by repeatedly pairing up two or more things until they form a bond. For example, if your child has problems attending in the presence of noise and if we pair up attention with a mild form of noise, his or her ability to attend within a noisy environment will improve.

Sneaking Up on the Goal

Although you probably want your child to have accomplished everything yesterday, learning just doesn't work that way. We want our children to learn quickly and often push them to achieve what we think will benefit them. Unfortunately, rushing to accomplish a goal is rarely successful. Both life and learning seem to have their own pace. Rarely is it as fast as we would like it to be. One of the hardest things for parents to develop is patience. By the time I learned it, my children were young adults. When we look at what our children are doing, we view it through the historical eyes of our experiences. Our children's vision is often similar to a blank slate. From our perspective, some of their actions may appear tentative, wrong, or slow. It can be hard to remember they don't have the knowledge and wisdom we've gained over a lifetime. They're doing the best they can. Wanting them to be rapid learners is not something we'll be able to do. Trying to rush them is rarely successful. You get frustrated and they fail. When I work with children, together we sneak up on goals, as if we're inching through the bushes on an unexpecting person. With each inch, we get closer, not even realizing the distance we're covering. Be a turtle in your teaching, not a hare.

Doing It Often

How many times should children be asked to do the same behavior before we're sure they can move on to the next step? It varies from child to child and from activity to activity. It's best to err on the side of too much practice, since each step builds on what precedes it. When I work with children, I usually use an 80 percent correct level.[55] Some clinicians insist on 90 percent, but I've found that to be overkill.[56] The purpose of these activities is for a child to learn something. With the slightest bit of inattention, it may appear the child hasn't learned it, but actually just became bored or distracted. I've found that 80 percent accuracy of 20 attempts usually assures me a child has mastered the task. Think about having one session for each step in an activity. Your session can be as little as 15 minutes or up to 30 minutes. These are only guidelines. With less than 15, there may not be enough repetition for children to retain information. With more than 30 minutes, their ability to focus may deteriorate. You'll need to adjust the time you spend on the activity based on experience with your child. Remember, we're not trying to change a simple learned behavior. We're trying to change a neurological pattern. Some interesting research has shown that sleep is necessary for transferring learning from short-term to long-term memory.[57] That would suggest your child needs time for whatever you are attempting to teach to settle. By keeping new material to a minimum, I would think it would be easier for your child to transfer it into long-term memory, especially after a good night's sleep.

Little Steps

Taking small steps toward a goal is the best way of arriving at a destination. To the amazement of many people, it's often quicker than attempting to take giant steps. In the 1950s, when the Chinese invaded Tibet, many of the monks, afraid for their lives, fled over some of the world's highest mountains, walking over 300 miles to find refuge in India. A very sick, elderly monk crossed the border after having endured waist-high snow, intense cold, and the knowledge his group was always within hours of being arrested by the Chinese, who were following them since the beginning of their escape from Lasa. An astonished Indian sentry, knowing who the monk was and what he experienced, bowed deeply to him.

Reverently he asked, "Dear Lama, how were you able to cross the Himalayas?"

Leaning on his walking stick and shaking with fatigue and illness, he looked up at the sentry, and slowly said, "One step at a time." Taking small steps is one of the most effective learning tools.[58] We will use it to teach everything.

Adults, just like children, often question their ability to succeed. They may look at a goal and see it as something so great; its accomplishment is thought to be out of reach. For a few, this can lead to a way of approaching all tasks with such trepidation, it immobilizes them.[59] Think of a goal you wanted to achieve. Something very big. The task appeared formidable if you approached it as undifferentiated whole. When I decided to learn a very complicated song, just listening to it from beginning to end was daunting. I put it away and went back to playing very easy pieces on my guitar. A week later, I looked at the song as if I was that monk fleeing over the Himalayas. It took me two months of constant practice, but eventually I was able to play a song I thought would be impossible to learn.

You'll be doing the same thing with your child. My son had a great deal of difficulty with organization when he was five. It didn't make any difference if it was his room, toys, clothing, or chores. His life was as chaotic as a child's birthday party. I used the successive approximation strategy to help him. My ultimate goal was for him to develop enough organization in his life so learning could proceed with the least amount of interference. That couldn't occur if he felt he was living in the middle of a whirlwind. I looked at the ultimate goal and tried to find just one little thing to start him on the path. I chose separating his cars from all other toys as the first step. He would keep the cars in a very special box we called the "garage." I didn't care where the hundreds of other toys were placed. We focused only on cars. It would be the first of many steps leading to a level of organization that allowed Justin to be successful in school.

Cueing

What happens when gradual steps don't work? That, in spite of designing a great program with very little steps, your child is still having problems. A mother with whom I worked did a marvelous job of helping her child improve her memory. Initially, her daughter had problems remembering instructions having three or more parts. She constructed a simple game where she would tell her daughter two things. If she did them correctly, her daughter received a point. After getting a certain number of points, they would spend the rest of the day in the park. It was a well thought-out game and the daughter loved it. The mother thought her daughter could progress to the next level after successfully completing five sets of a two-sequence direction. However, going to three directions proved to be a disaster. Rarely did the child get all three correct. Sometimes only one was done correctly. The mother was in a quandary. There was no number between two and three. She couldn't be missing a step. That's when she called me. My suggestion was to use cueing.

Cueing is nothing more than providing hints to your child. The hints are provided not only so children can succeed, but also to help them understand the strategy you are teaching. This method is very effective in learning.[60] The cues will eventually have to be phased out. Therefore, they're ordered in a hierarchy related to concreteness. What is more concrete is eliminated first. With this mother, I suggested we simultaneously use three cues, similar to the

Figure 5.11
Multiple Cues

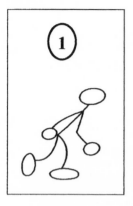  

ones appearing in Figure 5.11. These were displayed on three cards, each with a different color. The first card was a general picture of what the first instruction would be. For example, there was a stick figure moving. This implied the daughter had to go somewhere in the house. Above the picture was the number 1. On the second card, a picture depicted a toy. This meant she was to retrieve a specific object. It also contained a number, but this time 2. The final picture had a piece of food and the number 3. It meant she should find the food mentioned and eat it. This simple system, which took five minutes to develop, contained the following cues:

1. A picture of the type of thing to be done.
2. The number of things to be remembered signified by using three different cards.
3. The order in which it should be done, indicated by a number.

The system worked. Not only did the child immediately carry out the instructions in the order given, but proceeded to do an additional four sets of instructions perfectly. The cues obviously were working. However, the mother's goal was to have the child follow three-part directions without any cues. If she eliminated all the cues immediately, the likelihood of her daughter continuing to succeed would be remote. Her task was to gradually phase out the cues. The most concrete cues were the pictures. So they were phased out first, as shown in Figures 5.12 to 5.14. Now the child had only the numbers and individual colored sheets of paper to help her focus. When she was able to follow five three-part instructions, the mother then taped over the numbers, leaving only the cue of three blank cards, indicating the instructions had three parts. Finally, without any cues, her daughter was able to successfully complete the task.

Figure 5.12
Multiple Cues, Fade Out 1

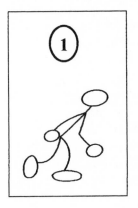

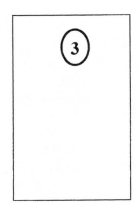

Figure 5.13
Multiple Cues, Fade Out 2

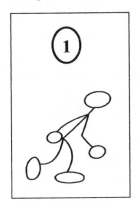
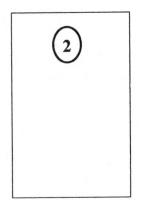
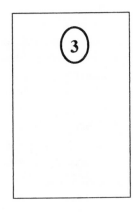

Figure 5.14
Multiple Cues, Fade Out 3

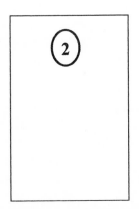

It may appear this is a very complicated and laborious method of teaching. It's not. First of all, the entire cueing sequence took less than three sessions of fifteen minutes to complete. Second, by using cues and then gradually phasing them out, the child became able to easily develop a new behavior that had eluded her. And finally, the child was almost always continually successful throughout each session. When the mother went on to four-part instructions she found her daughter was again having problems. This time, she just placed four cards in front of her daughter and repeated the strategy used in the three-card sequence. After a few problems, her daughter was eventually successful.

Cues provided to your children can take on many forms, some of which are more helpful than others. Color-coded cues result in faster response times than cues that rely only on shape.[61] This doesn't mean only color should be used in designing cues. It can be combined with shapes and interlocking pieces to emphasize differences and specific behaviors on which children should focus. For example, I once worked with a child who had problems understanding how words were placed together in specific orders. It's correct to say, "I see a green car," but not "I see a car green." Yet that was the way this child used adjectives, in a reverse order. To help her understand, my student and I constructed a series of word cards, each of which had a different color and could be connected in only one way to object cards (Figure 5.15). We used both a color cue and a connection cue to help this child learn how to use adjectives.

The cues you use can be tactile, visual, or oral. Often in kindergarten, as well as classes for older children, teachers miss wonderful opportunities to provide cues. When instructions or directions are given, they're usually only oral. The teacher might give children a list of things to do and expect them to be remembered and followed. Oral instructions should be paired with ones that are graphic. Pictures can be pasted onto the blackboard for younger children and words can be written for older ones. Visual and oral cues provide different degrees of help to children, depending on the task.[62] The longer, more difficult, and more complicated the tasks, the more reliance should be placed on visual cues.

We often rely on what we say to provide sufficient information when we want our child to do something requiring only a verbal response. Reliance on our words is not enough in many situations. The concreteness of visual cues provides a point on which children can focus. A variant of the visual cue is demonstration. Often what we are asking a child to do may be so complicated or involve so many steps, that our words become a tangled bush children can't work their way through. When that occurs, it's best to use demonstration, similar to our example of the soccer coach and the young child.

Sometimes we can't tell why some children take a long time to respond. It could be a problem in attending, understanding, working memory, short-

Figure 5.15
Connection Cues

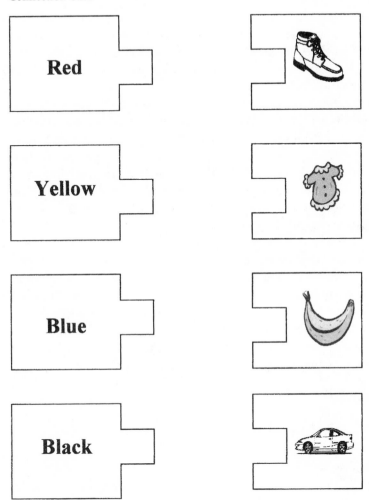

term memory, or retrieval. They may have a problem pulling out your auditory message from the sounds in the house, in the car, or on the street. Maybe the words or the length of sentence you used were difficult to understand. Possibly, your child has problems holding your words long enough in their mind to understand what to do with them. Or, finally, possibly the memory web wasn't rich enough for a quick and easy retrieval. Regardless what the source of the problem might be, we can increase the speed at which they process information by using visual cues. It can be as simple as a certain number of cards indicting the number of things to be done. Or more involved, such as having pictures of instructions with numbers indicating the order in which they should be performed.

I worked with a mother who was concerned about the very slow speed at which her three-year-old son would process what she said. I went to her house and observed what she was doing and how her son responded. She didn't speak particularly fast, nor were the words or grammar too complicated for her son to understand, and their house was very quiet. It didn't seem to make much difference what was being said to the child. It could involve his toys, getting ready for dinner, or even just having a conversation. Things appeared normal in other aspects of his behavior. He played appropriately with other children, appeared to attend without any problems, had sophisticated language for a three-year-old, and was a delight to be with. It just took him longer than expected to respond. I decided to do a little experiment. During my visit, I wanted the mother to ask him to get three things in his room. I noted the time it took for him to go to his room and retrieve the three objects. About 30 minutes later, we repeated the experiment, but this time, the mother showed him a simple drawing of each object. His response time decreased by 50 percent. We kept repeating the experiment, sometimes showing him the pictures first, and then later just using auditory instructions. The results were always the same; visual cued instructions almost always reduced the amount of time necessary for him to process information. I was never able to determine what part of the information-processing system caused the problem. Regardless of what it was, using graphic cues provided him with a detour that reduced processing time.

MONITORING AND FEEDBACK

Monitoring involves the use of anything that can help children stay on task. Feedback tells children if they are doing something correctly or incorrectly. Often it's not possible to differentiate between the two. If I'm helping my daughter monitor where she's placing her tongue when trying to produce a certain sound correctly, I'm also giving her feedback. While some therapists and learning experts make fine distinctions between monitoring and feedback, I think for parents, it makes sense to treat the two as related. Often they are so intertwined, you can't tell when one ends and the other begins.

Monitoring Techniques

Monitoring can involve visual or physical signals, which allow children to focus on a specific task. These can be initially supplied by the parent. When children are provided with a way of monitoring a new behavior, their performance improves.[63] It's important to monitor new behaviors in a very simple manner. It should require minimal concentration and effort. For example, a child can monitor the number of tasks carried out by checking a box for each one completed. Responsibility for monitoring should be gradually shifted from parents to children in three steps. The first is *parent monitoring*. In parent monitoring, parents continually monitor how well their children are using a strategy. The second is *shared responsibility*. In shared responsibility, the parent allows the child to use the monitoring device independently. However, at the first sign the device isn't being used correctly, the parent steps in and provides a correction. In the final stage, *child monitoring*, children are now responsible for monitoring their own behavior. Below is an example of how a parent shifted responsibility for monitoring a behavior from herself to her child.

"Michele, do you remember yesterday how we worked on keeping your room organized?"

"Yes Mommy."

"We placed all of your toys in special places (*what*). We did that by putting them on shelves (*how*). The reason we did that was so it would be easier for you to find things (*why*).

"I remember Mommy."

"Let's take this big pile of toys and put each one where it belongs. I put a picture of the types of toys that should go on each shelf. On this shelf is a picture of dolls."

"I see it Mommy."

"Good. Now let's look at the next shelf. I drew a picture of wheels. All of your cars, trucks, and trains go here."

"What about the tractor?"

"That's great Michele! I didn't even mention tractors and you knew it went there. If it has wheels, it goes there. Now, on the last shelf is a picture of a little box. You can put all your boxes of games here."

"Like Candyland?"

"That's right. Every time you put something on the right shelf, I'll tell you if it's right or wrong (*parent monitoring*)."

After having her daughter place numerous objects on the correct shelves, the mother was ready to begin sharing the responsibility for monitoring. She did it by simply saying, "Michele, this time let's do it a little differently. You put the toy on the shelf, and then look around to make sure it's right. Then you tell me."

"How Mommy?"

"Just say it's right or it's wrong."

"Okay."

After doing shared monitoring for a short period of time, the mother believed her daughter was ready to monitor independently. She relinquished responsibility to her daughter with a statement and a question.

"Michele, I need to start cooking dinner. Do you think you'll be able to finish putting the toys on the shelf by yourself?"

"Yes Mommy!" Michele said with a smile.

This mother not only gradually shifted responsibility for monitoring a behavior to her daughter, but also did it in such a gradual way, her daughter was mostly successful in her attempts, and when not, quickly understood how to correct it.

Another type of monitoring technique is known as "private speech" or "self-talk."[64] This is the speech children use to talk to themselves while engaging in an activity. When children are constructing a complex toy, they may be describing what parts should be selected in the construction and how each should be used. For example, a father asks his daughter to describe what she's doing as a Lego tower is being built.

"I'm getting the little green Lego and putting it on the red one."

"That's great honey. Tell me what you're going to do next."

"Now, I'm putting the really big green one on the side."

"How do you make them fit?"

"Well, I put one next to the other, and make sure these pimples go into the holes."

When young children use self-talk, they perform better.[65] However, for children beyond the age of five, self-talk is not very effective for problem solving.[66] As young children do a task, the parent can ask them to explain how each part of the task will be done. Although this form of monitoring is effective, parents may wish to supplement it by using a more permanent method of self-recording, such as a check-mark system for behaviors that lend themselves to it. For example, a mother may be working on having her daughter become more responsible for some self-help skills.

"Sarah, look at this piece of paper."

"Okay, Mommy."

"See, here is a picture of your toothbrush and here is one of your pajamas. In front of each picture is a box. When you brush your teeth, come into the living room and I'll give you a star to put in the teeth box. Then we'll do the same thing when you put on your pajamas."

Self-recording methods such as these significantly increase attending behavior and performance in children who have learning problems.[67] It allows them to continually monitor if they are doing expected behaviors.

FEEDBACK

Feedback tells children if responses were correct or incorrect, and the reasons why each occurred. Parents usually tell children whether or not a response was correct. Although this form of feedback is better than none at all, it may not provide the child with information critical for knowing *why* it was correct or incorrect. Imagine you're playing tennis with a friend who is an excellent player. In the past, you never won a set. Today, you're playing like a champion. Not only did you win the set, but your shots were incredible. "I can't believe how you played today. Every shot was either a killer or a defensive beauty," your tennis partner says.

You're glowing, not only because you won, but you also played brilliantly. Next week at your regular game, you lose just like you always did. Unfortunately, you have no idea why you reverted back to your "old self." Your partner last week only gave you simple feedback—you were awesome. But there weren't enough specifics to repeat your performance. Now imagine your partner gave you a different type of feedback.

"I can't believe how you played today. You set up way in advance of each shot. Then, you followed through on everything. As I hit my return, you were already placing your body in the right position."

This type of feedback is known as *instructional*, and it provides the type of information necessary to repeat your performance. It results in significantly better outcomes than simple feedback in both adults and children.[68] For example, a mother is working on helping her child develop hand-eye coordination. She observes her son perfectly bouncing a ball. "Bill that was great. You kept looking at the ball and you hit it very slowly."

Instead of just saying "great," the mother provided Bill with the reasons why he did it correctly. The same type of feedback would be provided when errors are made. For example, "Bill, the ball got away from you. You kept looking at it, but I think you moved your hand too fast." The more specific we are with our feedback the better children learn.[69]

Children like to know when they are doing things right. Feedback given to them will be perceived as positive if it reinforces the correctness of a performance or expression of an idea. Your feedback may be viewed as negative if it's instructive. Instructive feedback can be as subtle as suggesting something should be done slightly differently or as direct as an outright "no." Although we should be honest in our feedback to children, we also need to be aware of its effects. Negative feedback is more acceptable for children whose self-esteem is high than children whose self-esteem is low.[70] I worked with a child who was so unsure of himself that even mild criticism was devastating. He viewed even constructive comments as an attack on his personality. It was very difficult to provide any suggestions without him viewing it negatively. When low self-esteem children hear negative feedback, there's a tendency to over generalize even constructive criticism to other parts of their behavior or personality. Because a significant proportion of children with learning problems may have low self-esteem, negative feedback should be minimized if possible.

The feedback provided to children may serve as the primary way for them to know whether or not they correctly produced the learning goal. Often they're replacing something they've been doing for a long time with something brand new. At other times, what you're asking them to do is so minimal, they may not be aware they're doing something different. Given these possibilities, it's important that consistent feedback be provided. You need to get your timing and words right when providing feedback. By doing this, your children will be more likely to accept your comments.

I often watch parents giving their children stickers or other rewards at the end of a session for effort or cooperation. Although well intentioned, it's inappropriate. After working on a large number of behaviors for 20 minutes and not receiving feedback regarding their level of cooperation or effort, it's difficult, if not impossible, for children to know what specific parts of their behavior are being reinforced. It's not only important that there's a direct link between desired behaviors and rewards, but also there should be immediate feedback to children regarding all aspects of their behavior or attitudes. Immediacy of feedback significantly improves performance.[71]

SIX

Attention

*A*ttention is more complicated than most of us realize. We assume our children just need to listen or watch. But what does listening and watching require? For both, children need to pull out what's important from everything else.[1] In this chapter we'll look at four attending problems children may have in both listening and watching. Some children have problems only with listening, others with watching, and some have problems with both. In kindergarten, it's likely your child will have more problems with listening than watching.[2] Although there is much that's visual in kindergarten, it's in forms that are easier for children to attend to than things that are auditory.

The perspective of children is very direct and concrete. If they have attending problems, you can probably imagine them saying one of the following four statements.

1. There's too much noise.
2. I can't tell what's important.
3. I'm not ready to move on.
4. I'm too upset.

Children experience a problem, and then if able, they'll tell you what's happening. But sometimes, we can only indirectly know there's a problem. You rattle off four things for your child to do, and only one is accomplished. You might believe you gave too much information. Although that might be a reasonable conclusion, you may not have noticed your child was too upset to watch, or just as you instructed him or her, a loud truck went by the window. At times, we may not be able to tell which problem or combination of problems is occurring—we only see the result, not the cause. When you don't know, you have to assume the role of a clinical scientist. The first thing you do is to look for connections—what occurred immediately before the problem developed and the problem. Based on a possible connection between the two, guess which of the above four children's statements is a best fit. Working with children is not pure science. Guessing is a time-honored clinical technique practiced constantly by competent clinical scientists. When we guess, we make the assumption we don't know.

What differentiates the scientist from the charlatan is what happens once a guess is made.[3] Charlatans believe they and their ideology are infallible. They don't think they need to do anything beyond believing in themselves or a doctrine. They believe their wisdom and ideology are enough. Unfortunately, charlatans are not confined to strange faith-healing cults. We have some in all areas of education. While both the charlatan and clinical scientist guess, what distinguishes them from each other is what happens after a guess is made. While charlatans do nothing, clinical scientists *test* their guesses. And that's the next step in working with your child. Try one of the four programs I'll present later in this chapter and watch the results. If the program worked, you were right. If it didn't, just try another program. If none work, modify them.

Don't worry about getting it right the first time, or even the second or third time. I've been doing this work for 25 years and I still make mistakes—often. I've found persistence to be a more valuable asset than perfection. There are few times or situations when you can do something perfectly. But you can always persist, getting better and closer to your ultimate goal. When I work with children, I assume there is a great likelihood I'll get it wrong the first time—maybe even the second or third time. I don't get upset, nor do I take it as a rebuff of my competence. I developed some of my most useful techniques after failing numerous times with some children. It's similar to starting at the base of a pyramid. At the bottom there are many possibilities. But as you ascend it, the options become narrower, until you reach the pinnacle. Don't feel bad if you follow the same path. Professionals will make as many mistakes as you do, even if they're reluctant to admit it.

You'll have a choice of four programs to treat your child's attention problem. Each is broadly based on the strategies from Chapter 5 and can be equally applied to listening and watching problems. The only difference between each program is the goal.

1. Increasing attention in the presence of noise
2. Learning to tell what's important
3. Being able to move on to new activities
4. Learning in the presence of strong emotions

This will be the same format I'll use in the chapters on understanding and on storage and retrieval. Before starting on any intervention program, it's important to rule out physical problems. Often what may be easily corrected with a hearing aide or glasses is treated as if it was an attention problem.

Ruling Out Physical Problems

The first step in enhancing attention is to rule out vision and hearing problems related to the end organs—eyes and ears. Early vision problems have been associated with some types of reading difficulties that may be correctable by the intervention of an optometrist or ophthalmologist [4] These do not include the reading problem known as dyslexia. Current research views dyslexia as a processing problem of the brain, not as a purely visual problem.[5] Problems in hearing can cause difficulties with pronunciation and language learning if not identified early.[6] Both vision and hearing testing for preschoolers is usually done in a pediatrician's office during a routine visit. The type of testing is called *screening*. A screening test is one that is very general and designed to pick up actual and potential problems.[7] They are usually done by a nurse who may or may not have specialized training. A child who fails a screening test does not necessarily have a physical problem. The standards for failure are set low enough that a small percentage of children without problems fail. This is done intentionally. By setting standards low, the possibility of a child who has a problem remaining undetected is minimal.[8] Failing either screening test is a warning flag that says additional, in-depth testing should be done. If your child passes the screening test and you still believe there is a physical problem, seek out the appropriate trained professional for further testing. For example, if your child fails the hearing screening, a recommendation is made for a full evaluation by an audiologist or an otolaryngologist (ENT specialist). The audiologist will test the full range of your child's hearing ability. The otolaryngologist looks for the physical causes of the problem. Otolaryngologists will often have an audiologist on their staff. If your child fails the vision screening, a recommendation will be made to an optometrist or an ophthalmologist. The relationship between the optometrist and the ophthalmologist is similar to that of the audiologist and otolaryngologist.

Neither of the two screening tests is designed to evaluate attention problems. But if a physical problem exists and goes undetected, it's easy to assume it's an attention problem rather than a detection problem. If a child has problems detecting either auditory or visual signals, there will be problems with attention, though the hardwiring and software responsible for attending may be intact. A mother brought her three-year-old child into the clinic because she appeared to have a problem learning language and attending to auditory messages. In the clinic, we routinely do a hearing screening of all children. However, whenever we suspect something, a full test battery is administered. A decision was made to do a complete test for this child. After testing, the audiologist found the child had a significant hearing loss in both ears. Even if this mother used each of the strategies in Chapter 5 perfectly and implemented

the intervention programs exactly as I wrote them, her daughter would still have major problems attending. She just couldn't hear the signal, and no matter what type of intervention program was used, the girl would have failed. Fitted with appropriate hearing aids, this child quickly learned language and delighted in receiving previously unheard signals. Today, she excels in junior high school. She never needed any intervention with attention—she just needed to hear. If your child is three years old or older and has never had a vision or a hearing screening test, I would strongly encourage you to arrange for one either with your pediatrician or other professionals. If you have a university speech and language clinic in your area, they'll be able to do either a screening or full audiological test battery. Schools of optometry also provide a similar service for vision. Training facilities usually offer low-cost testing by graduate students who are supervised by qualified faculty.

THERE'S TOO MUCH NOISE

We need to broaden our definition of *noise*. We usually think of it as sounds that interfere with our listening, coming from cars, yelling, and the racket created by machines. It's better to think of noise as *anything* interfering with attending. Children talking when a teacher is speaking can be noise. A table cluttered with objects that interfere with a child doing her homework can also be noise. Using this broad definition, noise is an integral part of the kindergarten experience that can interfere with learning for some children.[9]

The Problem

To learn, children need to pull out important messages from the surrounding noise. For most children, it's not a problem. They seem to use some type of filter that allows only the important message to get in. However, some young children haven't developed this neurological filter. Without being able to filter auditory signals, noise can overwhelm what's important.[10] For many, the development of this neurological ability must wait until they're more mature.[11] Unfortunately, some children never completely develop it. Try the following experiment in order to experience what these children may have to cope with. Randomly choose a book from your local library. Preferably on a topic about which you know nothing. Take it home, and in total silence read the first page. Then summarize what you read in a single paragraph. Now, turn on the radio, preferably a talk show. With the volume set at a barely audible level, read the second page and repeat your summary activity. Then increase the volume slightly for the third page, once again summarizing right

after you finish reading. Finally, set the volume at a normal conversational level and *try* to read the fourth page and summarize. You probably found as the volume increased, you required more of an effort to concentrate. By the fourth page, your level of frustration may have reached a breaking point. What could you do to stop your frustrating learning experience? Obviously, just turn off the radio. Unfortunately, your child may not have the same option. Also, where you were probably able to easily tolerate a soft conversation on the radio, your child's threshold for noise interference may be crossed by even this low volume.

Not understanding that even small amounts of noise can interfere with attention can cause both parents and teachers to misinterpret why a child does certain things. When teachers request something reasonable and a child doesn't react, many assume the child is stubborn or defiant. It just could be the child couldn't distinguish the teacher's voice from the drone of noises reverberating off the solid floors and walls. A kindergarten teacher once complained to me about one child she thought was particularly disruptive.

"When I ask the children to do something, like get ready for lunch, Robbie just sits there. I know he can hear me, but I think he's just being defiant. When I go over to him and ask why he isn't getting ready for lunch, he gives me this look as if he has no idea I've already asked the whole class to get ready."

"Does he just do it for one activity, or does it occur in many different situations?" I asked.

Without any hesitation the teacher responded, "It happens all the time. It's so infuriating."

I thought for a moment and asked, "Does this disruptive behavior occur if you're close to him when you ask the class to do something?"

"Why, now that you mention it, no. When I'm close to him, he's fine."

"I don't think he's purposefully disruptive, I just think he's having a hard time listening."

"You mean he has a hearing problem?"

"It may be a hearing problem, but I don't think so. Look at his records to see the last time he was screened for hearing. If it was more than six months, we'll do a screening next week. But I think it's a listening problem." She looked confused.

"How noisy is your classroom?" I asked.

"Very," she said with an annoyed tone. "Bells ring, we can hear children screaming in the hallway, and those city buses every 15 minutes, they're the worst! The sounds keep reverberating back and forth across the room."

"I think your voice, which is high pitched, is getting lost in the voices of the children and the noises. Maybe Robbie can't filter them out. He can hear, but not listen."

She now understood the difference between hearing and listening. "But what can I do to help?" she asked.

"There are three easy things you can do. The first is to move Robbie's chair closer to you."

"That won't work," she replied. "The seating has already been set and it would be too disruptive for the other children if I move him."

"Then you may want to increase the volume of your voice and maybe even lower your pitch so it rises above the outside noise level and becomes more distinctive from the children's voices."

"I'm already speaking as loud as I can without getting laryngitis. That won't work either."

My suggestions were being met with the reality of the classroom.

"Would it be possible for you to move to a more central place in the classroom when you give oral directions to your children? You may even want to make a game of it. Somewhere in the middle of the room, you can have a box outlined on the floor. The children would know when you enter it, an instruction or request for the whole class would be given.

She thought for a moment and then smiled. "Yes, I could do that. I'll do it if it will help Robbie's listening. You know, it might even be helpful for some other children."

One week later we conferred again. Robbie had passed a hearing screening test only a month ago and the conversation the teacher had with the parents didn't indicate they suspected a hearing problem. The teacher said what I'd asked her to do was more difficult than she originally thought. It was hard to change such an engrained behavior in one week, since she had been doing the same thing for 15 years—standing in front of the class when giving instructions. With all the children watching her, she outlined a box with tape on the floor next to Robbie's table, which was near the center of the room.

"Children," she said, with 20 sets of eyes glued on her. "Whenever I'm in the box, I'm going to say something important and I want everyone to listen very carefully."

She jumped into the box and gave her first oral instruction. There was no talking and everyone, including Robbie, heard what she wanted them to do. I selected this example for three reasons. The first is to show how even simple changes can result in big differences. Instead of trying to shutdown the noise, we modify an activity to accommodate it. In this case, all it took was for the teacher to move 15 feet. The second is that sometimes it's necessary to propose alternative types of solutions. The first solution I offered the teacher wasn't acceptable and neither was the second. Finally, I found one that was. You'll usually be able to find something that'll work by staying flexible . And finally, if you are giving up a behavior or asking someone else to, remember old behaviors don't like to leave without a fight. Make sure the new behavior feels comfortable, is easy to do, and rewarding. In this case, I asked the teacher to just move with the implication Robbie's annoying behavior would diminish or stop.

Let's try another experiment, but this time one involving watching. Either visit your local museum's abstract art section, or use one of your child's *Where's Waldo?* books.[12] For the abstract art, find one that is particularly full. Stand back from either the painting or the page and try to identify its components. Most likely, both appear as a blur, with figures and objects blending into each other. Now move closer. Forms seem to emerge and what once was indistinct becomes identifiable. For children with visual processing problems, metaphorically, they may be standing at a distance more often than standing close. Just as in the auditory experiment, visually, there also is noise. A mother complained to me that her 4-year-old son was having difficulties doing simple activities. One was putting an easy puzzle together. A second involved the construction of a Lego toy. She also mentioned other examples involving visual organization activities. I agreed to visit them in their home and asked that the room and objects be in a configuration similar to the one when she noticed the problems. I entered a room that could only be described as a toy wonderland. Toys, games, pictures, and objects were everywhere. No matter where you looked, there was something—even on the ceiling. The table on which the puzzle was located was covered with unnecessary toys and objects. No matter what direction her son looked, the background was completely covered with objects. He was in a *Where's Waldo?* universe. I watched as her son attempted to complete the puzzle. Between glances at it, were furtive looks at other objects. Even I had difficulty watching the puzzle activity—there were too many interesting things to look at.

"Let's take the puzzle and put it in the living room," I suggested.

We all went into the living room and I found a space on the floor in front of a blank wall. I asked her son to face the wall and see if he could do the puzzle. With nothing to distract him, he was able to complete the puzzle with little effort. We eliminated the visual noise. Not all looking problems are treated as easily, but if you suspect a problem, first try to eliminate the visual noise.

The Solution

We can't tell beforehand the level of noise that will begin affecting a child's ability to attend. It's different for each child. Regardless of the level at which your child's attending ability becomes effected, our goal will be to gradually increase the ability to attend within a noisy auditory or visual field. We're going to build a bridge between the quiet of your house and the noise of a

Figure 6.1
There's Too Much Noise

Design Components	Auditory	Visual
Use a Good Design	Keep it simple Present it slowly Little time between saying and doing Short instructions and explanation Visual and concrete Many of the same Make it stand out Use familiar context	Keep it simple Present it slowly Little time between saying and doing Short instructions and explanation Visual and concrete Many of the same Make it stand out Use familiar context
Advance Organizing Statements	I want to listen to what Mommy says and try to do it. (*What*) I'll turn on the radio very quietly and let's see if you can still hear me. I'm going to tell you to get some things from your room. (*How*) You know how sometimes it's hard for you to hear what I say and then you can't do something? After we do this game, it will be easier for you. (*Why*)	I want you to watch what Mommy shows you and try to find what I ask for. (*What*) First I'll say what I want you to find, then I'll tell you to find it. (*How*) You know how sometimes it's hard for you to see some things? After we do this game, it will be easier for you. (*Why*)
Getting used to it	Desensitizing neurological behavior	Desensitizing neurological behavior
Make it Positive	Doing Completing Payoff	Doing Completing Payoff
Do It Often	Do a minimum of 10 attending activities at each sitting. Each sitting should be no more than 15 minutes.	Do a minimum of 10 attending activities at each sitting. Each sitting should be no more than 15 minutes.
Sneak Up On The Goal—Little Steps	1. Barely audible music from radio when you are requesting 2. Soft sound when requesting 3. Sound equal to your voice when requesting 4. Louder than your voice when requesting 5. Repeat entire sequence with voice on the radio	1. Picture or setting with minimal distracting objects 2. Some distracting objects 3. Many distracting objects
Sneak Up On The Goal—Cues	Use cards to represent objects to be retrieved or things to be done	Place markers on objects (e.g., little stickers)
Monitoring	Let child know if he or she is on the "right track"	Let child know if he or she is on the "right track"
Feedback	Use Instructive Feedback	Use Instructive Feedback

kindergarten class. You can do this by starting with something that is barely distracting and ending with something approaching a normal situation in kindergarten. For listening, begin with something barely audible and end with a signal that's as loud as your voice. For looking, have only one object act as a distracter and end with many objects present when your child is attempting to complete an activity. In Figure 6.1, a suggested sequence for listening and looking appears. It's a complete program starting with how to use a good design and ending with the type of feedback to use. Many of the components for the other programs throughout this and the next two chapters are identical. To avoid clutter, I'll only list the differences in the tables. However, you should still use all nine design components when developing something for your child.

In the *Sneak Up on the Goal—Little Steps* section of Figure 6.1, you'll see I've listed five steps for audition and four for vision. As children demonstrate they can attend at one level, move on to the next. Gradually they'll become desensitized to noise and increase their ability to attend in evermore distracting environments. However, it's important that you go slowly. The steps require only minimal amounts of additional attention. For example, going from (2) *Soft sound when requesting* to (3) *Sound equal to your voice when requesting* is not that great a step. Children shouldn't be able to tell any one step is more difficult than what preceded it. If it does pose a problem, the first possible solution is to just add a step. It could be an additional step we didn't anticipate is needed between two and three. Don't be afraid to experiment, either in this program or others. You can always add more steps without creating problems. But what if after you have added additional steps, your child is still having problems? You can include cues that represent the objects to be retrieved or the things to be done. If you are asking your child to retrieve two objects or do two activities, use cards to represent them. When your child is able to correctly follow the instructions, gradually remove the cues and proceed to the next step.

It will be easier for your child to be successful if the noise field is very different from the message. For listening, start with instrumental music (*no words*) for your noise field. For looking, the visual distracters should be very different from the target object (e.g., numerous dolls and a target of a car). We know when the difference between a message and its background is great, the message stands out.[13] And when the message stands out, children attend better.[14] But the greatest problems children face is when the noise field and the message take the same form. For example, the teacher is asking your child a question while 15 children are talking. Both the message and the noise field involve speech. An example of a watching problem is a teacher who, after writing something on the blackboard for a previous activity, leaves it there and places the new activity next to it. The teacher first asked the children to color a picture using crayons.

In order to help the children follow the order of coloring, she created a set of wonderful visuals on the board. It was very effective for all the children. The next activity involved using glue to create a macaroni man. Realizing the importance of using graphics, the teacher again drew them on the board. Unfortunately, she didn't erase the previous graphics. Although most children didn't have any problem with having both sets on the board, for a few children, it became confusing. Both sets of graphics were similar. The old graphics distracted the message of the new images. Your child's threshold of attention is rapidly approached when, just as in this example, the noise field and the message share common features. To prepare your child to deal with the reality of kindergarten, start with a noise field that differs greatly from the target, and then switch to a noise field that's similar to it. For listening, this would involve going from music to a speech background. For looking, it could be going from objects that differ greatly from the target objects (dolls to cars), to ones that are similar (trucks to cars).

The more familiar we are with the content of what is being said, the easier it is to follow.[15] The same thing applies to children. If you tried to have your child initially focus on an unfamiliar topic or object in the presence of noise, you will increase the likelihood of failure. Therefore, start with something your child is very familiar with and excited about. You can simply choose familiar toys or games. If you look at the *Advance Organizing Statement* section in Figure 6.1, you'll see the context in which children are asked to do something is very familiar—their room and toys.

I CAN'T TELL WHAT'S IMPORTANT

In learning, children are expected to focus only on speech sounds or visual configurations that are relevant. Some children can't distinguish between what is relevant and what isn't.[16] All parts of the message are treated as having the same importance. It's not something children consciously do. Rather, their neurological wiring is responsible for it.[17] When we as adults convey information, there are various things we use to indicate what's most important in a message. It may be the position of words (*Now*, I want you to get ready), the intonation pattern we use (Now I want you to *get ready*), or the nonverbal behaviors that accompany our messages (Now I want you to get ready [while frowning]).

The Problem

Sometimes even when noise is held to a minimum or is nonexistent, children may still have problems attending to the message. It's as if everything is flat;

nothing stands out. I remember when I was eight years old going to the 1953 3D movie *The House of Wax*.[18] By watching the movie through special glasses certain things stood out. They usually were objects that were frightening or amazing to the audience. In this movie, someone used a child's ball and bat game where a small rubber ball is attached to an elastic cord connected to a wooden paddle. With each whack, you thought you saw the ball move from the screen to within inches of your face. Seen as a regular non-3D movie, there was nothing interesting about the ball and bat. Yet to this day, when I think about 3D movies, the first thing that comes to mind is that sequence where I was sure the ball was about to enter my nose.

Children without attending problems can listen to incoming auditory or visual messages, and make distinctions between what is and what isn't important. Distinctions for some children with learning problems may be more difficult. I worked with a mother whose son had a great deal of difficulty matching up what his mother thought was important in a message and what he did.

"George, there's a slice of cake in the refrigerator. I left it there for your father since he didn't have any last night." The mother gave her son five distinct messages, all connected.

1. We're talking about cake.
2. The cake is located in the refrigerator.
3. It's not for you.
4. It's for your father.
5. Don't touch it.

The most important message the mother thought she conveyed was "Don't eat the cake." That not only was what the mother wanted her son to do, but also assumed he would be able to *infer* it by the words she used. She was wrong. What George heard was "there's a slice of cake in the refrigerator." Less than five minutes after she finished instructing him, he took the cake from the refrigerator and began eating it. When the mother returned she found her son smiling as he stuffed the last forkful of cake into his mouth. She assumed he was behaving badly and intentionally ignoring her instructions. When we conversed, she related other instances where the importance of one part of a message was not heeded.

The Solution

George and children like him don't intentionally disregard parts of messages. Despite many cues, they're unable to differentiate what's important from what isn't. There are various ways we can provide cues to what's important in a message. We can be very selective in the words we use. We can place the most

important parts of a message in the beginning of a sentence or request. We can raise the volume of our voice or the intonation pattern for the most important words. And finally, we can do something nonverbally to emphasize importance. In working on this problem the ultimate goal is to teach children to identify the cues people use for important parts of a message. The only two cues which seem to be consistently used are 1) loudness and intonation, and 2) some nonverbal behaviors.[19,20] Intuitively you might think whatever is most important appears in the beginning of sentences. If this was correct, it would be an easy cue to teach children. Unfortunately, the placement of what is thought to be important can occur anywhere in an utterance.[21] There just isn't enough consistency to teach children to rely on this cue. Therefore we'll focus on loudness, intonation, and facial behaviors. The program for loudness and intonation appears in Figure 6.2. In the figure, you'll see there are four steps in the auditory program, going from very loud to equal emphasis on

Figure 6.2
I Can't Tell What's Important
Intonation and/or Loudness

Design Components	Auditory	Visual
Advance Organizing Statements	I want you to listen to what Mommy says and try to do it. (*What*) I'm going to make the words that are very important either loud or I'll raise my voice, like this (do demonstration of both). I'm going to tell you to do some things. Listen for what's loud. (*How*) You know how sometimes it's hard for you to do everything I ask you to do? After we do this game, it will be easier for you. (*Why*)	I want you to watch what Mommy shows you and try to find what I ask for. Look for something that has more color than other things. (*What*) First I'll tell you want to find, then you look for it. It will be colored brigher. (*How*) You know how sometimes it's hard for you to see some things? After we do this game, it will be easier for you. (*Why*)
Do It Often	Do a minimum of 10 attending activities at each sitting. Each sitting should be no more than 15 minutes.	Do a minimum of 10 attending activities at each sitting. Each sitting should be no more than 15 minutes.
Sneak Up On The Goal— Little Steps	1. Very loud emphasis on main request 2. Loud emphasis on main request 3. Slightly louder emphasis on main request 4. Equal emphasis on main request	1. Picture or setting with minimal distracting objects 2. Some distracting objects 3. Many distracting objects

each of the words. In this program, you can use just a different pitch level, a difference in loudness, or a combination of both. It really doesn't make too much difference. Each of these cues highlights those things that are most important. We know both loudness and tone differences make parts of a message stand out and are easily identified by listeners.[22] But why, once you reduce the difference, do children do better at attending to the entire message? It's possible, by highlighting a neglected part of a message, increased attention is given to the entire message.[23] I've found in my practice the use of a cue for one part of the message increases attention to all parts. Sometimes, loudness works when increased intonation doesn't. Sometimes, nonverbal gestures work better than anything else. There doesn't seem to be one cuing system that works equally well for all children. Try one. If it doesn't work, move to the next and keep substituting until you find one that's most compatible with your child's learning style. In Figure 6.3, I've substituted facial cues for vocal intonation.

Figure 6.3
I Can't Tell What's Important
Facial Expressions

Design Components	Auditory	Visual
Advance Organizing Statements	I want you to listen to what Mommy says and watch my face. (*What*)	I want you to watch what Mommy shows you and try to find what I ask for. (*What*)
	When I say something important, I'll make a face like this (eyes wide open, eyebrows up, head moved forward. (*How*)	First I'll say what I want you to find, then I'll tell you to find it. (*How*)
	You know how sometimes it's hard for you to remember things I say? After we do this game, it will be easier for you. (*Why*)	You know how sometimes it's hard for you to see some things? After we do this game, it will be easier for you. (*Why*)
Do It Often	Do a minimum of 10 attending activities at each sitting. Each sitting should be no more than 15 minutes.	Do a minimum of 10 attending activities at each sitting. Each sitting should be no more than 15 minutes.
Sneak Up On The Goal— Little Steps	1. Use wide eyes, arching eyebrow, head forward 2. Use arching eyebrow, head forward 3. Use head forward 4. Don't use any nonverbal behaviors	1. Use wide eyes, arching eyebrow, head forward 2. Use arching eyebrow, head forward 3. Use head forward 4. Don't use any nonverbal behaviors

Similar procedures can be used for looking. Instead of highlighting the important words at the beginning of a sentence, the important features of the visual display can occupy the foreground, with less important things in the background. For example, take a child who often visually neglects the periphery of visual images. In the center of a blackboard is a picture of a child. On the periphery are cars and buildings. After looking at it for a few minutes he engages in another activity. You ask him what he saw on the blackboard. He says, "a boy," totally ignoring everything on the outer edges. Using figure-ground distinctions, you can recreate the same image, but increase the size of whatever is on the edges and decrease what is in the center. The target object can also be highlighted either by color or line intensity. The cars and buildings could be colored and the boy in the center only outlined. And just as with listening training, the difference between what is important and what isn't in visual displays is gradually reduced.

I'M NOT READY TO MOVE ON

Sometimes children, who have no problem with noise and can pull out the important parts of a message, still have difficulty moving from one activity to another. It may take them a while to get settled, but once on track, they do fine. Fine, that is, until they need to move on to something new. It's almost as if they just got settled in a nice comfortable chair, and someone asks them to move on to another one. Their difficulty engaging in a new task may take the form of reluctance to change or a poor performance with the second task.

The Problem

With some children, shifting from one activity to another can cause difficulties.[24] It's found in young children with and without learning problems.[25] This form of "attentional inertia" hasn't been shown to occur more often in children with learning problems.[26] However, correcting it may be more of a problem with children who have learning differences. I worked with a 3-year-old child who did beautifully when there was some time provided between activities. When activities occurred back-to-back, she would have difficulty doing the second one even if it was simpler than the first. It seemed while willingly engaging in the second activity, her mind was still on the first. The solution was fairly easy. I asked the mother to have a clean break between activities, during which time few things would be done. Often, it just involved a snack. When there were breaks between activities, she performed significantly better. However, both the mother and I knew when she went to kindergarten, activities would be continuous. Therefore, the program we designed was one in which the amount of time between activities was gradually decreased. She still required some downtime, but her performance improved.

The Solution

Researchers maintain for these children, things that are no longer relevant stay active in working memory, making it difficult for attention to be directed toward new activities.[27] For these children, the focus will be on enabling them to dump out of working memory what no longer is relevant. Before shifting to another activity, try to get closure on the current one. By doing this you can reduce the tendency of some children to fixate on an activity. For activities that could be endless, use a timer.

Figure 6.4
I'm Not Ready to Move On

Design Components	Auditory	Visual
Advance Organizing Statements	I know how much you like playing with this. I'm going to set the timer now. When it goes off, we'll stop and get a snack. (*What*) We'll stop playing and go into the kitchen for 10 minutes and get a snack. Then we'll play with the other game. (*How*) You know how sometimes it's hard for you to stop doing one thing and begin another? Doing this will make it easier for you to do other things. (*Why*)	I know how much you like playing with this. I'm going to set the timer now. When it goes off, we'll stop and get a snack. (*What*) We'll stop playing and go into the kitchen for 10 minutes and get a snack. Then we'll play with the other game. (*How*) You know how sometimes it's hard for you to stop doing one thing and begin another? Doing this will make it easier for you to do other things. (*Why*)
Do It Often	Do only a few attending activities after each outburst.	Do only a few attending activities after each outburst.
Sneak Up On The Goal— Little Steps	1. After stopping one activity, do something neutral for 10 minutes. 2. After stopping one activity, do something neutral for 8 minutes. 3. After stopping one activity, do something neutral for 5 minutes. 4. After stopping one activity, do something neutral for 2 minutes. 5. Go from one activity to another	1. After stopping one activity, do something neutral for 10 minutes. 2. After stopping one activity, do something neutral for 8 minutes. 3. After stopping one activity, do something neutral for 5 minutes. 4. After stopping one activity, do something neutral for 2 minutes. 5. Go from one activity to another.

We often want to rush our children between one activity and another, believing "more is better than less." For some children, the opposite is true. If you notice that your child seems to have problems when one activity is butted up against another, build in downtime. This can be as simple as having a snack between activities. The program for this problem appears in Figure 6.4, and starts with a significant amount of time between activities, then gradually reduces it until activities are done back-to-back. For some children, having a break between activities is enough to move them off onto another track.

I'm Too Upset

Feeling lousy affects everything we do. We have trouble interacting with others. We can't concentrate. We don't operate as efficiently as we'd like. Our children have the same problems, but they can't manage them as well as we can. Many of our problems can be reduced or eliminated through choices—we often have the option of not doing certain things when our emotions are running strong. The option doesn't exist for many children, especially once they enter school. All children will have some negative emotions in school, just as in other places. That's normal. What makes it difficult for the child with a learning problem is the additional negative feelings generated by not being able to learn as well or as quickly as other children.[28]

The Problem

When children are anxious, they have problems attending.[29] When they're sad, they have problems attending.[30] When they're angry, they have problems attending.[31] When they're disappointed, they have problems attending.[32] These and scores of other emotional states affect attending behavior for all children. For some children with learning problems, the effects may be magnified. Instead of just being annoyed while listening or watching, their emotions may make it impossible to concentrate.[33] Unfortunately, in kindergarten, these problems occur on a daily basis. I worked with a mother whose son was having a great deal of difficulty in preschool. The teacher would complain daily to the mother about Lee's behavior.

"It wasn't a good day for Lee," the preschool teacher said.

"What happened?" the mother asked with great apprehension. Maybe it wouldn't be as bad as yesterday's incident when he spent two hours crying in the corner.

"Everything was fine until he became angry with Laura. She wouldn't share the book I asked her to look at with Lee. He became so furious, he just wouldn't do anything else. It seemed even when I asked everyone to do a simple task, Lee either didn't do it, or couldn't do it right."

It was a familiar pattern with Lee. His problem attending had been noticed by his parents when he was three. Now at four, they were magnified. It seemed his ability to attend was fragile. Almost any strong emotion would cause the system to fail. The parents had tried to minimize those things that caused Lee to have emotional breakdowns. Although they could successfully manage it at home, their control vanished at the preschool door. The parents knew next year in kindergarten it would be even more of a problem.

The Solution

It would be lovely if we could massage our child's psyche so only positive emotions developed and negative ones vanished. Unfortunately, that's not possible. As a parent, you can either continue trying to "mellow out" your child, or teach him or her to attend when things aren't going well. While you've been able to control your anxiety, anger, disappointment, and sadness, you haven't been able to banish them. Those feelings are always there, some of which are below the surface while others continually erupt like a volcano. One of the problems with designing a program for enabling children to attend when they are emotionally charged, it that you can't schedule emotions. What you can do is look for opportunities. In other words, if your child has problems attending when he or she is angry or annoyed, use those situations for a learning activity. Hopefully, they won't occur that often. But when they do, be prepared. I worked with a father whose son wouldn't listen when he didn't get his way. The situations ranged from minor issues like not being allowed to have an additional serving of ice cream, to being made to go to his bedroom for saying something unacceptable to his mother. In general, this was a good kid. The outbursts occurred no more than once or twice a week. But the father was concerned if similar situations occurred in kindergarten, the consequences would be more negative than at home.

"I want more ice cream Daddy," Hal said to his father.

"I'm sorry Hal, you already had two bowls."

"But I want more!" he screamed.

"No Hal, you've had enough. End of story."

Hal's eyes started to tear as he walked away from the dinning room table and went into a corner of the living room to play with a toy. Though not disruptive, he was disappointed. The father decided to use this as an opportunity to teach Hal to attend while emotionally upset. On a range of negative emotions from 1 to 10, Hal's level was no more than a 3.

"Hal, I know you're upset, but I need you to do something simple for me now."

"What is it?" Hal asked, refusing to look at this father.

"I forgot my gloves and hat in the car. I'd like you to get them for me, please."

"Do I have to?"

"Yes you do Hal."

Hal shuffled out of the living room into the garage, and then returned with both of the items his father had requested. It was a very simple and natural exercise, but one that began the process of pairing attention with less than positive emotions. For the next three months, Hal's father continually looked for additional opportunities for Hal to attend while emotionally taxed. He gradually identified situations that were increasingly negative and used them as an opportunity to increase Hal's ability to attend while upset. The program appears in Figure 6.5. You'll notice that I only listed three gradations of negative emotions. I'm sure you can find more in your children. Use these steps only as guidelines.

Figure 6.5
I'm Too Upset To Listen

Design Components	Auditory	Visual
Advance Organizing Statements	I know you're upset, but I need for you to do something for me. (*What*) You know how sometimes it's hard for you to listen when you're upset? Doing this will make it easier to listen when you're upset. (*Why*)	I know you're upset, but I need for you to do something for me. (*What*) You know how sometimes it's hard for you to listen when you're upset? Doing this will make it easier to listen when you're upset. (*Why*)
Do It Often	Do a minimum of 10 attending activities at each sitting. Each sitting should be no more than 15 minutes.	Do a minimum of 10 attending activities at each sitting. Each sitting should be no more than 15 minutes.
Sneak Up On The Goal— Little Steps	Using a 1–5 scale of emotional upset. 1. Start an attending activity after a mildly negative reaction (1) 2. Start an attending activity after a more negative reaction (3) 3. Start an attending activity after a very negative reaction (5)	Using a 1–5 scale of emotional upset. 1. Start an attending activity after a mildly negative reaction (1) 2. Start an attending activity after a more negative reaction (3) 3. Start an attending activity after a very negative reacdtion (5)

SEVEN

Understanding

C hildren are born into this world understanding nothing—but wanting to learn everything. Amazingly, the process is very similar for most. In Appendix 2, you'll see there is a gradual unfolding of a child's ability to understand, and it seems to follow the development of intelligence. But sometimes, even when a child's intelligence is normal or above average, a problem may exist. There may be too much information being presented. It may be coming in too quickly. It may be too complicated, or in a form that's not understandable. The child may be able to get the big picture, but not individual facts. Or the reverse can occur—the facts are clear, but the child can't connect the dots to see the big picture. For some children who learn differently, only one problem exists. For others, there can be a combination of problems. In this chapter, we'll explore the most common types of understanding problems, not through the use of current cognitive theories, but rather through the eyes of children who have a hard time making sense of some things in a very complicated world.

There's Too Much Information

Have you ever tried to stuff a suitcase with more items than it really was designed to hold? Although clothes were bulging out of the unclosed zipper, you decided it could still hold one more dress. You slipped it in and while pressing down as hard as you could, you started to zipper it shut. With a great amount of effort, you finally closed it. Although you're getting very clear messages what you were doing might have dire consequences, you continued on, delighting in the fact you didn't have to carry another suitcase. As you looked at your overstuffed bag with great admiration, you noticed the stitching holding the zipper to the bag slowly is beginning to unravel. Sometimes the same thing happens with our children.[1] We try to stuff their little brains with too much information. If we proceed, they won't burst, but there may be consequences that can be as unfortunate as ruining a perfectly good suitcase.

The Problem

As children begin attending to something, they may understand the problem before them. But as the information piles up, they seem to understand less and less. Two reasons are offered to explain the problem. The first is as they learn something new, it takes a toll on the area known as working memory.[2] In Chapter 1, I explained working memory as what you need to manage and negotiate things as they occur. Children with this type of problem listen to what is being said and initially understand it, but eventually the ability of their working memory fatigues, making it difficult for them to move the information into short-term memory. It's almost as if you have been listening to a lecture for 45 minutes. When the presenter began, you were able to understand everything. But since he's incredibly boring, you found as he continued talking, it took an ever-increasing amount of effort for you to understand what he was saying. Imagine a similar process occurring with your child. However, instead of 45 minutes, it may be only 5. Instead of a boring lecturer, it could be a kindergarten teacher talking about something that is of no interest to your child.

A second explanation also involves working memory. This theory maintains for some reason working memory gets stuck processing one thing and can't move on to the next.[3] Imagine that you are playing the best tennis game of your life. You look at your watch and see in 30 minutes you have an appointment across town. If you immediately stop, you can still make it. But the intoxication of the game is so great, you decide to delay. You'll just be late. A similar process may be occurring with your child, although the level of conscious decision making may be minimal or even nonexistent. You're explaining to your child how to button his coat. When you move on to tying his shoes, his mind is still focusing on buttoning. He isn't consciously ignoring your new set of instructions, his mind appears to be stuck on the last activity. Although you chose to continue playing tennis, he didn't choose to stay with buttoning—his mind didn't allow him to move on.

We don't know which of the two explanations may be correct, or if even either one makes any sense. Regardless of the theoretical explanation, parents need to focus on what is contributing environmentally to children's difficulties in comprehending. You need to focus on what can be most easily controlled. In this case, it's the amount of incoming information.

When we instruct our children, we often provide more information than they need. During conversations and free play, the "extra" information serves as connective tissue holding together ideas, providing warmth, and conveying affection—all things that are important for children. However, when they are interspersed between specific instructions in a learning activity, they tend to obscure the central message.[4] There's basically too much information coming in for some children to process correctly.

The Solution

The most effective strategy is to just limit the amount of information. Jack Webb, in the 1950s, starred on television in the detective series *Dragnet*.[5] Often witnesses would ramble on about what they saw, interspersing observations with motivations and personal experiences having nothing at all to do with the crime. Webb, playing the Los Angeles police detective Sergeant Friday, would display this look of frustration to his partner, and then utter his most famous line, "All we want are the facts, ma'am."

For children who have understanding problems based on too much information, we need to keep in mind Jack Webb's line. We need to streamline messages. Streamlining, however, doesn't mean stripping things down to the bone. Just as scrap pieces of meat and grizzle add to the flavor of a good soup stock, so do some things surrounding the message. In previous chapters, I emphasized the importance of providing a "web" of things that help children retain and eventually retrieve information. The example I gave was of the little girl seeing the Ferrari. Because of the richness of the event, she was able to retrieve the name. Retrieval, after all, is the name of the game. It's the end product of all learning. We retrieve to do activities, form evaluations, and make sense of our world. Why do we teach our children things if we don't expect them to retrieve this information later on? When trying to help children who have comprehension problems based on too much information, we can't ignore the fact that eventually, they'll need to retrieve. Therefore, the trick is to create a streamlined model that still contains a web. Let's look at two listening examples. The first resembles the over-packed suitcase. I use italics to highlight only what was important.

Example 1
Too Much Information

Jimmy, I know how hard it is for you to button up your shirt. It can be very complicated, what with so many buttons and your little fingers. It's especially hard when the holes are very small and you don't have too much time. But, what we're going to do today is learn how to do it. *I'll show you how to make it easy.* We'll use your red shirt. You know the one with the roosters on it? First I'll show you how to do it by helping with the buttons, then I'll let you do it all by yourself. Show me your left hand. No, that's the right. The other one is the left. *The holes are always here* by your left hand. Good. Now show me your right. That's very good Jimmy. Take your left hand and wave it to me. Great. Now put it right next to the third hole on the left. No, that's not the third hole, it's the fourth. Let's

count together from the top to find it. One-two-three. That's it. *Now pull it just a little*, not too much and not too little. Do it just right, like the bed Little Red Riding Hood found in the story of the three bears I read to you last week. You remember that one don't you? We read it on Tuesday, right after your bath. One was too hard, one was too soft, but there was one that was just right. That's how I want you to pull the button hole—just right. Now wave your right hand to me. Very good. Hold on to the button opposite of the hole on your shirt and very slowly and carefully *pull it through the hole*.

In the second example, only the highlighted words in the first example are spoken, along with just enough information to create a retrieval web.

Example 2
Just the Right Amount of Information

Jimmy, I know how hard it is for you to button your shirt. I'll show you how to make it easy. The holes are always here, by this hand. And the buttons are always here by your other hand. Put your hole hand by this button and pull it a little and hold it. Now with your other hand hold the button and put it through the hole.

In the first example 291 words were used. In the second, only 68. By eliminating irrelevant things, children who have difficulty with too much incoming information have a better chance of comprehending what's important, and therefore increase the likelihood of a successful retrieval.[6] Unfortunately, for many children, life is closer to Example 1 than Example 2. You'll have to gradually increase the amount of connective tissue in your teaching in order to strengthen your child's ability to deal with an excess of incoming information. If there is a problem as you increase the number of irrelevant words you add to your instructions, use auditory cues. Simply increase emphasis or volume on the words that are most important. In the following example, the most important information is italicized and therefore spoken either at a higher volume or greater intensity: "Joey, I want you to *eat your breakfast* of corn flakes and *drink* the tall glass of chocolate milk *before* you *put on* your red *raincoat*.

Problems comprehending visual configurations are similar to listening problems. Children who have problems with too many visual stimuli should have their environment rearranged so initially only those things that are involved with the learning are visible. For example, your child may have difficulty doing something motorically when there are too many things to look at. You ask your child to bring four tablespoons and four forks to the dinner table. When she returns, she has three tablespoons, three forks, and tongs.

"Did you remember everything I asked you to bring in?" you ask.

Figure 7.1
There's Too Much Information

Design Components	Auditory	Visual
Advance Organizing Statements	I want you to listen to what Mommy says and try to do it. (*What*) I'll say only a few words at first, then later I'll use more (*How*) You know how sometimes it's hard for you to understand some things? After we do this game, it will be easier for you. (*Why*)	I want you to watch what Mommy shows you and try to find what I ask for. (*What*) First there will be only a few things to look at. Then later I'll use more things. (*How*) You know how sometimes it's hard for you to see some things? After we do this game, it will be easier for you. (*Why*)
Do It Often	Do a minimum of 10 understanding activities at each sitting. Each sitting should be no more than 15 minutes.	Do a minimum of 10 understanding activities at each sitting. Each sitting should be no more than 15 minutes.
Sneak Up On The Goal— Little Steps	1. Action + Object (*bring* me the *green doll*) 2. Action + Object + Location (*bring* me the *green doll* that's in the *living room*). 3. Gradually increase the length of your sentences. They don't have to follow a pattern similar to ones in examples one and two.	1. Action + Object (*point* to the *green doll*) 2. Action + Object + Location (*point* to the *green doll* that's somewhere close to *your bed*). 3. Gradually increase the number of objects near the target object. They don't have to follow a pattern similar to ones in examples one and two.

"Yes Mommy, you asked for three big spoons, some forks, and that thingy Daddy uses to pinch my nose when we play."

You can't understand what went wrong. She obviously remembered the words you used, but something changed from the time she left the dining room until she opened the drawer of the kitchen cabinet. Before asking your daughter to repeat it, you decide to look at the drawer. It's a jumble of knifes, forks, spoons, and all the cooking utensils you couldn't find room for elsewhere. Visually, it was as loaded as the listening example previously given. You decide to try a little experiment. Before reentering the dining room, you rearrange all of the eating utensils in their proper containers and remove everything else. You then go back into the dining room.

"Dear, I think these are a little dirty," you say, holding up what she previously brought you.

"Could you please go back into the kitchen and get me four forks and four big spoons."

"Sure Mommy."

Your daughter goes into the kitchen and in half the time it took her on the first trip brings back four forks and four tablespoons. You just did the equivalent of reducing the number of words used for listening problems. A model program for reducing the amount of information appears in Figure 7.1. In this program you start with short sentences in which the most important features become prominent. You can also emphasize specific words. Once your child is successful at this beginning level, gradually increase the length of the sentence. You will be repeating the same instructions you gave in step one, but now do a little embellishing. In step three, you again repeat the instructions from step one, but now put in additional information that's not relevant. This last step is the one most similar to the situations your child will face outside the confines of a protective home. By gradually adding more information, children begin learning how to effectively deal with larger amounts of it.[7]

It's Coming in Too Quickly

Our lives operate on quick speed. As adults, we've acclimated to it. However, for many children it's difficult to take information in as if they were a line of quick marching army recruits. I remember trying to learn Morse code when I was ten years old. I did fine when the speed was no greater than five words a minute. Listening to the slow tap of dots and dashes posed few problems. Anything faster became a nightmare. I would miss some individual words as the speed went to seven words a minute. As it approached nine words a minute, I never got a single word correct. For some children serial information becomes a problem when they perceive it to be moving at the speed of a freight train.

The Problem

Everybody's ability to process information is different. Some can process rapidly, while others may require a considerable amount of time. It's unclear whether or not processing speed is related to intelligence.[8] I worked with a child who scored in the upper 1 percent of children his age in solving math problems; yet, he had difficulty processing linguistic information at a reasonable speed. Randolph was a remarkable child. At seven years of age, he was experimenting with algebra. He'd look at a problem having three formulas and not only understood they were related, but could find the solution. However, he sometimes required up to one minute to respond when asked ques-

tions. His ability to process incoming linguistic information was painfully obvious.

"Randolph, your mother told me you went to Disney World last week and you went on the Wild Mouse. I remember going on that. It was a lot of fun. Can you tell me what it was like?

He glared at me and said nothing.

"Dear," his mother said, "Stan asked you a question."

"I'm still thinking," he said.

This pattern was present since he was three years old. When a question was asked, Randolph wouldn't respond. Usually, people thought he was just being shy. However, it became obvious to his parents that something was wrong. By five, he had been taught to say, "I'm still thinking." This response led listeners to think he was odd. Though thought to be just peculiar when he was a preschooler, it became a significant problem when he entered kindergarten. He was obviously very bright, but his learning problem isolated him from other children and adults. I was never quite sure where the problem was within Randolph. The first thing his parents and I tried with him was to slow down the speed of incoming auditory information.

The Solution

Slowing down the transmission of information is an important technique for solving this problem. There are two easy ways of doing this. The first, which was discussed in Chapter 6, is to slow down your rate of speech. That procedure not only increases attending ability, but also comprehension. The model program explained in Chapter 6 can be applied just as it is for comprehension problems. Another technique for slowing down information is to keep one thought to one sentence, separating each with a brief pause. By doing this, you allow your child to process only one thought at a time. If they are having problems processing too much information, your pauses may allow sufficient time for their working memory to "catch up." For example, you want your child to get ready for school and there are three things she should do.

In the following example, everything is fired off as if your speech came out of a machine gun. There is no delay between thoughts: "Andrea please go upstairs and in the hall closet get your jacket then go into the kitchen and get your lunch."

In the next example, you're acting more like a sharpshooter on a practice range, where after taking one shot, you count to three before squeezing the trigger again.

"Andrea, please go upstairs." (pause 1-2-3)

"Open the hall closet." (pause 1-2-3)

"Inside you'll see your jacket." (pause 1-2-3)
"Bring it downstairs." (pause 1-2-3)
"Then go into the kitchen." (pause 1-2-3)
"When you're in the kitchen, bring out your lunch." (pause 1-2-3)

By keeping one thought to each sentence and pausing between sentences, you give a child the extra time needed to process information. The same thing can be done for visual problems. Just as with the previous strategy, you can gradually change the conditions of the activity. Here, you may eventually want to put more than two ideas in a sentence and decrease the amount of time between them. However, regardless whether or not a child has a comprehension problem, I usually choose to keep one thought per sentence. I've found it increases attending, comprehension, and retrieval in both children and adults.[9] The model for keeping each thought separate appears in Figure 7.2. When you start, there should be a considerable amount of time between your sentences. Gradually, the amount of time between sentences is reduced until one occurs immediately after the previous one ends. For children who also have problems retaining serial information, start with one sentence, and then gradually increase the number.

Figure 7.2
It's Coming In Too Quickly

Design Components	Auditory	Visual
Advance Organizing Statements	I want you to listen to what Mommy says and try to do it. (*What*) I'm going to tell you some things to do, but I'll stop after each thing. Then when I'm done, I'll raise my hand and you'll do them. (*How*) You know how sometimes it's hard for you to understand some things? After we do this game, it will be easier for you. (*Why*)	I want you to listen to what Mommy says and try to do it. (*What*) I'm going to tell you to look at some things, but I'll stop after I say each. Then when I'm done, I'll raise my hand and you'll point to them. (*How*) You know how sometimes it's hard for you to see some things? After we do this game, it will be easier for you. (*Why*)
Do It Often	Do a minimum of 10 understanding activities at each sitting. Each sitting should be no more than 15 minutes.	Do a minimum of 10 understanding activities at each sitting. Each sitting should be no more than 15 minutes.
Sneak Up On The Goal— Little Steps	1. I want you to (...) pause 1,2,3,4 2. I want you to (...) pause 1,2,3 3. I want you to (...) pause 1,2,2	1. I want you to find (...) pause 1,2,3,4 2. I want you to find (...) pause 1,2,3 3. I want you to find (...) pause 1,2,2

IT'S TOO COMPLICATED
TO UNDERSTAND

Sometimes just the words you select can be enough to make a difference for understanding.[10] I worked with a father who tried to increase his son's vocabulary by routinely using new words. He thought by minimizing the words his son already understood, he could increase his vocabulary. Intuitively, the approach makes sense. In fact, if new words were never introduced, children couldn't expand their vocabularies.[11] However, there can be too much of a good thing. Instead of gradually introducing new words and grammatical constructions to his 4-year-old son, this father would spew them out as if he was engaging in the practice used in World War II know as "carpet bombing," where tons of bombs rained down on an area. With enough tonnage, the small ball bearing factory located in the middle of a town would be destroyed. Unfortunately, so would every building surrounding it within two miles. Out of the ten new words he would use in his interaction with his son, possibly only one might be recognizable. However, because so much was incomprehensible, much of the father's message was lost. He needed to be selective in the use of new words and grammatical constructions.

The Problem

You don't need a degree in linguistics to determine what your child can and cannot understand. Start by just listening. You may even want to begin developing an audio collection of your child's language. Once a month, do a simple activity with your child, one that involves conversation rather than question and answers. Fantasy games work very well. Start playing the game with your child and record your conversation for a minimum of ten minutes. Then put it aside until the next month. Each month repeat the same activity. Over a three-month period, you should begin seeing how your child uses and develops language. Not only is it a wonderful tool for both you and other professionals if a problem is suspected, but what a terrific wedding gift when your child marries!

There are some technical language constructions you should be aware of that may cause problems. Younger children have difficulty with structures known as compound and complex sentences.[12] A compound sentence consists of two or more equals joined together in a sentence: I want to eat ice cream and I want to go for a walk this afternoon.

A complex sentence is one that has a main idea and another that is subordinate to it: I want to eat the ice cream (main idea) that's next to the strawberry flavor (subordinate idea).

By five years of age, many children not only understand these structures but routinely use them. Surprisingly, children as young as four-years-of-age do relatively well understanding casual or "if-then" relationships: If you don't eat all of your vegetables (if), you won't be able to watch television tonight (then).[13]

In general, young children's ability to understand the meaning of a word precedes their use of it by a few months.[14] They'll listen to a new word and then make some hypotheses about what it means. After hearing it often, they may try it out.

"Daddy, my new toy is so *scrumptious*."

The father is confused. He knows his daughter's use of the word is incorrect, but her intent is obvious. This is a toy she really likes, and the use of *scrumptious*, while incorrect, is in the ballpark of meaning. He has no idea where the word came from even though he used it over 30 times during the last month when describing his wife's cooking.

"Honey, do you mean that you really like it?"

"Yes Daddy. I like it as much as you like Mommy's spaghetti."

Now he remembers. His daughter has overgeneralized the meaning of the term. "Honey, we only use scrumptious when we talk about food."

"Oh. Okay Daddy."

The little girl goes back to playing with her wonderful, not scrumptious, toy. This is how children learn new words and concepts. They listen and watch, form theories, then test them out. They act like little scientists, always questioning what they think they know. If they're correct, they continue using the new knowledge. If they aren't, they scrap it and form a new hypothesis. The process works remarkably well until too many hypotheses need to be formed in one situation too quickly. It's like eating exquisite Belgium chocolate. One small square is wonderful. A half-pound eaten at once will send you into the bathroom. The equivalent in language is if what is being presented to the child is too complicated to understand, the child will become confused or simply ignore the message.

"Marty, we will *commence* our game by *indulging* in your mother's *whims*. You'll *assume* the *character* of Pinocchio and I'll be the *puppeteer* who is his *surrogate* father."

The father was very proud of himself. During this short conversation he introduced seven new words to his son. Unfortunately, when four-year-olds listen to something totally confusing, their first impulse isn't to say, "Daddy, there are seven words you said I didn't understand. Could you please explain them to me?" No, what children do is become confused. What is being said is in a form that's too complicated for them to understand.

The Solution

I become easily confused with all the bells and whistles on new electronic equipment. When I bought a new digital camera, I asked the sales person for a "Ph.D. camera." He looked quizzically at me.

"I'm sorry sir, we only have Nikons, Fujis, and Cannons. We don't carry the Ph.D. brand."

My attempt at being humorous was a bust. "No," I responded. "A Ph.D. camera is a *Push Here Dummy* one. You know, the type that's so simple it only requires me to push one button.

He smiled. "Oh, yes sir, we have many models for people like you." So goes the inappropriate use of humor.

The use of a simple model of comprehension may be the key to helping a child who has difficulty with complex relationships. You'll need to use alternative methods of conveying ideas without losing their essential meaning. This can be done by using more familiar words, less complex grammatical structures, and making abstract relationships more visual and concrete.

Using Familiar Words and Grammatical Structures

You don't need to be a linguist to effectively choose words and structures your child can understand. All you have to do is simplify them. Let's take the example we used above of the over-zealous father who wanted his son to become a Rhodes Scholar by five, and modify it so he can understand what the father is saying. "Marty, we'll *begin* our game by *doing* what your mother *would like*. You'll *be* Pinocchio and I'll be his *daddy*."

Not only did we simplify the choice of words, but also used fewer of them and arranged them in a form much more understandable to 4-year-olds, especially those with language difficulties. Just by simplifying, he now understands what the father wants to do. Children feel good about themselves when they can make sense out of what is occurring around them.[15] They don't when things are too confusing. Remember the piece of Belgium chocolate. A little bit is fine, but too much and you may get an upset stomach. Introduce new words and grammatical constructions slowly to children. Words are learned more quickly than grammatical constructions. A benchmark can be one new word every day or two, and one new grammatical construction every two or three weeks.

Simplify Relationships

In 1944, the famous comedy team, Abbot and Costello, broadcast their classic radio routine "Who's on First?"[16] Bud Abbot tries to explain to Lou Costello the names of the members of a baseball team. Each ball player has a nick-name, like *Who, Why, I Don't Know,* and *Maybe.* As Costello asks the names of the ball players, Abbot responds in classic exchanges such as these:

ABBOT: Who's on first, What's on second, I Don't Know is on third
COSTELLO: That's what I want to find out.
ABBOT: I say Who's on first, What's on second, I Don't Know's on third.
COSTELLO: Who's on first?
ABBOT: Yes.
COSTELLO: I mean the fellow's name.
ABBOT: Who.
COSTELLO: The guy on first.
ABBOT: Who.

Throughout the routine, Abbot continually confuses Costello by not fully explaining the bizarre nature of the ballplayers nicknames. To our children, our explanations often resemble the Abbot and Costello *Who's On First?* routine. When we explain things, they can be as simple as describing the colors of an object, or as complicated as explaining how 10 different relatives are connected to each other. A child's ability to understand abstract connections develops over time.[17] For some children, it takes longer than for others. I worked with a child who had a basic understanding of how things were connected, such as the rules that are used in school, if-then relationships, explanation of how things worked, and why certain items were combined into groups such as "fruits." However, when the connections jumped up a level, he was lost. For example, although he knew all of the items in a bowl on the kitchen counter were "fruits," he couldn't understand why some would become softer over a three-day period of time and others remained hard. And even more difficult to understand was why some fruits were fine to eat when hard and others weren't.

Show It Differently

The reoccurring theme of this book is every child's learning style is unique. Although there are similarities between children, each may have their own individual learning quirks. For some children, just changing the format (visual or auditory) used to convey information is enough to increase accuracy.[18] We know these preferences are neurologically based.[19] It's not necessarily a clean choice children make. For example, even if a child's learning preference is auditory, if the auditory message is coupled with visuals or graphics, they may do better.[20] Finding the best presentation mode may not be that difficult.

Over time, you've probably noticed your child learns better when you demonstrate what you would like him or her to do. Not only is understanding increased when you find the best presentation mode, but material is better retained, more quickly retrieved, and used more frequently.[21] Additionally, children's confidence in themselves increases, and learning becomes more satisfying.[22] Find the right way of presenting something, and magic occurs.

I GET THE BIG PICTURE, BUT NOT THE FACTS

How often have you watched a very long movie and then tried to explain it to someone? While you may have left out many of the details, you remembered the plot. Most movies are designed so you can do that. They're written with a beginning, middle, and end. Plots move in predictable patterns in most movies. In some of the worst cases, such as in many action movies, it's written according to a formula. By the end of the first ten minutes you can probably predict who gets the girl, who dies, and how it will end. Often there is little development of the characters; it's the overall plot that dictates how the movie will progress. Although the facts and minimal character development add to the movie, they aren't crucial. Instead of a robotic cop from a distant planet who saves the world, it could be a mechanical dog from Detroit that saves Michigan—either scenario moves the plot along. You can enjoy action-adventure movies even if you don't remember all the facts. The facts aren't that important in these types of movies. Unfortunately, many of the situations we find ourselves in don't mirror the movies. While we may have a grasp of the overall picture, a lack of knowledge about the facts can get us into trouble.

I was supposed to meet a friend at a car return location close to an airport. As I came close, I could see the planes ascending and descending, but didn't know which road led to the off-site destination. I decided to get off the highway and ask at a gas station.

"Oh, that's easy. Get back on the highway, head north until you see state route 45, not federal highway 45, then take the east exist, go for two miles until you see the Arby's sign on the left. That'll be three traffic lights and two stop signs. Turn left at the last stop sign and head south. You can't miss it."

Since I am easily confused when driving at night and having had minimal sleep, it was a nightmare. For two hours, my friend waited at the car return terminal while I circled and zigzagged around the airport. For two hours I was never more than three miles away. Yet, because I couldn't follow the facts, I remained confused. I had the big picture, but not the individual facts. Sometimes the actions of children resemble my efforts at finding my friend.

The Problem

There are some children who have problems with facts. They can see the big picture, but can't grasp details. As long as there is a match between their ability and what they are trying to understand, everything is fine. However, problems occur when children lack whatever is required to understand a situation.[23] Some researchers believe children who have difficulty with facts are unable to derive cues from the context.[24] For example, a child is in a kindergarten class and the teacher is showing the children how to cut a piece of paper with scissors. With little effort, the scissors cut through the paper. For many children, this would imply scissors are sharp, and they should not put their finger between the blades. The context was watching the scissors effortless cutting through the paper. The individual fact was the sharp blade. Let's assume the teacher forgot to say, "Don't put your finger on the blade, it's very sharp." While some of the children would have been able to understand the blades were sharp because of the action of the scissors (the context), other children may not have been able to deduce that fact.

The Solution

Let's take the scissor-cutting example to show how children who have problems with facts can be given the support they need. If the teacher understood that some of the children in her class had problems with individual facts, she could explain it using a graphic similar to the one in Figure 7.3 At the top of the graphic is a representation of the entire scissor-cutting act. Below it are the individual facts that comprise it. She could explain cutting with scissors in the following way.

"Children, can you see this card? On the top is a picture of a pair of scissors (points to the picture of the scissors). We'll be using them today. Here is a picture of a piece of paper (points to the picture of the paper). We'll be cutting it. We start on the edge of the paper, but we need to be careful because the scissors are very sharp (points to the picture of the scissors cutting the paper). If you're not careful, you can cut your finger (points to the picture of the finger)."

You might be wondering why I didn't suggest using real objects, such as scissors, paper, and bandages. The purpose of using graphics is to have things concrete and enduring. Part of this sequence involves an action—cutting. Since actions have starting and ending points, they are fleeting. Since I want the child to remember "cutting," I can make it concrete and lasting by depicting it on the card. In some learning activities it is possible to depict all of the facts using real objects. For example, "car," "truck," and "airplane." For those situations, there's no problem. However, it's hard to show categories of facts using

Figure 7.3
Cutting with a Scissors

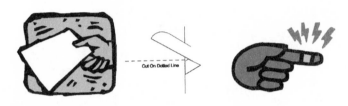

Figure 7.4
I Get the Big Picture, But Not the Facts

Design Components	Auditory	Visual
Advance Organizing Statements	We're going to talk about _____. (*What*) There are lots of things we know about it. I've drawn a box for each one. After I tell the story, I want you to tell me what goes into each box. (*How*) You know how sometimes it's hard for you to remember some things about stories? After we do this game, it will be easier for you. (*Why*)	We're going to talk about _____. (*What*) There are lots of things we know about it. I've drawn a box for each one. After we look at it, I want you to tell me something that goes into each box. (*How*) You know how sometimes it's hard for you to remember some things about what you see? After we do this game, it will be easier for you. (*Why*)
Do It Often	Do a minimum of 10 understanding activities at each sitting. Each sitting should be no more than 15 minutes.	Do a minimum of 10 understanding activities at each sitting. Each sitting should be no more than 15 minutes.
Sneak Up On The Goal— Little Steps	1. Have three cards, each representing a characteristic of the story (i.e., who, what, where) 2. Cover graphics on one card. 3. Cover graphics on two cards. 4. Cover graphics on all three cards.	1. Have three cards, each representing a characteristic of the story (i.e., who, what, where) 2. Cover graphics on one card. 3. Cover graphics on two cards. 4. Cover graphics on all three cards.

real objects. For example, Figure 7.4 is a complete program for increasing a child's ability to remember facts. In this program, the child will be asked to remember three individual facts about a story. They could be something about *who* was in the story, *where* the story was located, and *what* was done. While these three categories of facts are easily depicted with graphics, they may pose problems if real objects are used. It would be possible for the child to mistake the category for the real object.

I Get the Facts, But Not the Big Picture

One of the problems with big pictures is they rarely are visible or concrete. We don't see big pictures—we infer their existence. For example, you can't show your child a *family*. What you can show them are individuals somehow connected, like "mommy," "daddy," brother," and "sister." You don't see a *family*, you see its members. The same is true for other types of relationships, such as causal—"*If* you eat your asparagus, *then* you can have ice cream."

Your child can see the asparagus and the ice cream. But where are these *ifs* and *then* things? Big pictures are things we as adults *infer*. They have no objective reality of their own. Rules fall into this category. We can't see the rules, only the consequences of following or not following them. We create big pictures and hope our children can understand them. Unfortunately, some can't. In which case, if we can't make them real, we need to give them a quasi-reality. The easiest way of doing this is to use graphics.

Imagine being told you have to draw a duck, and you're not a very good artist. You struggle with the outline, getting much of what you drew totally out of proportion to what the animal looks like. It sort of looks like a duck, but it could also be a dog or a moose. What if you were asked to do the same drawing, but this time, the outline appeared as a series of dots? By connecting the dots, your drawing would come much closer to what a duck looks like. If you have a child who can't see the big picture, you'll need to construct activities that are similar to the connect-the-dots pictures. You'll need to provide varying degrees of outlines, depending on the severity of the problem.

The Problem

Not being able to see the big picture is the flip side of not being able to see individual facts. They are not separate problems. Rather, they fall along a continuum, where sometimes facts come easy and big pictures don't, while at other times the reverse occurs. It's very difficult to determine where a child's problem lies.

When my daughter was young and I read her a story, she could easily identify the plot, theme, and the story's moral. It was an amazing thing to watch. However, it was difficult for her to remember the names of the characters or where the action took place. If I assumed this meant she had problems with facts in all situations, I would be wrong. When doing an art project, Jessie would be able to articulate her vision of the final product (big picture) and what would be necessary for achieving it (individual facts). You'll find the same things may occur with your children. First assume there is variability in their ability to use facts and understand the big picture. If situations indicate that there is a more consistent pattern, then you can change your beliefs.

The Solution

For children who can't see the big picture, you need to make it explicit. This can be done graphically. The graphic representation takes the same form, but in reverse, as in the previous section when individual facts were the problem. A complete program appears in Figure 7.5.

An explicit example appears in Figure 7.6, which depicted individual facts related to food.

There are three different food categories: fruits, desserts, and fish. An arrow from each food group leads to a boy eating. Regardless of the number, they are all related. They are all foods. This list could be increased or made smaller, depending on a child's ability to group individual facts. For example, instead of there being a boy in the center, there could be a picture of fruit, and instead of fruit, dessert, and fish on the top, there could be pictures of an apple, a banana, and a pear. In each of these situations, we are teaching children concepts: fruits, desserts, fish, and food. These are all big picture items.

Not all big pictures involve relationships between individual facts and concepts. Sometimes the problem exists between different types of relationships, like if-then consequences. These often appear when children have difficulty understanding the rules of play or social interaction. I worked with a preschooler who, while understanding and occasionally following the rules used in preschool, didn't understand their purpose or how they were all connected. He was a bright child, having a vast command of individual facts in many areas, but couldn't see the connections between things. He knew the five rules the teacher believed were most important for her classroom. She made graphic representations for each on the blackboard. Although there were other rules, violations of these would cause grief for the teacher, and therefore for the child and parents. The rules were:

No yelling.
Raise your hand before speaking.

Figure 7.5
I Get the Facts, But Not the Big Picture

Design Components	Auditory	Visual
Advance Organizing Statements	We're going to solve a puzzle. (*What*) I'm going to talk about something and I want you to tell me what it's about when I'm done. To make it easier for you, I'll show you three cards and you choose which one solves the puzzle. (*How*) You know how sometimes it's hard for you to remember some things about stories? After we do this game, it will be easier for you. (*Why*)	We're going to solve a puzzle. (*What*) I'm going to show you something and I want you to tell me what it's about when I'm done. To make it easier for you, I'll show you three cards and you choose which one solves the puzzle. (*How*) You know how sometimes it's hard for you to remember some things about stories? After we do this game, it will be easier for you. (*Why*)
Do It Often	Do a minimum of 10 understanding activities at each sitting. Each sitting should be no more than 15 minutes.	Do a minimum of 10 understanding activities at each sitting. Each sitting should be no more than 15 minutes.
Sneak Up On The Goal—Little Steps	1. Have three cards, each representing the theme of the story (the big picture) 2. Cover graphics on one card. 3. Cover graphics on two cards. 4. Cover graphics on all three cards.	1. Have three cards, each representing the theme of the story (the big picture) 2. Cover graphics on one card. 3. Cover graphics on two cards. 4. Cover graphics on all three cards.

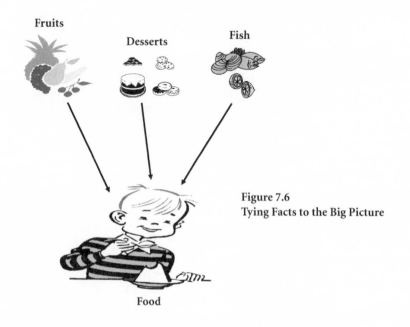

Fruits

Desserts

Fish

Figure 7.6
Tying Facts to the Big Picture

Food

Sit in your own chair.

Tell the teacher if you need to use the bathroom.

No hitting.

While the teacher did a terrific job of making sure the children understood the rules, she assumed they would also know why they were important. For most children, it was enough simply to know the rules must be followed. But for Wayne, he didn't see how these were related to his daily life in preschool. Sometimes he would follow the rules. Other times he would just ignore them.

"Why does your teacher tell you not to do these things?" I asked, pointing to each graphic on the blackboard.

"I don't know," Wayne responded.

"Would you like to know?"

"I don't know," he repeated.

I proceeded to pull out a large piece of paper and copied on to it each of the graphics depicting the five rules. Then I began drawing the big picture for each rule. A similar drawing to the one I used for "no yelling" appears in Figure 7.7.

"If you yell Wayne, the teacher will become angry and so will the children. And if you yell, the teacher will have to tell your mother and father. And then they will become upset. Now do you understand why you shouldn't yell?"

"Yes," he said, as if something completely new was being shown to him.

"Do you think you'll yell anymore in class?"

"Oh no! I don't want to make people not like me."

Although Wayne still had occasional yelling episodes, their occurrence lessened after the lesson on

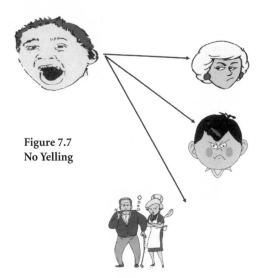

Figure 7.7
No Yelling

behaviors and consequence. You can use this same format for any relationship that may be difficult for your child to understand. It can be particularly effective for children who have trouble understanding the rules of play. I worked with a child who clearly understood rules, such as taking turns. However, he didn't know what was an appropriate action when another child violated the rule. His parents and I taught him "options" for when rules were ignored. For example, if someone takes an extra turn, you can:

1. Ask him nicely to follow by the rules: "You took an extra turn. You shouldn't do that."
2. Ask an adult for assistance.
3. Play with another child.

Each option was graphically depicted on a card. Then, we all participated in a game in which one of the players violated the rule and Steven was asked to choose an appropriate response. We successfully repeated this process for each of the rules. Rules and options are abstractions. Your child will find them easier to understand if you make them concrete through the use of graphics. Also, your life will probably become less stressful.

EIGHT

Storage, Retrieval, and Usage

You may be wondering why I lumped storage, retrieval, and appropriate usage into a single chapter. The reason is, even though all three are separate, they're treated identically when it comes to intervention. Storage is something we can only know indirectly.[1] We assume our children store information, but we don't really know until it's retrieved. Retrieval is the child's ability to bring past learned material to a conscious level. Appropriate retrieval is the end of information processing—using the retrieved information in the way it was taught. If you begin worrying about memory problems after information is stored, you're too late. It's like hoping a tap dancer who didn't practice enough will remember each of the moves in a performance. If you worry about retrieval as it is occurring, you're also too late. That poorly rehearsed dancer will most likely be out-of-sync with the rest of her fellow dancers during the performance, no matter how much she tries to retrieve the correct movements. What we do while getting our children to attend and understand has a direct relationship to how information is stored and eventually retrieved.[2] In this chapter, we'll look at strategies that help storage, retrieval, and appropriate usage. Most of these strategies are applied during the attention and understanding stages.

I CAN'T SEE HOW THINGS ARE RELATED

Imagine you need to retrieve both facts and relationships. Let's assume you are in Las Vegas, and have just learned the rules of a poker game called Texas Hold'em. Although the rules are simple, the way in which you bet your cards isn't. There are various types of plays you can make depending on the cards you're holding and the cards laying face up on the table. You also have to factor in some of the strategies used when certain types of bets are made. Although you spent 30 minutes learning everything about the game, there was so much to learn and remember, you couldn't retain everything. Worse, the way in which the game was taught to you was not very organized. Instead of teaching you how cards, betting options, and opposite player moves are all connected, your well-meaning teacher jumbled them together in a very disorganized manner. But since you want to try out your new skills, it's off to the casino. The evening ends with the sweet little old lady at the end of the table cleaning out your wallet. Some children constantly face a Texas Hold'em game in their everyday lives. For these children, relationships that may be inherent to others are invisible to them.[3]

The Problem

Life requires children to retrieve both individual facts and relationships. For example, when children go onto the playground, they not only have to retrieve information about individual activities, but also how children play with each other.[4] The rules of children's play are very complicated. There are rules for turn taking, conversing, sharing, withholding, and a multitude of other interactions most children just pick up through experience. What makes it even more complicated is for every rule there are exceptions and rebuttals. This rule applies in all situations except *a* and *b*. If a child breaks the rule, then you can either do *c* or *d*, but not *e*.

Problems with relationships are not limited to play situations. In the last chapter, we discussed children who could identify individual facts but had problems with the big picture. Think of problems with relationships as similar to lacking the big picture. What's missing is an understanding of the logical relationships between individual facts. If it was never stored with the connections, it won't be retrieved with them.[5] Let's take the use of a painting kit. It contains small and large tipped brushes, cups, paint, canvas boards on which to paint, a smock, and 12 different paints—each in a black jar with colors on the screw-on lid. You demonstrate how to use the kit, believing your child will be able to do so alone next time. You show her how to use each item and the order it should be used.

1. She puts on the smock.
2. Newspapers are laid down on the kitchen floor.
3. The easel is set up on top of the paper.
4. One canvas board is put on the easel.
5. Paints are selected then placed on a small table next to the easel.
6. Brushes are selected.
7. Only jars of paints to be used are opened.
8. Painting begins.

Your demonstration of what your child should do is perfect. Not only are you pleased with yourself as a teacher, but your child loves the activity and does extremely well at it. Two days later, your daughter asks if she can paint again.

"Of course dear. I'll get out the paint set and lay it out for you in the kitchen."

Your daughter's delighted. You begin to lay out everything. Just then you receive a phone call. You take it in the other room since it's from a relative and it concerns your daughter's cousin.

"Mommy can I start?" your daughter asks.

Deeply engaged in your conversation, you nod, unaware of what you just agreed to. Twenty minutes later the phone call ends and you come back into the kitchen. There's your daughter, laying on the floor covered with paint from her hair to her shoes. Every jar of paint is opened, some of which are on their sides on the floor. Your daughter has four brushes in her hand and is making a swirl design on the canvas that somehow manages to continue onto your new tile floor. What went wrong? Basically, although your daughter was able to retrieve all of the information you taught her during the learning process, she lacked the organizational structure necessary to save your kitchen from becoming an incredible mess. Many of the problems could have been eliminated if advance and retrieval organizers were used.

The Solution

To solve the problem, we introduce organization during attention and understanding, and again during retrieval. In order for some children to understand abstract concepts (e.g., vegetables, fruits, meats, et cetera.), they need to be made aware of connections during the attention phase of learning. A child who can see connections before you even start teaching will have less difficulty learning than if she first encounters them during the understanding phase of learning. Let's say that we want to teach a child abstract concepts by showing him examples. So, for fruits, we use an apple, pineapple, orange, and banana. For meats, we will use chicken, pork, and beef. We can place all of the items together, as in Figure 8.1, and pull out examples of items from each concept category. In this scenario, the initial visual configuration doesn't add anything to the child's understanding. They're just a bunch of items. Attention is not being used as effectively as it could be. But if we arrange the items, as I did in Figure 8.2, the child begins to see the

Figure 8.1
I Can't See How Things Are Related (No Grouping)

Figure 8.2
I Can't See How Things Are Related
(Grouping)

items are connected even before the understanding activity begins. In this example, attention is being used to facilitate understanding concepts. We now make concepts more explicit in the understanding phase.

"Ruth, can you see how all these things are together (pointing to each group in Figure 8.2)?"

"Yes," she answered.

"What are they?"

"An apple, a pineapple, an orange, and a banana"

"That's right. Do you know why I put them all together?"

"No."

"They're together because all of them grow on trees. If it grows on a tree, we call it a fruit." A symbol card with a tree is placed over the group as in Figure 8.3.

"Oh."

"What are all these things, Ruth?"

"Fruit."

In this simple teaching model, we've done three things to help with retrieval of the word "fruit." The first thing was to use attention to begin teaching the concept. Second, during the understanding phase, we emphasized the relationship graphically between objects. And third, we created a template for retrieval. If later in the day we wish to see if Ruth still understands the concept, we need to have her retrieve it. If we use the same format that was used in understanding, we greatly increase the possibility of an accurate retrieval.

"Ruth, do you remember how we learned a new word earlier today?"

"Yes."

Figure 8.3
I Can't See How Things Are Related
(Fruit Grouping)

"Let's look at the card again (Figure 8.3). What's the name we used for all things that you can eat that grow on trees?"

"Fruit."

You can use this model both during active teaching activities, such as working with concepts and rules, and also with teaching that's passive. An example of a passive teaching model would be physical arrangements in your house. For example, besides using the card to teach the concept of "fruit," you could also put all of the fruit in your house in a large bowl on the counter or designate a drawer in your refrigerator just for them. You could also place the teaching graphic next to the bowl or on the drawer. The same approach can also be taken for teaching organization of other items. Store all jars in one area of your kitchen, all tools together, all personal hygiene items on a specific shelf in the bathroom, et cetera. These passive forms of teaching organization can also be used for relationships. For example, clothing items can be arranged in the order they are to be put on. As your child learns things from both forms of teaching, each template is stored along with the individual items. In the presence of an organizing device, retrieval is made easier. And just as with all other learning programs, the role of the organizing device is gradually phased out. For example, the bowl in which the fruit was stored could initially be removed and the fruits remain on the counter. Then, fruits could be placed inside the refrigerator on various shelves and your child asked to bring you a piece of fruit.

Advance organizers are templates used for laying down information in memory.[6] Retrieval organizers take the same form as advance organizers but are used immediately before you ask a child to retrieve information.[7] Let's reexamine our painting disaster and see if the use of advance and retrieval organizers could have made any difference. When the painting activity was first taught, the mother could have graphically shown the order in which each part of the painting activity was to be done, such as in Figure 8.4. Instead of just having her daughter engage in the activities, as the mother initially did, it would have been better to use the template and have the child identify each activity by herself.

"Amy, do you see these pictures of all the things we're going to do?"

"Yes Mommy."

"How many are there?"

"One, two, three, four, five, six, seven, eight! There's eight Mommy!"

"That's right. There are eight things. Let's look at the first one. What do you think that's a picture of?"

"It looks like a coat."

"And is the little girl wearing it?"

"Yes Mommy."

Figure 8.4
Painting Sequence

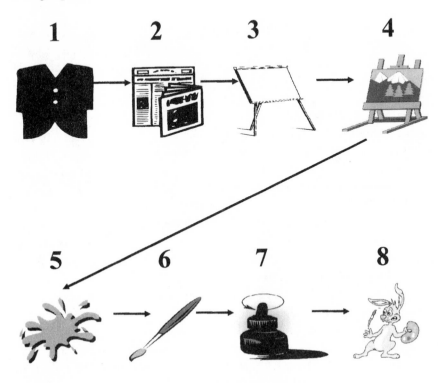

"I want you to do whatever we see in the picture. So, find the coat and put it on."

"It's here Mommy."

"That's terrific. Now I want you to tell me everything you're doing, as you do it.

"Okay. I'm putting one hand into the coat. Now I'm putting in the other. Now I'm pushing the snap things so the coat closes. Did I do everything right?"

"Yes, you did. Do you know why you should put it on?"

"No Mommy."

"Because when we paint, I don't want you to get any paint on your shirt. Since we did the first thing, on the card, why don't we put a big star on it so we know it's done."

"Great. Then can we do the second?"

The same sequence was repeated until all eight steps were completed. In this simple activity, the mother initially created the structure into which the activity was ordered. For children who have difficulty seeing the organization

of ideas, this strategy is very effective. It creates the holes into which individual facts are placed. Not only are individual facts stored, but the structure is stored that connects them. Connections can take many forms. In this case, it had to do with sequencing. But it can apply equally to relationships between objects, such as how parts of a toy are related to each other. In addition to supplying a structure, this mother did a number of things that greatly enhanced her daughter's memory. First, she actively involved her in learning the sequence. She not only told her what she would be doing, but had her demonstrate each of the steps.[8] The more involved a child is in an activity, the greater chance the information will be retained. The mother added an extra boast to her daughter's memory by having her say what she did as she did it. It seems the retention of words used to describe a learning activity makes it easier to retrieve the activity itself.[9] Finally, to give importance to each step of the activity, she explained why they were doing it.

If everything worked as planned, it would be easier than in the first example for the child to remember the activity. When the comedian W.C. Fields was dying, a good friend visited him and found him reading a Bible. Since everyone knew Fields was an atheist, his friend was astonished.

"Bill, why are you reading that?" his friend asked incredulously.

"Insurance," Fields responded.

Just like Fields's attempt to get that extra edge, we should do the same thing with children who have problems with organization. We could just have them retrieve the information we taught them using the templates we developed and hope it was rich enough to allow them to be successful. Or, we, just like Fields, could take out insurance. We do this by simply repeating the use of the advance organizing strategies immediately before we ask them to retrieve.

"Honey, I'm going to let you set up your paint all by yourself."

"Okay Mommy, but there are a lot of things to do."

"I know. That's why we'll use the same pictures on the card again. I'll just watch you do it all by yourself. And do you remember when I taught you to use the paint set, I asked you to tell me what you were doing as you did it?"

"Yes Mommy."

"I want you to do the same thing again."

We've loaded the situation in favor of our child. We provided a structure during learning, and then used the same strategy for retrieval. What we've described is only the starting point in enabling children to develop a sense of organization. While you will be successful in using this method, eventually your child will need to function in a world that doesn't lay out things as well as you do. The first step is to phase out the retrieval cues, much as this mother did it in Figure 8.5.

Figure 8.5
Painting Sequence—Phasing Out Cues

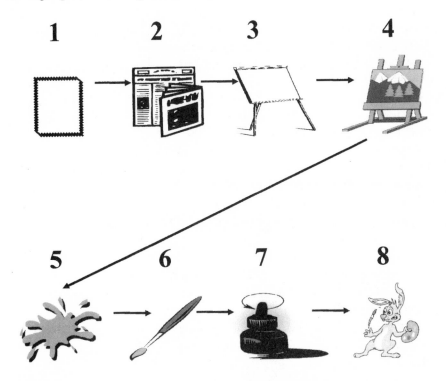

"Amy, you did so well yesterday when I allowed you set up the paint by yourself. We'll do it again today, but this time, I'm going to put a blank card on the first thing you need to do. Do you think you can remember it?"

"Yes Mommy!" she said as she grabbed the coat and put it on.

Gradually, the retrieval cues are phased out and the child is still able to successfully set up the paint set and use it appropriately. With children who have organizational problems, I would be more cautious in phasing out the advance organizing cues. Since appropriate retrieval is dependent on organized memory, a too early phase-out period may result in problems.

Simulations can be very effective devices for retrieval when used in teaching.[10] To be effective, the simulation needs to incorporate all of the important features that will be present during the retrieval. Simulations can be used for teaching different types of things. It's best to begin with those that are more concrete and then move onto abstractions.[11] This would mean beginning with simulations that are pragmatic, then progressing to those that are inferential.

I Can Store It, But When I Retrieve Parts Are Missing

When I go to the store for groceries I sometimes forget my shopping list. When I rely just on memory, I often return home with one or two items missing. Instead of the nicely trimmed rack of lamb, I get a pork roast. I look at all the condiments laid out on the counter for my lamb and wonder how I could have forgotten it. A senior moment? Or just something that happens when you rely on memory for too many items? I think the latter. Think about the last time something similar happened with your child.

"Marjorie, tomorrow we're going to visit Grandma. I know how important your train toys are for you. I want you to put them into your suitcase tonight so you'll have them at Grandma's."

"Okay Mommy," your daughter says as she bounds up the stairs.

The next day you leave and begin the four-hour drive to your mother's house. Fifteen minutes away from Grandma's, your daughter begins crying.

"What's wrong dear?"

"I forgot my trains."

This wasn't anything complicated about what you asked her to do—simply to put three objects into the suitcase. She clearly understood your request and had no difficulty storing it in her memory. Why then did she forget? You'll probably never know. But what you can do for a child who routinely forgets things is to look back at how she attended and learned those things before storing them in her memory.

The Problem

When children have trouble correctly retrieving, the reason for the problem can often be found by just looking at what was forgotten or distorted. Was the thing something that was too complicated? Did it receive too little emphasis when it was being learned? Did it involve something abstract? By trying to determine the type of error your child made, you can identify what went wrong during the understanding phase. When my son was three, we visited his grandparents and uncle in South Florida. As we drove, he asked me where his uncle was.

"Tom went to see the Miami Dolphins."

He thought a minute and then started to cry. "He went to see your fish? Why couldn't I go to see your Ammi Dolphins?"

I was initially baffled. Why was he crying? And how did you go from Miami Dolphins to fish that I owned called Ammi Dolphins? Then I realized what happened. "Miami" wasn't a word Justin had ever heard. And "Dolphins" to him were a kind of fish. When I said "Miami Dolphins," he heard "My Ammi Dolphins." Never having heard the word "Miami," he reasonably misinterpreted it as "My Ammi." If you look at the errors in retrieval your child is making, you might not find anything similar to Justin's problem, but you will see others. Sometimes, the errors are isolated events, as was the misinterpretation of "Miami" for "My Ammi." However, you might begin seeing patterns. For example, I worked with a child who had problems correctly retrieving the speed of objects.

"Was the car going fast, Joey?" the father asked his son as he was trying to recall the events of the morning.

"I don't know."

After the father noticed that it was a pattern, he came to see me. In our discussions, it appeared that Joey was having trouble retrieving things that weren't concrete. The speed of a car was just one example.

The Solution

Once you have identified the type of item your child has difficulty retrieving, you can use the strategy of making the element more distinctive. By doing this, your child will have a better chance of retaining the item.[12] I developed a very simple program for Joey, in which the father and son would initially focus on the speed of objects and people. Although the problem cut across anything that was abstract, I decided to start on speed. Once Joey was able to consistently recall this abstraction, we would move on to others. In general, it's best to only work on one problem at a time. The game I developed was called "How Fast?" Joey and his father would walk around the block and find 20 things whose speed could be described before circling back to their house. If the speed of 20 things were identified, Joey was rewarded with a trip to the ice cream store. Joey delighted in the activity. I developed a card on which graphics depicted three speeds—slow, medium, and fast. Joey's father would point to something and ask Joey to touch the graphic that best described the object's speed. The father selected objects moving at different speeds. The game worked very well. Joey consistently identified the correct speed of objects and completed the 20 trials well before returning to the house. On the drive to the ice cream store, the father began the following conversation.

"Joey, do you remember that very big white truck we saw on our block?"

"Yes Daddy."

"How fast was it going?" the father said as he pointed to the card in front of Joey.

"Like this," Joey said as he pointed to the slow graphic. "It was so slow!"

Throughout the 15 minute ride to the store, the father talked about what they had just seen and asked his son to describe the speed of various objects through the car window. He was consistently correct. Later that day, the father asked Joey to recall some of the earlier events, again using the card. This time, only 80 percent of the retrievals were correct. But it was a significant improvement. We started the activity with the assumption Joey could differentiate different speeds as he saw them. The problem was the way in which they were stored did not facilitate retrieval. By using the graphics, whatever was missing during storage was provided. The activity continued for a week, gradually reducing the use of the speed card. First the graphics were taken out, leaving only the numbers. Then the entire card was eliminated. When retrieval for movement was no longer a significant problem, we proceeded to Joey's problems with sequencing. Using the same format, we effectively treated that problem as well.

You Waited Too Long to Ask Me to Do It

Our memory often appears to resemble a pebble dropping into a pond. Close to the impact, the ripples are definable. But as you move away from where the stone entered the water, the size diminishes, eventually leaving the water as flat as it was before you dropped in the stone. Think of the pebble as what you will eventually want to retrieve and the receding ripples as time. The closer the retrieval activity is to the learning activity, the greater the accuracy of the retrieval.[13]

The Problem

Unfortunately, we often don't have the opportunity to retrieve what we learn until much later. It's as if you are required to wait until the ripple reaches the shore, where it's barely discernable. If the time you need to wait is fixed, is there anything you can do to make it more likely that you will retrieve the information accurately? Yes. Use a 500-pound boulder rather than a pebble. If you dropped a 500-pound boulder into the water, instead of a ripple, you'd have a wave. While the pebble's ripple fizzled out by the time it reached shore, the boulder's wave crashed 10 feet over the shoreline. The greater the impact of what is being learned, the longer it will be retained in memory. For some children, using boulders rather than pebbles is the key to increasing the accuracy of retrievals.

The Solution

Throughout this book, you've learned a number of techniques that will make information stand out, such as figure-ground distinctions, highlighting, and cues. These are your 500-pound boulders. There are other techniques that can supplement them. The first is called restatement, and when used during learning, it helps retrieval.[14] In Chapter 5, I emphasized the importance of beginning each activity with the advance organizing statements of what, how, and why. These three statements set up the child to focus on the activity. It's analogous to sharpening knives. To make your knives very sharp, you start by putting a grinded edge on them. That's the advance organizing statements. However, the sharpening process isn't over until a fine edge is honed. That's the equivalent of restatements. A restatement happens at the end of each activity. It's merely taking everything you and your child did, and restating it in simple terms. For example:

"Mark, you did so well today. We started by putting parts of the story in the right order. I would ask you to tell me which came first, then second, and last. You had the pictures in front of you and as I read the story you looked at them. When I finished, I asked you to put the pictures in the right order. And you did it perfectly! The story I read you was of a fisherman who went out in a very stormy ocean. And the reason I had you put the cards in the right order was so when your teacher tells you things to do, you'll remember them."

It's hard to imagine how this simple 30-second summary of a 15-minute activity helps memory, but it does. It's as if you're trying to get something that requires gelatin to set. It's just a bowl of liquid until the gelatin enters it and it goes into the refrigerator for a while. The same thing seems to be taking place when restatement is used. It's a very simple technique that takes only seconds to perform.

Another boulder is the use of familiar words during the teaching portion. The more familiar the words, the better the retrieval.[15] Think of each word you use as a potential retrieval hook. If the words aren't familiar, most likely they won't be of much help in retrieving. Compare the following two descriptions of how to pour milk given to a four-year-old.

"Mary, I'm going to demonstrate for you the proper way of pouring milk. It has a three-part sequence. The first is placing the glass approximately in the middle of the table. Then, firmly gripping the container with both hands, gradually pour."

"Mary, I'll show you how to pour milk. Put the glass in the middle of the table. Hold the milk in both hands, and then slowly pour."

Not only did the first example have too many words, but many of the words were either unfamiliar or barely familiar. By making it simple and familiar, such as in the second example, retrieval is helped. The use of familiar words falls into the area of prior knowledge. When children have prior knowledge, not only of the words that will be used, but other parts of the learning activity, memory is enhanced.[16]

There are two other techniques you can use to help retrieval. Though slightly different, in practice they are used similarly. The first is called *scaffolding*, and just like its construction counterpart, it holds things together. When the term is used in learning, it means that actions are related to objects.[17] A broader use of this technique is known as *elaboration*.[18] Elaboration not only includes what you would be doing in scaffolding, but also can involve any other connection. The use of either strategy results in the creation of memory webs containing hooks. An example of a scaffold would be the following.

"George, that's a garbage truck."
"Garbage truck?"
"Yes, a garbage truck moves very slowly on the street."

We'll take the same example, leave the scaffolding, and add elaboration.

"George, that's a garbage truck."
"Garbage truck?"
"Yes, a garbage truck moves very slowly on the street. Can you smell it?"
"It's yucky."
"Yes it is. You know all of the stuff we keep in the can under the sink?"
"Yes."
"Inside the garbage truck is our stuff and the stuff of everyone in the neighborhood."

In my practice I've found both techniques help with retrieval, but elaboration seems to have a greater effect since it is more inclusive.

The last technique which helps retrieval is context. The more familiar the context of what is being taught, the greater the likelihood it will be retrieved.[19] The context becomes the canvas upon which the thing to be remembered is placed. Let's look at above example of the garbage truck. The father could have easily taught the words "garbage truck" just by looking at a picture of the truck in a book. The only context would have been the picture in which the truck appeared. If context is important for retrieval, we don't have a very strong element here. But the father took his son outside and actually watched the garbage truck come lumbering up the street, making a lot of noise, occasionally dropping rotten fruits out of the back, and leaving behind an incredible smell as it moved up the block. What a great context! The child now has an enormous number of hooks to use when trying to retrieve the name of this vehicle.

I DID IT JUST LIKE YOU TOLD ME, SO WHY ARE YOU UPSET?

There are times when our kids retrieve beautifully. Unfortunately, it doesn't always occur during the right time or place. In Chapter 2, I gave the example of my son urinating on the sidewalk. Every single thing he did in the retrieval of individual behaviors was perfect. Why then was it totally inappropriate? Obviously something was missing. And whatever that was had to do with the way I originally taught him how to go to the bathroom. You may find that your child has the same problem, and it mystifies you. You're absolutely sure you not only taught the specific behaviors, but also the context in which it should be used. Although, that's a possibility, most likely, you, just as I, forgot something.

The Problem

When things are accurately retrieved, but not appropriately, there can be two problems. The first possibility is that when the teaching took place, there was minimal emphasis on context. For example, when I was teaching Justin to use the potty, I focused on waiting until his bladder just began feeling full, unzipping his pants and pulling them down, dropping his training pants, holding his penis in both hands, taking aim, and letting go of the urine stream. A very systematic and logical approach. And he learned it perfectly. But never in my instructions did I indicate the importance of the action occurring in the bathroom, although that's were he was trained.

The second reason things may be accurately but inappropriately retrieved is because there is a set of rules or assumptions that remain hidden. A good example is the rules of children's play. When you watch children play, things seem to evolve. It's like a jazz improvisation piece, in which the musicians take a basic melody and perform endless variations. Billy Strayhorn wrote a wonderful jazz number called "Take the A Train." As the number begins, you can easily hear the melody. But as the piece progresses, it seems to fade. Notes are thrown all over the place. You struggle to hear the melody and become frustrated when you can't find it. Then suddenly, there it is! Just a few notes, but it's definitely the melody. Then without warning, it's gone again. Sometimes our children approach play in the same way, continually trying to find the melody. If the listener understood jazz improvisation, he would have realized the melody was always there. If children understand the rules of play, they would know that what they are witnessing are either the rules or their variations.

The Solution

Since there are two problems, there are two solutions. The solution to the first problem of lacking the appropriate context is to emphasis more cues during teaching. Think about the situation as having two interrelated components. The first is the behavior you wish to teach. The second are the contexts in which you want it retrieved. For example, you're trying to teach your child not to interrupt. You develop a simple "interruption" game in which you teach him the nonverbal and verbal cues he can look for signaling, "Don't interrupt." The activity is successful, but unfortunately, you only do it in your home, with the two of you as players. What you should do is identify as many types of contexts as possible that he will find himself in, and either simulate those situations or actually train in them. For example, you may wish to teach your son not to interrupt in a classroom, when adults are talking to each other, and when adults are talking to him. By training in all three contexts, your child is more likely to retrieve the "no interruption" behavior appropriately.

The second problem of appropriate retrieval is more difficult. Here, your child needs to be taught things that are hidden, like rules and if-then relationships. Though more difficult, it's still possible. Your main task is to develop graphic representations or abstractions. For example, your child has difficulty with turn taking. She knows she needs to use this rule in preschool, if she wishes to have children play with her. She can understand the rule, but has problems with its variations. For example, what do you do when your playmate won't give you a turn? The rules say, you should have a turn. But you don't. What do you do? Should you spit, hit him, or just grab the toy away from him? None are appropriate behaviors. You as a parent will need to teach your child the options that are available when a rule is violated. You do this in a simulated situation that still contains many of the elements of the ones in which your child has problems. By simulating not only the rule but also its violation, your child begins to store appropriate responses. When a violation does occur, it is easier to retrieve an appropriate response if the scenario was practiced through simulation.

Part III

Family and Friends

The journey you're taking is not limited to you and your child. Many others are coming along for the ride. Some willingly and others grudgingly. In this final part of the book you'll first learn how to enlist the help of family, friends, and teachers. While their involvement may not be as great as yours, it will be important.

Then we'll look at how the problem affects the entire family. Having a child with a learning problem can be draining. There is a natural tendency to devote so much time to a child with a problem, other family members feel they're being ignored. We'll talk about ways of preventing this. You're vital to the growth of your child. To function best, you need to remain whole and emotionally healthy. Some of the ways of doing this involve simple methods, such as stress reduction. Others, such as dealing with your emotions, may be more difficult.

Finally, we'll look into your child's future. Not so much planning what he or she will do or become 15 years from now, but what you can do now so that, in 15 years, your daughter or son can have a larger number of options.

NINE

Getting Others to Help

If we hold out our hand to a dog, it may approach us, expecting food or friendship; but if we raise our hand to it, the same dog will run away, suspecting that we mean it harm. In the same way, every move, sound or thought we create has some effect on others. We have only to look around to confirm that this is so.

Akong Tulku Rinpoche[1]

Y ou can't get other people to help by reproaching them. When people feel a part of their personality is being attacked, they become defensive.[2] To understand other people's reactions think about what happens when you get defensive. It doesn't make a difference whether the tactic used against you was a head-on assault or the subtle use of guilt. Defensive reactions can take many forms, none of which will be beneficial to either you or your child. You shouldn't bully people into helping. Even if it's subtle, the resentment it creates never leaves. On one popular television comedy show, the husband, though a loving father, rarely takes any responsibility for his children. On one episode, the wife creates a scenario in which, through guilt, she gets him to take care of the kids for a Saturday afternoon, rather than playing golf. He takes care of the children, but at the golf course. His idea of an appropriate activity was allowing them to dive for golf balls in a pond on the fifteenth hole.

Sometimes we repeat the sitcom's plot, trying to get family members to help. Often we also use guilt. A mother I was working with told me about her unsuccessful attempts to get her husband to become more involved with their child's learning.

"It's hard for me to do it alone, what with the other two children. And I don't get home from work until after 5 P.M." she lamented.

"And your husband, when does he get home?" I asked.

"Usually about the same time. I know he's exhausted, but so am I. When he tries to help out with Bobby, it's always half-hearted. He just doesn't care."

I didn't think the father was uncaring. I believed his reactions had more to do with the relationship with his wife. There were four reasons it was important for this father to become involved in teaching his son. The first is when both parents are involved, children perceive a stronger family structure. When children see a more cohesive family, they tend to view themselves more positively.[3] And with a more positive self-image, children with learning differences do better. The second reason is having only one parent being responsible may create psychological problems that interfere with positive outcomes.[4] Being totally responsible, a single caregiver eventually builds up a significant amount of stress. As the stress increases, the ability to deal with the child diminishes. The third reason is as exhaustion develops, a person's ability to accurately observe what is occurring dwindles.[5] An emotionally and physically worn-out person can't see things as clearly as someone who is well rested. Behaviors that are only mildly disturbing when a person feels good can become intolerable when they're exhausted. The fourth reason is the child may also see the family as fragmented, with only one parent concerned enough to be involved.[6]

"What types of things do you say to your husband about helping out with Bobby?" I asked.

"Well, I tell him that he *should* be equally responsible. That it's his *duty* to help. After all, this is his son."

What she was doing was the same as raising her hand to an approaching dog. Yes, this father should believe he's equally responsible for helping. Unfortunately, how he should act is not the same as how his does act.

Requesting help from teachers, though not as direct as those used by this mother against her husband, may also involve the use of guilt, or worse, a threat to the teacher's competence. Yet, we see the most effective change occurring when a positive relationship between two people is developed, rather than one based either on guilt or a threat.[7] Resentment is not a good way to establish a helping relationship. In 1997, there was a wonderful documentary about Monty Roberts who became known as a "horse whisperer."[8] He believed in breaking wild horses through minimal control and lots of love. While unorthodox, the results of his training style are incontrovertible—they worked. Not only are they effective for horses, but also people. As you approach people to help, imagine they are a reluctant horse whose trust you need to gain. Not by being abrasive or demanding, but rather through compassion and understanding.

People Want to Help

All people have the innate desire to help. They just need to be shown how to do it. Sometimes, by indicating a commonality of interest or need, the person will feel a greater compulsion to help.[9] There are many misconceptions regarding helping. Often when you approach someone, they view the effort required as an inconvenience or something requiring them mentally to go to a psychological place where they may feel uncomfortable. Your job is to show them that neither will be necessary.

"Dear," the mother in the above example said to her husband, "Bobby needs to finish his work in three minutes when the buzzer goes off. Can you make sure he's completed it by then?"

"I guess so," he reluctantly said from behind his newspaper.

"Great, I'll be outside in the garden weeding. I know you don't like doing that and you're tired, So just sit and read your paper, and let me know when the buzzer goes off. I won't be able to hear it in the garden."

The husband's involvement required virtually no time and he benefited from it—he didn't have to do any weeding. He could help his son and wife, and still read his newspaper. This mother took the first step in allowing her husband to develop responsible actions and compassion. It's similar to the old carnival sideshow men who traveled from town to town when I was a child. Standing outside of a big tent they promised you could see the two-headed lady for only a quarter. After giving a quarter, you went inside and saw her. But she was wearing a coat covering the other head. For an additional quarter, you could see more. And then for another quarter, still more. Almost without realizing it, I gave up my whole weekly allowance. That's exactly what this mother did with her husband. She slowly stripped away those things from her husband's heart preventing responsible action—not by raising up her hand, but by offering him what he needed.

Sometimes, you need to be as sneaky as this mother was in your approach. Instead of thinking about your needs and your child's, start with thinking what your designated helper needs. Then offer to take care of it. Eventually, the father looked forward to working with his son and took immense joy from each new success. A similar approach can be used with others. The teacher who is loaded down with 20 children may need a little comfort during the day. Offer that in your request for help. A relative who has never been given respect should be offered it as you request her help with your child. The administrator who hates the adversarial relationships his job forces him into should be offered understanding and friendship within your request. Find what each person needs, and fill that void.

As much as we would like certain people to help, they may not be suited, either by temperament or the way in which they teach.[10] One father complained to me even though his wife wanted to be continually involved in the education of their son, her level of anxiety was so high, he thought it would place undo pressure on him. I agreed after I observed the mother and son interact. She wasn't giving her child time to respond and would act incredibility disappointed when he didn't do something correctly. Learning for her son became something filled with anxiety. I diplomatically gave her two options: She could either change the way she interacted with her son, or step aside during learning activities. She agreed to change, but after one week found it too difficult. When it became apparent she would never be calm enough to facilitate her son's learning, we all agreed she shouldn't be involved in any structured activities. Her son was delighted.

INITIATING CONTACT

We have a natural tendency to want to decide things first, then ask others to help us achieve our goals. In Chapter 2, I emphasized the importance of involving your children in the planning of goals and activities. The same principle applies to involving others. Ask for input before you decide what you would like someone to do. Compare how you would feel if you were *told* how you were going to be involved or if you where *asked* if you wanted to be involved and how extensive you wanted your involvement to be.

Although the actions coming from both may be identical, the approaches result in radically different attitudes. We know the more involved someone is in the initial design of an activity, the greater their involvement and, usually, the more successful it will be. This not only applies to children, but anyone who is involved in an activity. However, before asking for input, decide on the parameters. Just as with children, never provide a choice you're not prepared to accept. Take, for example, the following conversation between a child's mother and grandmother.

"Mom, I've been working on Jerry's memory problems and we're making real progress."

"That's great Dorothy. I know it will be important for him when he enters kindergarten."

"I was wondering if you could help him when I bring him here to visit with you?"

"Of course dear, he's my grandson. Whatever I can do to help."

"What kind of things do you see him having problems with when he stays with you?"

"Well, when he stays over, sometimes it takes me forever to get him ready for school. He just seems not to remember the things he needs to do to get ready in the morning."

"I think that's a very good point Mom. Would you like me to show you how it can be easier for him to get ready in the morning and take less of your time?

"That would be wonderful!"

"You have no idea how important this will be to Jerry's development. I'm so grateful."

In the above example, the mother set the parameters of the involvement—anything involving memory. She then asked the grandmother for input. Whatever problem the grandmother identified would be the one the mother would focus on. Once she had input, she asked the grandmother if that's what she wanted to do. If it was, then the mother would design a simple program for the grandmother to use. Basically, the mother used five simple steps in her solicitation for help.

1. Set the *parameters* of what is to be worked on.
2. Ask for *input*
3. Indicate how working on the problem would *benefit* the child and caregiver.
4. *Reconfirm* this was what the caregiver would really like to do.
5. Indicate how *grateful* you are and how important the person's involvement will be for your child.

The same five steps should be used with other family members, friends, and teachers. Although with teachers, there are additional concerns, most of which involve misperceptions. Some teachers believe parents want to be only minimally involved in the formal education of their children.[11] When parents show initiative it can come as a surprise to some teachers. While they may initially suspect an ulterior motive for parent involvement, such as questioning their competence, if presented right, teachers too become willing participants. There can be great misperception between how parents and teachers see each other.[12] Often misperceptions are created by past experiences, false beliefs, and cultural differences. As a parent, you can bridge the gap, regardless of how small or large it may be, by demonstrating to the teacher your commitment to help both her and your child succeed. Perceptions are strange creatures. Often they can develop a reality of their own that may not be even remotely related to what's going on. It happens often between elementary school teachers and parents.[13]

WHAT SHOULD THEY DO?

Once you have a willing helper, you'll need to decide what you want them to do. In making the decision, view learning as having two major parts: learning something new and then applying it. You teach the new behavior or attitude. Let your helper assist with its application. Throughout this book, I've emphasized the importance of teaching behaviors in settings in which they're used.

For example, if you want your child to become organized, you start in a small area in the house, then gradually expand the area of organization. Expanding the settings in which behaviors will be used is called *generalization*. The more relevant the generalization activity, the more likely it will be learned and retained.[14] Generalization can be greatly enhanced if other people become involved. For example, your child may now have her room very well organized, but has never been asked to use the same skill at her grandfather's house, or in kindergarten. The more often she has an opportunity to practice the skill, the more automatic it will become, and eventually be a part of her life.[15] That should be the role of helpers—to help your child expand something he or she already knows. It's also less intimidating to the potential helper—they know the child is already familiar with the behavior. Just like your child, it's important that your helper is successful. The principles and strategies highlighted in Chapters 2 and 5 for using with your children are also useful techniques to employ with your helper.

Take Care of Their Needs

Start by understanding the needs of your helper. If it's a relative and she has limited time or feels most comfortable with your child in her home, that's were you start. A dichotomy is often made between self-interest and altruism. People either act out of self-interest or because they really care for another person. Those who act out of self-interest are often thought of as crass and motivated by less than ethical reasons. Those who act altruistically are viewed as saintly. Their only desire is to help make a child "whole."[16] Something's missing in the life of the child, and they are being given an opportunity to correct it. It's a powerful incentive for helping—especially if the person is a relative. But the line between self-interest and altruism is not as neat as some people believe.[17] It's been argued that the most powerful and beneficial actions occur when the two merge.[18] I've found this to be true in my practice. I've had the greatest success when I can couple a basic desire to help with a benefit to person who is helping.[19]

A number of years ago, I worked with a student who tried to enlist a classroom teacher to help with a child. The student had prepared endless lists of instructions, almost as if they were part of a training manual. Although concise, when she handed them to the teacher, the annoyance on the teacher's face was evident.

"Here are the things I would like you to do with Jimmy. If you can do these, it will greatly help me out in my therapy."

"If I have time, I'll try to do them," the teacher curtly replied.

The student came to see me after two weeks, during which time the teacher never seemed to have any time to do the activities. She showed me the materials she had developed and explained how she approached the teacher.

"She's a real witch. She doesn't care about the kids," my student said.

"Why do you say that?" I asked.

"She won't do any of the things I suggested that'll help Jimmy."

"Help Jimmy, or help you?" I asked.

"I don't understand," my confused student responded.

"Look," I said. "You presented the materials and emphasized what she would be doing would help *you*. Why would someone who already is responsible for 25 children put herself out to help another person who has the luxury of working with children one-on-one?"

Her focus was wrong. In order for this teacher to become involved, she had to believe three things. One was what she was doing would benefit Jimmy, not the speech-language clinician. The second was it wouldn't add any time to what she was already responsible for doing. And finally, whatever she would be doing with Jimmy would also benefit her. This is how my student should have approached the teacher.

"I know that Jimmy can be disruptive in class. I've developed some materials I think will help and make it easier for him to follow you. It just involves putting numbers on the board when you instruct the kids. Would you be interested in using it? I can show you how it's done and it won't take any additional time."

If my student hadn't already burnt her bridges with her prior comments, the above scenario probably would have worked.

Give Praise, Accept Blame

"Give all profit and gain to others. Take all loss and defeat on yourself."[20] This old Tibetan saying pertaining to humility can also be used as a guiding principle for enlisting the help of others. People need to know they are appreciated and their involvement makes a difference. Often we just assume they know the contribution they're making. Unless explicitly stated, there's a possibility they don't know. They may think they're contributing, but unless you tell them, they won't know what you think. The difference between what people believe and what is real is often as great as between how two people from different cultures view a common experience. You need to be clear, direct, and magnanimous in your praise—regardless of the contribution's importance. I was asked to change the attitudes of elementary school teachers in a troubled school. The principal knew the negative feelings his teachers had were affecting how children were learning.

"Who is your most receptive teacher?" I asked the principal.

"Ms. Gray. She always seems to want to try new things.

"Alright," I said, "Then that's the only teacher I'll start working with."

"I don't understand," the principal said, "You're being paid to change the entire school, not just one teacher. Why would you want to work with the only teacher in the school that is already onboard with what I want to accomplish?"

"Because she's the only teacher onboard," I replied.

"I don't understand," he said.

"I want to work with the person most likely to be successful. She'll be our spearhead for getting the other teachers to change."

For the entire semester, I only worked with Ms. Gray. I developed a simple program for her to use with a child being seen by the speech-language clinician. The clinician was instructed to give feedback to the teacher.

"Thank you so much for what you did with Kevin. You have no idea how much of a difference it made in therapy and also at home. His mother asked me to thank you."

It was just a small behavior and there wasn't anything untruthful in the clinician's praise. She exaggerated only slightly. We were working on the correct production of "r." Three times a day, Kevin would walk up to the teacher and practice saying sentences using words that began with "r." The only things the teacher had to do was to listen and place a checkmark on a card Kevin carried with him indicating that he said the "r" words correctly. Her involvement was important for generalizing Kevin's new behaviors—just maybe not as important as the clinician indicated. However, the potency of the compliment had far reaching effects. Everyone likes to believe they're doing important work. And they like to be acknowledged for it. Every time we worked on a new behavior and complimented the teacher, she would share the information and accolades with her fellow teachers during the lunch break. One month after we began involving Ms. Gray, two other teachers approached the clinician asking if there was anything they could do to help. Eventually, more teachers asked to be involved. By the end of the semester many were asking for help with a variety of problems.

Not everything we did with Ms. Gray and the other teachers was successful. When it wasn't, we tried to minimize failures and remove blame.

"It was a disaster yesterday when Kevin and I worked on those new words."

"What happened?" I asked.

"Well, half of the time he couldn't remember them. And when he did, he didn't use them correctly. I tried to figure out what I did wrong, but I'm not sure."

"Now that I look at the program, I realize the mistake was mine. You didn't do anything wrong. I forgot an important step. Let me fix it, and we'll try again. Sorry for the problem."

Give all credit to others, place all blame on yourself. It doesn't make any difference if the situation warrants it. You need to provide nurture and reinforcement to your helper in the same way you do for your children.

Active Rather Than Passive

Train your helpers to use an active rather than passive learning style. The active learning approach you want your helper to use consists of two parts. The first is the activity. Hands-on activities are not only more exciting to children, but also result in better and more lasting learning.[21] The second type of active learning involves feedback given when an error occurs. A mother I trained had a very difficult time convincing her child's grandmother she shouldn't be giving the correct answer to her son when he didn't get something correct in the training program she developed.

"Mom, when he doesn't bring the correct item to you, don't tell him what to get."

"But he made a mistake," the grandmother said. "Why shouldn't I just tell him the right answer?"

"Because it doesn't help him as much as making him think it through."

"I don't understand," the grandmother responded.

"When I just watched you, I saw you ask him to go into the laundry room and bring you the three things you needed to clean the carpet."

"Yes, just like you told me to."

"And you did it perfectly. But instead of bringing you the pail, the washcloth, and the cleaner, he only brought the pail and the cleaner."

"That's right. That's when I told him he forgot the washcloth."

"That was fine Mom, but it becomes more helpful if you would have said, 'Jim I asked you to bring in three things. You only brought in two. Can you remember the third one?' If he couldn't remember, then I would have given him a choice. 'Did you forget the cleaner or the mop?' By giving him choices when he makes mistakes, he learns better."

You can use the above dialogue as a model for explaining the differences between passive and active feedback. Most of the time, it's best to demonstrate the changes you'd like your helper to make, rather than just using words.

Provide a Single Typed Sheet of Instructions

When we try to teach something new to a person, we assume it will be remembered—exactly as it was delivered. That rarely happens. It's best not to rely on memory but rather simple instructions typed on a single page. Having something typed results in better results than just oral explanations.[22] An example is provided in Figure 9.1. The simpler the instructions, the more comfortable your helper will feel. At the top of Figure 9.1, you'll find three orientating questions for your helper. Next you'll see clear instructions. This is followed by the cue you want them to use. Finally, at the bottom of the page is a simple system for recording how well your child did. The activity you design should be enjoyable and successful. In this example, Wayne has already demonstrated he could recall objects he played with and where the activity occurred. This activity simply reinforces an already acquired skill. If the activity you design is enjoyable to the helper, it's more likely he or she will want to continue on with other activities.[23] Set up the activity so that nobody takes themselves too seriously and keep it simple. As you demonstrate it to your helper, do it slowly, gradually involving them in working with your child. There should be minimal time between what they will be saying and your child's

---

Figure 9.1
Example of Written Instructions

What We Are Doing: We are working on having Wayne remember things.

How We Are Doing It: 10 minutes after Wayne has done something, ask him to recall it.

Why We Are Doing it: This activity improves short-term memory.

Have Wayne do something in a specific room. Wait 10 minutes then say "Wayne a little while ago you were moving around on something in one of the rooms in the house. Can you tell me what it was (point to the bicyclist as you say this) and where you held it (point to the house as you say this)?

Do this three times while he's at your house. If he retrieved it correctly, draw in a smiley face. If he didn't, put in a neutral face.

response. Whenever possible, show them how to initially use things that are visual and concrete. In our example, we used cues. The more often an activity is done, the more likely it will become automatic. Initially, only have your helper do it a few times. As they feel more comfortable, you can suggest doing it more often, if they haven't already requested greater involvement. Always have them track your child's responses. In our example, we use a smiley face and a neutral face. Others can be used as long as they don't require more than a checkmark or star. In our example, only one simple behavior is worked on. Keep your program to one behavior. The first behavior you select should be one you're reasonably sure your child will do perfectly with little resistance.

Always ask for feedback. It will serve three important functions. First, it lets you know how well your child did. Second, it provides an opportunity for helpers to feel they not only did something worthy, but also their input is viewed as valuable. And finally, when helpers are asked how they can make the program better, their commitment to the learning process increases significantly.[24]

TEN

And What About You?

*I*n this chapter, we're going to explore your and your family's needs. We'll look at both your intentions and their outcomes, practical methods for reducing stress, and the acceptance of your feelings about your child's limitations. We may be opening a door that contains hidden thoughts, some of which you've never discussed with anyone. At times the hardest thing to do is to begin. But the journey in educating your child can never be completed until you start. We'll now look inward to take that first step.

INTENTIONS AND OUTCOMES

When you look at your actions, you can evaluate them in two different ways: what they were intended to accomplish and what they actually achieved. Good outcomes are easy to determine. You did something, and because of your action, your child benefited. You feel great about what occurred and your child learned. But what about when the outcome wasn't that great, although the intention was terrific? What you tried didn't work in spite of your whole-hearted effort? What did you feel about yourself then? If you're like most parents, guilt or despair may have begun creeping into your thoughts. They shouldn't. Even though you didn't succeed, your intentions were good. Never forget that. Intentions are as important as outcomes for your psychological well-being. Some would maintain, even more important. Sometimes the transition between intentions and outcomes can be quite complicated and messy. In many of the previous chapters we looked at things that could prevent good intentions from becoming successful outcomes. In this section, we'll look at others that are generated by your and your family's needs.

When Things Get Out of Hand

Have you ever been in a small boat during the middle of a storm? If you have, you already know the image I'm about to create. If you haven't, imagine sitting in a ten-foot rowboat in the middle of a lake. You're only one hundred feet from shore when a squall line approaches from behind. Since you never turned your back to see it, its ominous black clouds come upon you without warning. From a beautiful blue windless sky, something really terrifying develops. You know you can't outrun it. It's moving at fifteen miles an hour and your rowing ability is limited to two miles an hour. From a placid surface, waves in excess of four feet develop. What do you do? Trying to outrun the storm is useless. Moving about the boat will make it unstable, maybe even leading you to capsize. The only thing to do is sit quietly in the middle of it, keep the boat balanced, and wait for the storm to pass. Sometimes in our lives, that's also what we need to do. Just sit quietly and wait for the chaos to stop. If we just act, rather than wait, our behaviors arise from thoughts that are riddled with illogic, anger, fear, or confusion. A scholar once said, "It is useless to try and change the object that is seen-it is the eyesight that has to be improved."[1]

For Akong Tulku Rinpoche, actions coming from unclear thoughts lead to behaviors having the same characteristics. Rather than continuing to act when you can't see things clearly, his suggestion is to stop and develop new thoughts. I've found this also to be true in my work with parents. I was helping a mother who waged the "the good fight" against public school administrators who resisted providing the services she knew were needed. It went as far as a hearing before a district administrative officer. Unfortunately, even with the assistance of an advocate and an expert on learning problems, she lost. It was difficult for all of us to accept. The mother wanted to immediately take legal action against the school district.

"I know this disability lawyer who'll sue the pants off them. I have his number right here, I'll call him now on my cell phone."

Her anger was so pervasive, it affected her thoughts, words, and actions. It was as if everything was being seen through a pair of tinted glasses—everything became red, regardless of its true color.

"Let's wait a few days," I suggested.

"No. What's the point? I won't let those bastards do this to Jerome and me."

We sat down and talked. I tried to explain the adversarial path she wanted to pursue might lead her to a place she may not want to go. Worse, it might result in the opposite of what we wanted for her son. I suggested we do nothing for a few days. Just relax and wait until the anger we all felt subsided. Reluctantly she agreed. When things become chaotic, few people have the capacity to think straight—including me. A period of calmness is needed. We spoke in two days and went over what would be the best approach to deal with our inability to have the mandated services provided we knew Jerome needed. With calm minds, we carefully analyzed everything that had transpired from the first IEP (individualized educational plan) meeting and evaluated our options. I knew the school district had a multitude of problems ranging from the misappropriation of funds to personnel shortages. With an expensive lawsuit we probably would win. However, there would be no assurance winning would result in what we thought Jerome needed. It would be like winning a case for damages from a company that had declared bankruptcy. We needed to look elsewhere. His classroom teacher was always present throughout our confrontations with various levels of administrators. It appeared to me she was always on the verge of saying something, but resisted whenever she glanced at the administrator. There was something in her demeanor suggesting she might be what we needed. I suggested the mother invite her to lunch or dinner to discuss Jerome. Just the two of them, two concerned adults. The teacher was delighted and accepted the invitation. Over dinner, the parent and teacher discussed what could be done in the classroom without involving the principal or learning specialist who sided with the administration. Together, the mother and teacher, with my assistance, developed a simple program that would help Jerome. By sitting in that rowboat until the storm passed, this mother was able to do something beneficial for her son. If she had tried to row through the storm, the boat would have capsized, leaving her son in turbulent waters. Sometimes, it's just best to do nothing, at least until things become calmer.

Living Through Our Children

You are not your child, nor should you be defining yourself through your child's accomplishments or failures. In an earlier chapter, I related the story of the mother who kept comparing her son's accomplishments to my daughter's. For whatever reasons, she kept defining herself in terms of her son's accomplishments in grade school. Unfortunately, when your identity is tied to another individual, your self-worth is also dependent on them. It wasn't a problem throughout junior high school. Her son excelled both academically and athletically. His social life was full, and it appeared he was becoming everything his mother had hoped for. Then, in his junior year in high school, things began falling apart. First it was the drugs, then the vandalism. He was thrown off the basketball team, and finally his grades began to slip. Instead of the Ivy League school his mother envisioned for him, both had to settle for the local junior college. By being joined at the hip, this mother's life suffered the same trauma as her son's. We all derive great joy from what our children do, but also suffer from the pain they experience. It's only natural, they're *part* of us. But if we become our children, we lose our own identity. We're pulled into a realm of emotions we have no control over. It's almost as if we are placed in a prison, where our freedom is limited and our children control our lives.

Often we use our imagination to develop future scenarios in which our children are successful, and we live out our dreams through their accomplishments. Our imagination and needs are so intertwined they gain a reality of their own, acting like a blunt instrument with the potential of hurting all who come within its clubbing distance. In the 1800s, a wise man, Patrul Rinpoche, commenting on imagination said, "Do not rule over imaginary kingdoms of endlessly proliferating possibilities."[2] Likewise, as we try to imagine what are children's lives will be like in the future, we need to keep our own dreams to a bedroom activity. You are not your child. Your aspirations are yours. Theirs are theirs.

Guilt—The Most Useless of All Emotions

When we make mistakes, we cannot turn the clock back and try again. All we can do is use the present well.[3]

His Holiness, the Dali Lama

Successful parenting is not always possible, and we often feel guilty because we can't achieve the mythical image of the "perfect" parent. I remember my mother telling me, how when she arrived at Ellis Island in 1910, everyone was required to walk up the stairs in the Great Hall. At the bottom of the staircase one official observed physical problems people had as they ascended. At the top, another watched the official below. If someone had problems walking, a signal went to the top official and that person was sent to another area to receive a more in-depth examination or summarily sent back to the country of his or her origin. When I work with parents, I wish I could identify guilt as easily as those officials did physical problems. I've never met a parent who didn't harbor some guilt. They blame themselves no matter what the problem may be with their children—if not completely, then partially. It can often lead to serious consequences for the entire family.[4] Parents feel guilty because of what they think they did or should've done for their child. With some parents, the guilt can be overwhelming.

During a stressful period in my life a number of years ago, I felt guilty about not being able to provide emotional support to my children. As a solution, I decided to spend a weekend at a Buddhist monastery in northern California. I thought, if I couldn't figure out how to make things right with my family, maybe someone else could. I had been studying Eastern philosophies for over 20 years, but had very little direct experience other than an occasional meditation session. After everyone had arrived at the monastery, the abbot gave an introductory welcoming speech.

"Thank you for coming. We will be doing meditation throughout the weekend. There's sitting meditation, walking meditation, eating meditation, and working meditation."

In the past, I found even 15 minutes of meditation exhausting. Now, I was expected to do it throughout the weekend.

"Between meditations," the abbot continued, "there will be talks on the principles of Zen Buddhism."

Between meditations? It seemed *everything* would be meditation. How would there be any time for teachings? I gave up a week of fishing the pristine waters of northern California to do this. I wondered if I made the right decision.

"I know many of you have specific problems. Since they may be of a personal nature, you may schedule time with Reverend Master Asako."

He gestured to his right and I saw the Reverend Master was probably in his early twenties. How could I possibly discuss my family problems with someone who only recently began shaving? Maybe this wasn't such a great idea. But I decided to stay. My appointment time was on the second day. My resistance by then had been lowered, and I was at least willing to present my problems to someone who was half my age and probably knew as much about family life as I did about the cloistered life of a monk. He compassionately listened as I discussed many of the poor decisions I made and their effects on my family. Instead of jumping in when I paused between thoughts, like a good therapist, he patiently waited for me to continue. For almost 30 minutes, I unloaded my burden, rattling off a litany of transgressions I regretted. Finally he spoke.

"Stan, people do the best they're *capable* of doing, given the circumstances of their life." He then rose and left the room, leaving me to think about his response.

I sat there for 20 minutes until I understood this simple, yet poignant thought. He was right. Given the turbulence surrounding me, there was no reason to feel guilty because I didn't do other things. What I did was what I was capable of doing, given the *circumstances of my life*. In my practice, I've found the same to be true when working with parents. I've never met a parent who willfully did hurtful things to their children. Yet, every parent I've worked with has some regrets.

"If only I did…"

"If only I started sooner…"

"If only I saw…"

Dwelling on what *could have been* is a futile exercise. We conjure up images of things that never were and allow them to shape a reality of what never could be.

Parental guilt is one of the hardest things I've had to deal with professionally. But, overcoming guilt may be the first step in self-healing and the creation of a positive attitude necessary for helping your child.[5] We handle guilt in a number of ways, few of which are beneficial. Because we feel responsible for problems our child is having, we may overcompensate, often doing more damage than good. I worked with a single mother whose crack addiction during her pregnancy led to severe attention problems in her child. From the moment of his birth, she dedicated her life to making him whole. While noble, it resulted in her burning out and losing her own identity. Providing 24-hour care for her son resulted in her utter exhaustion. Until he was six-years-old, she refused any help. She felt since she created the problem, she should shoulder the entire burden. It took a team of dedicated social workers, teachers, and a psychologist to convince her that "going it alone" may be a worthy penitence, but it was destroying both her and her son. She was perpetually exhausted and in spite of trying to do everything she could to help him become more attentive, he failed. They convinced her that shouldering all the work was selfish. Although it may take care of her needs to be punished, it wasn't helping her son. Finally, she allowed others to help. Only after regaining some balance in her life did her son have significant improvements, and she became whole again.

Another way we as parents handle guilt is through anger, much of which is self-directed.[6] We view what we have done as so fundamentally wrong, it's unforgivable. Worse, every time we see the effects of our poor decisions when our children do something inappropriate, we're reminded of our past actions, and in not so subtle ways. Our children's problems are constantly thrust in our face. Often, instead of compassion and positive actions, we may feel anger. Nobody likes to be constantly reminded of what they believe they did wrong. The father of a six-year-old had refused to seek help for his son since the age of three. Now, at six, the boy was having serious social problems. The father's explanations to his wife and relatives in the past were always the same.

"He's normal. He's fine, just a little slow at understanding how to play with kids. We need to find him better friends."

Worn down by his insistence, eventually, they would just nod in agreement. He refused to see what was in front of him.

"He's not going to see no god-damn shrink, nor any of those other people. My son's okay."

Well, he wasn't okay. His inability to know how to play with other children led to serious consequences. He was continually rejected by other children and became a loner. By six years of age, he had become violent. He would torture small animals and hit other children for no apparent reason. The father believed his decision not to seek help was the source of his son's problems. Not only did he feel guilty, but he also became angry with himself. He thought what he did was unforgivable. Anger is an interesting phenomenon. It doesn't like to be contained. Rather, it's like those "free-range" chickens that are allowed to roam about and eat anything that moves. Anger does the same thing to one's personality.[7] You can't confine it. It will poison everything and every relationship you have. And that's exactly what happened with this father. Although he was angry with himself, it flowed out of him like sweat after a hard exercise, touching his son, wife, and friends. It destroyed his family, and until he was no longer a part of it, his son never improved. Now, four years after he left, his son's social behaviors are almost normal.

Guilt can also take the form of withdrawal.[8] The guilt can be so strong we believe no one can accept or love us. A friend of mine is a physician whose skill was responsible for saving the lives of many children. His dedication to the well-being of his patients often interfered with how much time he spent with his own children. As an adult, his son confronted him about the choices he made to spend time with patients rather than him. As a child, the son struggled with learning new things and always felt if his father was there, things would have been better. Now as an adult, he wrongly blamed all of his many failures on his father's absence. My friend was devastated. He believed if he had made different choices, his son's life would have been different. He felt what he did was unforgivable. If he couldn't forgive himself, how could anyone else? He withdrew from friends, family, and colleagues. Yes, the choices he made had negative consequences. But they weren't enough to make his actions unforgivable. Given the circumstances of his life, he did the best he was capable of.

Balancing Your Life

Thich Nhat Hanh tells a wonderful old story about a monk in the Tang Dynasty.[9] The monk was practicing sitting meditation continuously day and night. His goal was to practice harder than anyone else in the monastery. Day and night he sat as a mountain waiting for his suffering to be transformed into enlightenment. But it was to no avail. One day a teacher, curious as to what the monk was doing, sat next to him and said nothing for a few minutes. Then he spoke.

"Why are you sitting so hard?" the teacher asked.

"To become a Buddha," the monk replied.

The teacher looked around on the floor and found a rough clay tile. With great effort, he began polishing it with a dirty rag. Eventually, the monk saw what the teacher was doing, but didn't understand.

"What are you doing?" the monk asked.

"Making a mirror," the teacher replied.

"How can you make a mirror from a tile?" the confused monk asked.

"How can you become a Buddha by sitting?" the teacher replied.

The accomplishment of many things is based on the right selection of techniques and strategies. Hoping that by devoting all of your time to your child will result in a better life for the both of you is like trying to polish a tile to turn it into a mirror. Some parents believe their role in life is that of a sacrificer. As one parent said to me, "I would *give* anything; I would *give up* everything, I would *do* anything if I could get rid of my child's problem." When parents truly believe this is a viable option, they focus their entire life on their child. The notion of balance is lost. Many believe to do anything other than devote their lives to their child is selfish. As they spend more and more of their time with their child and less on other activities and with other people, they change. They develop a cocoon in which they live, protected from other people and even their own feelings. Only their child is let in. What is thought to be a total commitment is actually an isolating move. By withdrawing from the world, they deprive their child of a complete human being. It's difficult helping your child develop a balanced life when yours is one-sided.

Striving for Sainthood

I've never known a parent who was a saint, although I've known many who made their lives miserable trying to be one. I knew a woman who strove to be the "perfect mom." Someone who could handle the problems at a stressful job, a family of four, a child with a moderate learning problem, and community commitments. Her husband, who was perpetually involved with his business, rarely helped with the family responsibilities. She never thought about herself. The needs of everyone else came first, especially her child with the learning problem. It was as if she was a pot with a small hole in the bottom into which water was being poured. As long as the amount entering was no greater than the amount leaving, the pot didn't overflow, and she was able to "handle" everything. Eventually, what was poured in the top far exceeded what dripped out the hole. She broke down and was no longer able keep things under control. The "perfect mom" was no longer perfect, and couldn't even function as a mom. It was even difficult for her to get out of bed. The care she spent on her children diminished. The love she had for her husband evaporated. And her ability to function at work decreased significantly. The only thing that happens to saints is they eventually loose their halos. The higher you place yourself on a pedestal, the greater will be your fall. I've never met the perfect mom or dad. However, I've seen many tragedies created by those who tried.

DEALING WITH STRESS

Lake Tahoe is one of the most pristine bodies of water in the world. From a boat, you can look down through 50 feet of clear blue water and see the bottom.

Whenever we visit the area, I like to go to a high ledge and peer down into it, imaging the calmness to be a reflection of my life. Rarely is it. My life is more like what I see standing on the Riverwalk in New Orleans, looking out onto the turbulence of the Mississippi. By the time it reaches New Orleans, the river is churning with strong currents and has the color of coffee with a little cream. Having a child who has a learning problem can place us more often on the banks of Mississippi than on the shores of Lake Tahoe. As we try to deal with the needs of our child and family, an enormous amount of stress can be created. You need to relieve it. In this section we'll look at a number of ways of doing it. Some you'll find more to your liking than others. It really doesn't make a difference which one or combination of techniques you use. The only important thing is to widen that hole in the bottom of your bucket.

Take a Break

Some people view stress as something good and necessary for action to occur. After all, they reason, if there were no stress, they wouldn't be motivated to achieve as much as they do. For us ordinary mortals, stress is not something that's positive. The more stress there is in the lives of parents, the less helpful they are to their children.[10] As they try to handle one current problem, three others are on their mind. It's as if they are a support beam on which an ever-increasing amount of weight is placed. With sufficient weight, the beam will break, regardless of its strength. Some years ago, in an attempt to reduce the weight of my own support beam, I attended a panel presentation on stress. The first three presenters were well known and had published extensively. Their presentations were scholarly, with each seemingly trying to outdo the other in the number of research citations they gave. It was very educational, but thoroughly boring. The last panelist was a psychology professor from a local university. He was a replacement for a distinguished researcher who had to cancel at the last minute. The "fill-in" took his place behind the podium and began to speak without any notes.

"I'm not going to cite any of the literature or refer to any of the theories on stress-reduction, as important as I know they are. I'm just going to tell you what I do when things go bonkers."

He immediately captivated everyone, including myself. This is what people had come to here. Not *what* stress was. Everybody already knew that. They wanted to know *how* to reduce it. For the next 20 minutes, he related to the audience types of stressful situations he found himself in and what he did to limit it. For example, if he allowed it, his students would make appointments to see him for problems every day. Even if there was only one student, the issues were sufficiently negative for him to feel uneasy for the entire day. Since stress made him feel uncomfortable, why not limit seeing students to one day per week? Why ruin the entire week, if misery could be confined to one eight-hour work day? Above his office door he had a sign printed in large letters: *Problems only on Tuesdays.* Neither colleagues nor students were pleased, but they abided by the sign's instruction. After using the rule for one month, he found rarely did anyone's problem require immediate attention. Knowing he would only have to deal with stressful issues on Tuesdays not only gave him four stress-free work days, but also gave him time to prepare for the difficult day. Although this may be too radical an approach to life with a child who has a learning problem, you can modify it to give yourself a few stress-free days or hours. Another technique he used during very stressful situations was the "call of nature." He often found himself in the middle of a difficult interaction that was either reducing his ability to respond or placing him in an unfair position. He knew whatever decision he made would have immediate and often important consequences.

"Excuse me, I know what your saying is very important, but I need to use the bathroom now. I'll be right back."

He would leave people in mid-sentence, often shocked by his abruptness, and occasionally disappointed that their line of attack was being interrupted. Sometimes he would go to the bathroom. Other times he'd just walk in the hallway or go outside the building. The few minutes he took to regain his composure gave him the calmness to continue with a clear mind. There is nothing wrong with breaking off an interaction when you know your ability to respond is impaired. Bathroom breaks are fine, but you can also be more forthright.

"I'm sorry, I really need a break now for a few minutes to clear my head," one of my parents would often say when dealing with school administrators and teachers.

Not only did this statement provide her with the time she needed to refocus, but it also gave an important message to those people she routinely interacted with. It said, "Stop trying to bully me with forceful speech. Go over the line, and I'll take a break."

It's similar to a tactic some football teams will use when the score is close, there's only a few minutes left, and the kicker can win the game with a successful punt. The opposing team will call time out to disorientate the kicker. Often the tactic is successful. Call time out whenever you need it.

You don't always have to completely stop stressful situations to function better. You can simply redirect the negative energy that is being hurled toward you. There is a martial art known as Aikido. One of its main principles is instead of resisting force, use it as a way of disarming your opponent. When an opponent lunges toward you, don't resist, but use his forward movement to throw him off balance. It's not only an interesting form of self-defense, but also a metaphor for life and stress reduction. I often find myself in professional situations, in which there is anger directed toward me because of an advocacy position I've taken. It doesn't make any difference how passive I am at the beginning of the interaction or my choice of tone or words. Everyone knows the position I've taken and it's one that's threatening. It usually involves services I believe a child should have. Those opposing my position are usually people who feel what I'm asking for is excessive.

"What you're expecting from the school is totally unreasonable," an irate administrator said to me at an IEP meeting. "We have neither the money nor personnel to do it. And it goes far beyond what the law requires."

As he forcefully thrust forward his position, he expected me to parry back, as if I was a swordsman in a medieval fencing dual. But I disappointed him.

"I can see the dilemma you're in. The school doesn't have enough money to even buy sufficient books and I know how hard it is to hire enough teachers. You have a serious problem."

He was stunned. Instead of me starting the battle with an aggressive statement, I commiserated with him. If I had done what he expected, undoubtedly, my stress level would have risen, maybe making me less effective in advocating for what I knew the child needed. By not playing the game, I remained calm and confused the administrator. Think about the situations in which you met anger or defiance with resistance. What happened? Was it effective or did you come away so angry you spent endless hours reliving the incident? And with each remembrance, your stress level increased. These situations remind me of some of the after-point antics of professional football players. In the end zone they face each other and charge, banging their chests and recoiling back two feet. They continue doing it, but never seem to get anywhere. That's what often happens when you meet another person's anger with your own. But what would happen if as one of the football players lounged forward, the other moved to the side? Think about that scene the next time you're in a situation where someone is trying to overwhelm you. Become an Aikido master of your emotions and words.

Get Organized

Disorganization becomes a fertile ground for stress. It can be internal, external, or both. Regardless of its location, it can be a real pain. Not knowing what you want to do or having your thoughts disorganized can cause endless grief. I worked with a family of five whose lives were out of control. They had one child with a learning problem, another who was on the way to becoming a juvenile delinquent, and the jobs of each parent required extra hours away from the home. There was much in their lives that couldn't be changed. It was impossible to schedule "problem days," like the psychology professor. Taking breaks in their occupations wasn't possible. He was a surgeon and she was a trial lawyer. Open-heart surgery and embattled court interactions are not the places to say, "I'm sorry, I need to go to the bathroom now." Although there was much they had no control of, it was still possible to reduce stress. Their lives were more like a child's room after every toy had been played with. I suggested even though they couldn't do anything about the amount of things they were required to do, they could become more organized. Being organized reduces the energy necessary for doing things. The same amount is done, but you've spent less emotionally and physically accomplishing it. Both being in fields requiring a great deal of precision, I asked them to take their sense of organization required to perform effectively in the work setting and apply it in the home. We started with simple things, such as, how they got ready for work, how they ate, and even how they drove. They did the same number of things, but now they were done more efficiently. Instead of wondering what would be made for dinner each night and then running out to the supermarket to get ingredients, I suggested the menu for the week be planned over the weekend, and all ingredients bought on Sunday. Some of the prep work, such as cutting the vegetables could also be done in advance when they had more time. Since at least 60 percent of the time required to complete a meal involves preparations, Monday through Friday meals would become less stressful and time consuming. Instead of deciding who would be responsible for household chores when the need arose, everyone would have a weekly assignment. There were other suggestions, all of which were designed to increase organization. By creating an organized house, they found their daughter was better able to function in a wide variety of activities. The organization surrounding her made it easier to do a number of things that her learning problems made more difficult.

Having disorganized thoughts can be as distressful as living within a disorganized environment.[11] You're trying to deal with ten different things, each having a different deadline and varying demands. As you try getting closure on one, the others start impinging on your time and thoughts. You never seem to feel that you have a handle on anything. When your disorganization is both internal and external, chaos reigns. It's as if you have no place to find peace. However, when there is both internal and external peace, a magical condition arises that is greater than the sum of the two. With internal organization you feel whole and at ease with your body. It was described as a warrior wearing a suit of armor.[12] External organization is the creation of an environment in which everything is in harmony with what you need. When both external and internal organization exists, you are in control and your stress level decreases.

Rest

Have you ever noticed how poorly you function when tired? Our minds just don't seem to function very well with minimal sleep. When we can't handle things well, stress can build. Often it's not that you're doing too many things, you just may not be doing them efficiently. A mother I worked with always looked tired.

"Mary, how much sleep do you get every night?" I asked.

"Oh, I don't know, maybe four hours, sometimes more, sometimes less."

"How do you think it affects your ability to deal with Bruce's problems?"

"I don't know," she responded. "I don't think it affects it."

I had developed a very simple checklist allowing her to rate how well she was dealing with her son's learning problems. There were only ten items, such as "patient with Bruce's difficulty in remembering things." Beside each item was a five-point rating system.

    1 = very
    2 = somewhat
    3 = a little bit
    4 = not very much
    5 = not at all

"I'd like you to honestly check off the items," I said.

She completed each and we looked at the results. There were a few "1's" and many "4's" and "5's." I suggested some of her problems with her son might be related to sleep deprivation. She should try getting at least six hours of sleep at night—more if possible. If over-the-counter medications didn't work, I thought her family physician could prescribe something a little stronger. We would meet again in two weeks to see how increased sleep affected her interactions with her son. When we again met I asked her how much sleep she had been getting.

"My doctor gave me a prescription for this sleep medication I took for the last two weeks. It was terrific. I slept at least six hours, sometime seven each night."

"That's great," I said. "Has Bruce been acting any differently over the past two weeks?

"What do you mean?" she asked.

"Well at our last meeting, you described some of the memory problems he was experiencing."

"No, it's been about the same," she responded.

"I'd like to use the rating sheet again."

"No problem," she said. After completing the sheet we looked at the results. There were only a few "4's" and "5's". Most were "1's" and "2's". Although her son's behaviors had not changed significantly over the two weeks, her ability to tolerate them did. Never underestimate the power of a good night's sleep.

Meditate

For many people, the thought of meditating brings images of 1970s with hippies sitting in Golden Gate Park in San Francisco, smoking pot and swaying back and forth while uttering words like "groovy" and "love." Meditation can be viewed as a superficial aspect of a strange cultural movement, an integral component of some eastern religions, or just an exercise to rest the mind. We'll focus here only on the last version. The technique of meditation is a valuable tool for both organizing what's in your mind and also releasing what's no longer needed. Think of your mind as if it was a file cabinet. Within each drawer are a number of files, some useful and others useless. They're so full, it's impossible to place new ones inside. Or if there is any room, it squeezes the files together, making it impossible to easily pull out ones you need. Think of mediation as a process of weeding out those useless files. By just resting the mind while in a wakeful state, much of what no longer is useful can be thrown away.

Unfortunately, meditation, just like any other skill, is not something that can be done once and whose effectiveness is evaluated immediately.[13] That would be like an overweight person eating one low-fat meal and expecting to drop ten pounds by the next day. It requires practice and consistency.[14] Think of it as a daily multiple vitamin pill. You shouldn't expect to see much positive benefits from meditation for at least two weeks. Start slowly, and gradually build up the time of your meditation. Five minutes is a good start. Then add one minute each day. There are many different forms of meditation. This isn't the place to explain or teach any of them. There are organizations, mostly Buddhist, that offer free classes on meditation. A quick search on the Internet will reveal many in your area. Also, most bookstores have books on how to meditate. Although they'll describe the process step-by-step, I would first try to find a class. There's nothing like a hands-on activity and the guidance you'll get from someone who is experienced. The classes are nondenominational, with no attempts at spiritual conversion. Usually a single session is enough to get you started. Most are offered on weekday nights and weekend mornings. Rarely, are there any charges.

You don't need to subscribe to any religion to meditate. I've known Catholic priests, Orthodox Jews, and devout Muslims who have embraced meditation techniques to settle their minds and reduce stress in their lives. Meditation has been described by some as similar to preparing a field for planting. Some studies have shown that following meditation, there are beneficial physiological differences, including a reduction of blood pressure and a strengthening of the immune system.[15] Prior to doing a presentation, I'll find a few minutes to meditate; it allows me to be calmer and more focused. When time allows, I also meditate prior to my sessions with clients. Sometimes, even a few minutes of quiet mindful walking from my car to my client's house is sufficient to establish focus. The purpose of meditation is not to add anything to your life. Rather it is to reduce the fuzziness of one's thinking, leaving you with a natural clarity of thought. It's like cleaning the surface of a mirror in order to see what is reflected without a haze.

Continually dealing with a child with a learning problem adds stress. It may not be much on a daily basis, but it can be cumulative. I have a dog that sheds—a lot. Daily there are only a few hairs covering the hardwood floors. Not much, but unless I vacuum them, they just stay there. Each day, the number of hairs increases. By the fifth day, the floors look like they have a multitude of white specs painted on them. Stress is analogous to my dog's hair. Unless you get rid of it, it just sits there, growing even bigger. Meditation acts like a vacuum cleaner.

Just Breathe

One of the simplest ways of reducing stress is to just breathe slowly and deeply.[16] The next time you find you are in a very stressful situation, notice your breathing. Is it slow and regular or fast and irregular? As we experience stress, our body reacts. It produces the "fight or flight" pattern. Muscles become tensed, reaction times are shortened, and breathing becomes shallow. Not good for our thinking or our body. You'll find by consciously slowing down your breathing to a gentle and deep pattern, the physical stress you are feeling is also reduced.[17] It's not only a wonderful technique to reduce stress, but also one that effectively prevents it.[18] If you know you are about to enter a stressful situation, begin breathing slowly and deeply. Before having major surgery, I asked my surgeon if it would be helpful to him if I could reduce my blood pressure during the operation.

"Of course," he said, thinking that my question and its implied action were quite bizarre.

"Alright then, I'll lower it for you."

He didn't even ask how I intended to do something he was certain had no relationship to someone's will. The morning of surgery, I started my day at home with 45 minutes of meditation during which time I focused on slowing down my breathing and relaxing. On the way to the hospital I did my breathing exercises, continuing them right into the pre-op room. When the nurse came in to take my blood pressure, it was 100 over 60. Normal pressure should be 120 over 80. Mine was usually 122 over 85.

"I'm sorry, the blood pressure meter is broken, I'll get another one," she said.

She left before I could tell her I was practicing lowering my blood pressure in order to help the surgeon. She came back with another meter and proceeded to take my pressure again. Same results. Same confusion on her part.

Before she could go for a third instrument I said, "I've been practicing deep breathing for the last two hours. It lowers my blood pressure."

She looked at me unconvinced. "Right. *Nobody* has a lower blood pressure before surgery. *Nobody!*" She left and began looking for a third blood pressure meter.

If this simple technique can lower blood pressure immediately before a very stressful event, think how effective it could be with run-of-the-mill daily situations. You don't need any special training to breathe—you do it all the time. Just do it a little slower and deeper, and try to relax your body. After a few minutes you'll notice your mind settling, your blood pressure goes down, and stressful situations lose some of their strength. Some people believe that life isn't measured in years, but rather breaths—everyone has a specific number of breaths. When they're used up, death follows. This may be little more than a folk tale, but what if it isn't? Now there's a reason to slow down your breathing!

ACCEPTANCE

Letting go of expectations is the beginning of freedom. Letting go does not mean giving up, but rather an acceptance of what is possible and what isn't. There will be some things that you can change about your child and others you can't. As hard as it may be, you need to learn to accept those things you can't change and take glory in those in which you did everything you could, regardless of the outcome. A mother I knew wanted her daughter to become a ballerina, something she aspired to when she was her daughter's age. Unfortunately, the daughter had hand-eye coordination problems and difficulties in organizing visual configurations.

"Alright children," the ballet instructor would say, "I'm going to show you a very simple sequence. It has three parts. First I'll demonstrate it to you, and then I want each of you to do it in turn."

With that, she did the simple sequence. Even doing it very slowly, the child couldn't hold the fleeting visual images in memory. It became a blur. As each child repeated the sequence, the instructor would provide them with words of encouragement.

"That was wonderful Estelle. Just a little tighter on the turn."

There was always just a little adjustment each child needed, until it was time for Martina to show the steps. Not only were they clumsily executed, but two of the three weren't even similar to the ones he demonstrated. Instead of moving to the right on the first step, Martina moved to the left. On the second step, she bowed forward instead of lifting her arms upward. The teacher saw the futility of this child attempting ballet. Unfortunately, the mother didn't. In spite of a conference with the instructor, the mother insisted the daughter continue. The torture lasted for six months, until Martina would become hysterical at the mere thought of going to ballet class. Sometimes as parents we need to accept things as they are.

Dealing with Disappointment

Having a child with a learning difference can be disappointing. Parents look at their children and compare them to others—sometimes even their own. They may have had intricate plans for their child's future—a doctor, lawyer, politician, or corporate executive—and now realize they'll never materialize. When we plan for others, especially our children, we often disguise our own aspirations as goals they should aspire to. We're not our children and they shouldn't have the burden of meeting our unfulfilled dreams, regardless of how much disappointment we may feel. Unfortunately, disappointment resists confinement. It can become a malignancy that invades many aspects of our lives in strange and unique ways. When we are disappointed in our children, we often can't see the wondrous parts of their personality. They're doing the best they know how, and all we're seeing is what they can't do.

When we are disappointed in our children, our personality changes. Instead of seeing life as something good, we view things through a black mesh that puts a depressing darkness on things not even related to our children. I knew a research scientist whose dream was for her child to continue in her tradition. She had received numerous international awards and was considered to be the best in her area. When her child was born, she already envisioned which university she would send him to, the field of research he would study and the joint papers they could write together. It never happened. By the age of four, it became painfully obvious her son would never be the person she wanted him to be. His difficulty with both short- and long-term memory dashed her plans. He was a sweet child, who while having memory problems, was wonderful at interacting with people of all ages. She could only see what he wouldn't become. Her disappointment became a template for shaping both her thoughts and actions. She no longer took joy in her research or new awards, and the love she had shown her son was muted after realizing he could never become a colleague. The joy she initially experienced as a top researcher and a new mother became a distant memory. She bore little resemblance to the person she was four years ago. When we are disappointed in our children, our relationships with other family members change and our negativity may effect how we interact with everyone.[19] When we are disappointed in our children, we may seek joy and comfort from other sources, often neglecting the child who didn't meet our needs.

Giving up things, identities, and activities is easy compared to the aspirations we have for our children. Giving them up for some people is as difficult as burying a child. Unfortunately, the burial is not the end of the process, but its beginning. A number of years ago, I was a consultant at a community center for children with moderate to severe learning and cognitive problems. Elizabeth Kubler-Ross, the noted author on death and grieving, generously offered to give a workshop for the parents. She likened the emotions of parents whose children have significant impairments to those whose children have died. There was only a small group of parents, Elizabeth Kubler-Ross, and myself. As she spoke and made the analogy, there were tears in the eyes of many parents. Then the conversation began. For many years, most had felt the emotions Kubler-Ross talked about. Some had felt it from the birth of their child when they were immediately told about the problem. But few ever expressed the enormity of their grief to anyone. By the end of the two-hour session, the faces of the participants were visibly changed. There was an expression of calmness and acceptance I'd never seen, in spite of contact with them three times a week for over one year. They were beginning to grieve not the loss of their child, but of their own aspirations. For some, it was as powerful as grieving the death of a child—the one they never had. But a marvelous thing began to happen over the next few months. As they came to accept their children, along with their limitations, their involvement in their child's learning grew. Parents who in the past would just drop off their children at the center and leave now wanted to know what they could do to help. It's natural to grieve and may be the beginning of getting on with your life. Instead of denying it, you need to get in touch with it. Dealing with the death of aspirations is not an intellectual exercise. The loss may never go away. But it can be diminished to a background hum.

Anger towards Others

There is an old saying that anger is like a hot coal. Although you may hurt the person you hit with it, you'll also burn your hand when you throw it. Anger is not an emotion that can be isolated. When you're angry you can't be compassionate. When you're angry you can't be forgiving. When you're angry you can't be happy. When you're angry you can't think. Thich Nhat Hanh said, "Anger is a fire burning inside us, filling our whole being with smoke. When we are angry, we need to calm ourselves."[20] Some have suggested the best thing to do when you're angry is to refrain from speaking. Allowing your anger to subside does not necessarily mean you don't have a right to negative thoughts about someone's actions or speech. You can and should express them, but in a way that's compassionate. Harmful actions almost always indicate something lacking in the originator—usually an unfulfilled need. For example, some faculty at my university engaged in a number of behaviors I initially felt were both hurtful and inconsiderate. I was furious, since I felt it was undeserved. The longer I viewed it in this way, the angrier I became. The angrier I became, the more consumed I was by the events. It was only when I changed my view that my anger subsided and changed into compassion. Each of these faculty members were acting out of their own needs. They weren't trying to be mean-spirited, their lack of wholeness drove them to act the way they did. They were just trying to fill their own needs.

The lives of these faculty members, just like many people, are often like a rolling meadow. When it rains, water puddles into those areas that are the lowest. I believe the same thing occurs in people who are viewed as mean-spirited. Just as the field can't control where the water will eventually rest, these people often can't control their actions. Their unfulfilled needs dominate. Given the circumstances of their lives, they're doing the best they can. As you look at what angers you, try to change your perspective in the same way I did. Hurtful behaviors are rarely directed at other people. They usually are a reaction to an inadequacy or need. Let others throw the hot coals. Like the Aikido master, duck. You have more important and positive things to do than burn your hands.

Growing through Our Problems

There's an old Zen Buddhist saying, "Barn's burnt down—now I can see the moon." Having a child who learns differently can change how parents perceive the world, how they interact with other family members, and how they view themselves. For some, the feeling of loss is so overwhelming; it colors everything they do. For others, it allows them to see the moon. The Dali Lama said, "Unfortunately events, though potentially a source of anger and despair, have equal potential to be a source of spiritual growth. Whether or not this is the outcome depends on our response.[21]

I knew an individual who spent 25 years working for an organization. Throughout this period, she went far beyond what was required. When taking on administrative positions, she not only effectively managed her division, but also was supportive of every person for whom she was responsible. She defended them even when their position was questionable. She did it out of loyalty and a sense of commitment—often putting her own position at risk. During the last few years of her employment, she became involved in some controversies in which she believed unethical positions were taken for reasons of expediency by members of her division. When she announced her upcoming retirement, she initially received the normal round of congratulations. During her last month, she expected to be asked about her preferences for a retirement party. But there was nothing. Possibly a surprise party was being planned? On her last workday, her supervisees and colleagues presented her with a bouquet of roses. Hardly something worthy of spending a lifetime defending people whose actions were often indefensible. She was crushed and angry.

"Those ungrateful sons of bitches. After all I did for them," she said to her husband.

He listened compassionately but didn't know how to comfort her. He knew during the 25 years his wife had worked for the company, everyone who retired had received a retirement party. Many had even been organized by his wife and were held at their house. For months her anger colored everything she did. Eventually, he suggested his wife speak with me. Not because he thought I had any unique insights, just that sometimes speaking with a good friend can result in a little relief.

"I couldn't believe it. I saved the jobs of four of them, was responsible for having two others hired in spite of opposition, and brought the division to a position of leadership within the company. How could they have been so ungrateful?"

"Looking back, would you have done anything differently?" I asked.

"No, absolutely not. Even if I knew how ungrateful they'd be."

"Why not?"

"Because what I did were the right things to do. I did them because they were necessary and ethical."

"If what you did was the right thing, why are you so upset because you didn't get your party?"

She thought for a minute then responded, "Because I deserved it."

"That's what you would have done. Given a party to anyone who retires?" I asked.

"Absolutely, that's the *right* thing to do."

"So what you're saying is your colleagues *should* have acted the way you would have."

"You're damn right!"

"But how can you be angry at people who don't have the same values as you? How can you be angry at people who have giant holes in their personalities?"

"Why? Because they should be decent human beings!"

"They are. They're just different. Would you be angry at a blind person for bumping into you?"

"Of course not. I'd feel sorry for him, and maybe even help him get to where he wants to go."

I just smiled and waited for the realization to set in. For the first time in three months the anger subsided. For three months my friend looked at everything through her pain, taking the actions of her colleagues as a personal rebuke of everything she did for the past 25 years. Now the anger changed to compassion. She understood how the needs of these individuals were so great they found it necessary to hurt her to make themselves feel whole. They didn't deserve her anger. What they needed was her compassion.

Throughout your life, there will be things that have the potential of hurting you. The actions or words may be directed towards your child, other family members, or from people you think are preventing your child from receiving appropriate services. Righteous indignation is a natural reaction against people who are acting in a way that's antithetical to your values. But remaining judgmental doesn't allow you to grow beyond the pain. Understanding the purpose of hurtful behaviors does. Just as a blind person doesn't justify your anger when bumping into you, neither should the inconsiderate actions of people who are in need. Barn's burnt down—now you can see the moon.

Finding Happiness in Your Child

What do you think about when someone says "happiness?" Usually, what comes to mind are things, or outcomes. Happiness can be a four-car garage in the suburbs, a high-paying job, an expensive new car, or a child who becomes a successful professional. We have a tendency to externalize happiness. It becomes something intimately involved in a thing or event. It becomes a *goal*. Unfortunately, the path to that goal is often ignored. You had to have two backbreaking jobs just to afford the mortgage on the house with the four-car garage. That high-paying job was only possible by doing things in the workplace you would find unethical in social situations. The new car could only be purchased if you denied yourself simple pleasures over two years in order to afford your new status symbol. And what about your child? What would be required in order for you to feel happiness about what he or she achieves academically, socially, or professionally?

Once you associate happiness with goals, both you and your child are primed for a fall. The goals, many of which are unobtainable, become traps; if they can't be reached, neither can your happiness. And by focusing on the goal, the path is often ignored. I worked with a parent whose whole life was focused on getting her daughter into a prestigious university.

"It'll be worth it if I can get her into Stanford or U.C. Berkeley. Maybe she could even go to Harvard."

The mother was aware her daughter had a moderate learning problem. Since three, she had enrolled her daughter in as many enrichment classes as could fit into a day: sensory integration, speech therapy, physical therapy, occupational therapy, music, cognitive focusing, and others with questionable legitimacy. Her daughter enjoyed few of these activities.

"Does Anita like doing these things?" I asked.

"That's irrelevant. I want to give her the best chance possible to be accepted at a good college."

"But she's only five," I said.

"Yes," the mother responded angrily, "But if I don't do everything I can now, she'll never be successful.

"But do you get any pleasure *now* from what Anita is doing?"

"That's not important," she said, "Only the future is."

Unfortunately, I wasn't able to make any headway with this mother. Actually, she thought my understanding was so off base, she sought someone else to work with her daughter. Anita never made it to Stanford. Actually, Anita never made it through high school. She viewed each of the things her mother wanted for her as goals, most of which she wasn't interested in. The journey was so arduous the goals became unimportant. She had no joy or happiness in any of them. If you shift your search for happiness from the future to the present, from what your child *may* be able to do in the future to what he or she *can* do now, from goals to journeys, you'll find the happiness that eludes many parents. Happiness is not something that's external to you. It's not the successes your child has, or the intrinsic value of their accomplishments. Happiness is something totally dependent on how you view things. There's the old joke about two boys looking into a barn and seeing an empty stall filled with manure.

"Ugh," the first child said. "Look at all of that crap. It stinks."

"Wow," the second child said. "I know there must be a pony here somewhere!"

Very rarely is something inherently good or evil, ugly or beautiful, depressing or joyful. It's our values and how we view them that attach meaning to events and things. In Chapter 11, I'll tell the story of a mother of an autistic child. For her, having her child raise her arm to put on her coat had as much importance as the possibility of her child graduating with honors from Stanford. Happiness for her was internal. Who could get unspeakable pleasure from a child lifting her arm, unless it was generated internally? By not being tied to external validation, this type of happiness has the capacity of spreading and touching many aspects of your life. It has been described as a magic fire that continues to burn brightly even when cold water is poured onto it.[22] The search for happiness, based on what your child can offer, is not one that becomes fulfilled in the future. It's something that happens every day, during every interaction.

ELEVEN

Your Child's Future

I t's hard to fit in when you know you're different. So it's no surprise some children with learning problems are at risk for adjusting socially.[1] As they mature and reach adulthood, sometimes the differences, though hidden, pull them away from others. However, it's not inevitable that your child will have social problems. There are things you can do now to reduce the likelihood problems will occur. One of the strongest antidotes is to develop a strong connection with your child.[2] Connectiveness shouldn't be confused with overprotection. It involves the development of a bond between you and your child that is both helping and accepting. You do what is necessary to help your child succeed; yet, you are prepared to accept both what they can and cannot do. In this chapter, you'll learn how to strengthen the bond. We are going to explore what it means to let go, how to focus on what is important, learn to accept your child for who he or she is, prepare your child now for college, and understand the relationship between learning problems and career choices. What you do in the next few years may have a fundamental impact on the life of your child.

LETTING GO—THE OPTIONS

One of the hardest things for parents to do with children is to let go. In the process of wanting to protect them, we often do the opposite.[3] As we build even harder and larger shells around our children, we prevent them from growing. We do this, not for selfish reasons, but because we fear our child's learning problem will lead to pain. These are reasonable fears. The more severe the learning problem, the greater the likelihood your child will have difficulties.[4] Parents have four options when it comes to letting go:

1. Hold on tightly now.
2. Let children experience failures now.
3. Protect them forever.
4. Help them develop independence.

Each choice results in a very different outcome, both for children and families.

Hold On Tightly Now

Often parents live in a time warp called *tomorrow*. Tomorrow, I'll let her do more. Tomorrow I'll give up control. Tomorrow is soon enough for her to become more independent. I knew a mother who believed this was the best option. She had a wonderful humorous daughter. There were many things she did flawlessly, such as anything involving physical coordination, artistic activities, interactions with other children and adults, and being compassionate. Unfortunately, she had difficulties with understanding. When someone began explaining anything complicated, she would often miss portions of what was said. Although she could understand logical relationships, it took her a while to process them. While having a significant learning problem, she appeared no different from other 14-year-olds. Her grades in school were mostly C's, even with the help of a tutor she worked with every day after school. She wasn't excelling, but she was succeeding. Her mother viewed her level of functioning as less than adequate, as something requiring protection. Until she was 14 years old, her mother would explain everything to her, rarely allowing her daughter to make mistakes on her own. This mother, just as many others, believed that because her daughter had a learning problem she needed additional protection in areas such as drugs, sexual conduct, smoking, and boy-girl relationships.[5] The daughter resented her mother's overprotectiveness, which made it difficult for her to develop the social and intellectual skills necessary to function as a normal teenager. She wanted an opportunity to be hurt.

"No, Maria, you can't go to the dance. There are boys there who will take advantage of you."

"No, Maria, I don't think it's wise for you to do an overnight with those girls. You may have some problems understanding what they're talking about."

"No, Maria, the class trip to Washington isn't a possibility. It requires too many things you have difficulty doing."

Maria's life was punctuated with a series of "no's" from her mother. Not because she didn't love her daughter, but because she loved her too much. She wanted to prevent Maria from experiencing the failures she knew would happen. It was an act of love that forced Maria to rebel. At 14, she began refusing to listen to anything her mother said and started engaging in risky social behaviors. Whatever bond had developed was broken. This was followed by a series of disasters. At 15, she began experimenting with drugs. At 16, she was pregnant. By 17, she was out of the house and living with someone twice her age. She was a good kid, but felt she had few options left for expressing her need for independence.

Experiencing Failures Now

The second option is to allow children with learning problems to immediately feel the failures often associated with having a learning problem. Failures, according to some people are necessary for growth. Unfortunately, too many failures, too quickly, can lead to disastrous changes in a child's personality. Although they can be addressed in counseling, it's best not to have created them.[6] A father I knew believed the only way his son could prepare for the future was to experience failure now. He had always experienced a great amount of difficulty with attention. It was diagnosed early and specific suggestions were made to the parents, such as to reduce the amount of noise present when instructing him. The father, who was a career military man, viewed all of the suggestions as coddling.

"That's not how life works," he said to the educational psychologist. "No one stops the noise for anyone in the real world. Ralph needs to deal with the real world. Not something so artificial it bears no resemblance to reality."

He refused to do anything special for his child when it came to increasing his attending abilities. If the television was on when he asked his son to do something, it stayed on. When he explained something to his son, it was irrelevant if Ralph's sensory system wasn't prepared to process it. From the ages of 4 to 12, this poor little guy experienced an endless series of failures. Instead of becoming more proficient by facing reality, as his father thought would happen, he began developing emotional problems that interfered with everything. Eventually, a psychologist convinced the father that rather than preparing his son for the future, he was preventing him from experiencing it. The boy had chosen to withdraw rather than continually fail. At 12 years of age, Ralph had few friends, choosing to spend all of his time outside of school on the computer. He felt safe there.

Protect Forever

The third option is to protect children—forever. One of the most poignant movies on parental protection is *Best Boy,* the 1979 Academy Award-winning documentary by Ira Wohl chronicling his attempts to have his aging aunt and uncle begin thinking about what would become of their son when they died.[7] At the time of the filming, they both were in their seventies Their son, Philly, was in his fifties. Philly had always lived at home and never received any training. For parents whose children were born in the 1940s and 1950s, few options where possible.[8] For severe disabilities, you either placed children in an institution or kept them at home and hoped for the best. Although the situation has drastically changed, the attitudes of some parents haven't. I worked with a family whose love for their daughter was unquestionable. While able to do simple things, anything complicated caused her confusion. As a result, the parents were very protective, always trying to prevent their daughter from experiencing anything painful. They would answer for her in stores and restaurants and even go so far as to interrupt conversations she was having with adults so her problems wouldn't become evident. They tried very hard to protect their daughter—too hard. One of the most difficult discussions I have with parents involves their child's future. This one was no exception.

"Where do you see Lisa as an adult?"

"I don't understand," the father said to me as he turned to his wife.

"Lisa has problems that won't go away," I said. "Problems that will restrict what she can and cannot do as an adult."

I could tell this was an uncomfortable topic for both parents. But I felt one that needed exploration.

"Lisa has difficulties when things become too complicated. As a 7-year-old, it may not be a problem. But what will happen when she's 20, 40, or 60?"

"We'll help her as long we're here."

"And what will happen when you're no longer here?" I asked. "When neither of you are alive?"

This is the question many parents with children who have disabling conditions are afraid to answer. We spent over one hour dancing around the question. As I would approach a discussion about what their daughter would do after they died, they ran in the opposite direction. Avoiding dealing with the problem doesn't make it go away. It only delays it, sometimes beyond the point at which anything can be done. Eventually, they stopped running away and through tearful eyes began looking at what they feared.

"I know we'll both die before she does," the father said. The mother shook her head in agreement.

"We can do everything to protect her now, but I'm terrified of what will happen after we're gone," she said.

These parents were dealing with a gripping fear. There was no way I could make them feel better about the situation if Lisa didn't receive training. After they both died, Lisa would need assistance with independent living. However, we did have the option of changing the situation.

"Maybe it would be better if we could think about what she'll need to do when neither of you are here. Maybe we can start working on things now that will be helpful when she becomes an adult."

I introduced the fourth option to them. Instead of trying to avoid dealing with the inevitable, we were going to do something positive—we were going to teach their daughter coping behaviors that would begin a transition from dependence to independence.

Developing Independence

There is a middle ground, in which a child is neither held too tightly nor let go too quickly. It involves gradually letting go of children and allowing them, with guidance, to become independent. In Chapter 2, I wrote about teaching my son how to ride a two-wheel bicycle. I would gradually let go of his seat, yet kept my hand close, immediately replacing it when he lost balance. It's a good analogy for the transition between dependence and independence. The difficulty in letting go wasn't just a problem for Lisa's parents; it's a persistent problem for many parents of children with learning problems, regardless of its severity.[9] Although it took these parents several years, they gradually learned to let go. First, simple controls were relinquished; then those that weren't terrifying to the parents were released. With each new freedom, Lisa blossomed. As she became more independent, her parents' anxiety diminished. She was capable of doing more things than they could have ever imagined. They knew she would need the assistance of an independent living organization, but they could prepare her now, rather than having her start preparing years from now. They did things at seven that prepared their daughter for adulthood and for a time when they would no longer be able to protect her. Letting go can ease the passage between dependence and independence. The support provided by parents softens the edges and makes the transition a wonderful journey rather than a drop over a precipice. Children must grow and in the process unavoidably experience pain. That pain can be uncontrolled or measured, and as parents, we have the opportunity to guide and limit it.

FOCUSING ON WHAT'S IMPORTANT

At times, things can become overwhelming. We want to do everything for our children. Often we overschedule, overload, and overplay. We believe by being the super mom or dad, we can compensate for the problems our children have. Although our efforts are well intentioned and often do help our children, we may end up doing too much or trying too hard, and in the process hurt both ourselves and our children.[10] As we try to do more and more things, our children's lives become an unending schedule of events. We often loose our focus, giving everything equal attention. Instead of having sharply delineated activities, we create a stew for our children. It makes more sense to focus on what's important. The first step might be to just stop everything and take an inventory of what's happening. Let children identify those things they are passionate about. Don't worry about the quantity. As in most things in life, it's quality that matters.

When my children were young, I felt my entire life revolved around their activities. Three days a week I drove my daughter to rowing practice at 5:00 A.M. Three days a week, I drove my son to soccer practice at 4:00 P.M. Once a week at 6:00 P.M., I drove my daughter to her Spanish tutor. Then there was the Tuesday and Thursday math and English tutoring at our house for my son. On weekends there were soccer matches and rowing events. I thought my life was controlled by my children's needs until I spoke with a mother with whom I was working. My schedule was a romp in the park compared to hers. Her daughter was involved in music lessons, math tutoring, ballet, soccer, computer skills, and learning-enrichment programs. This was a child who had short-term memory problems that were exacerbated by too much stimulation. Virtually every minute of nonschool time was scheduled up through bedtime—seven days a week.

"Why?" I asked her mother.

"Why what?" she responded.

"Why do you find it necessary to fill every bit of your child's free time with activities?

"I know she has problems with memory," she said. "I need to give her everything she'll need now."

"I'm not sure that's the best approach. If you want her to improve her memory, you need to have her do less."

I called in her daughter and we began talking about everything she was doing.

"Emma, what's the favorite thing you do?"

"Soccer," she said without any hesitation.

"Why?"

"Because I'm good at it and it's fun."

"What don't you like?" I asked.

"A little or a lot?"

"A lot," I said.

"I hate my piano lessons."

"Why?"

"I feel so stupid. My teacher shows me how to play notes, but I can't remember them."

I suggested the piano lessons be eliminated, at least for the time being. Not because it wasn't enriching, but rather, by continually engaging in something Emma believed she couldn't do, the belief she couldn't be successful was reinforced. We know children will often generalize their feelings from one activity to another.[11] If she couldn't be successful playing the piano, should she expect the same type of results from the enrichment program? We eliminated half of the after-school activities, leaving only those Emma truly loved and at which she was successful. By reducing the amount of information she needed to process and providing her with downtime, her memory problems improved. It wasn't a cure; we just eliminated some of the hindrances.

When we see a problem in our children, our first reaction is to overcompensate. We think if we only can do a little extra, the problem will go away. And if a little extra works, why not a lot extra? Sol Stein, a noted editor, would lament about the amount of words aspiring novelists used. We would continually repeat the mantra, "Less is more." [12] When we attempt to provide our children with everything we think is necessary to help, fewer activities may be more beneficial than a frenetic schedule where they are running from one activity to another. Less may be more.

BEING WHAT THEY ARE

There is a tendency on the part of some parents to make their children become someone who they aren't and never could be. The author G.K. Chesterton said, "Do not go about . . . encouraging triangles to break out of the prison of their three sides. If a triangle breaks out of its three sides, its life comes to a lamentable end." [13]

The same holds true for our children. As parents, we often want our children to become someone they'd rather not be. [14] I knew a father who insisted his son take advanced English in high school. For years he struggled with reading problems, yet still managed to get straight A's. Based on his performance, he qualified for any advanced course he wanted to take. If it was up to him, he wouldn't have taken any. He was very successful, but at a great cost. Rarely would he finish his homework before midnight, in spite of beginning his studies right after getting home from school. His father viewed it as a sign his son was committed to learning. The son did it only because, without the extra time, he wouldn't understand the material. And without understanding the material, the A's would drop to C's. With C's he knew he would disappoint his father and maybe even loose his love. He had few friends and didn't do any extracurricular activities—he didn't have the time. He continued not to disappoint, in spite of the cost to his emotional well-being. In his first year of college, everything fell apart. Living in a dorm 400 miles from home, he faced a world for which he wasn't prepared. He knew how to study, but not how to be a complete person. The experience was so bad, in spite of still getting good grades, he dropped out of school.

Instead of trying to make your children into something they aren't, accept them. Acceptance doesn't necessarily mean you like it; rather you've come to accept the existence of something that may not be changeable. Focus on the wonderful things your children are capable of doing. That should be your source of joy. Forget about those images of what they can never become. If you hold onto them, nothing but disappointment will follow. Trying to force them into a hole, in which they can't fit, may produce something you want, but not what will make your child happy.

WHEN IT CAN'T BE FIXED

For the past ten chapters, I've explained how you can help your child learn. Implicit is the belief that when a problem exists, we can either fix it, or provide alternative paths. But what happens when it can't be fixed or we can't develop detours? What happens when the problem is so fundamental or severe, nothing works? In spite of the best efforts of you and your child, the problem doesn't go away. I recently attended a hospice volunteer training program led by Frank Ostaseski, the founder of the Zen Hospice Project in San Francisco. Frank's a remarkable person whose life work is serving the dying and training people to do the same. One of the exercises we did on the first day of training involved a direct encounter with death. Frank opened a box of black-and-white photographs and matter-of-factly explained that the 100 photographs were of adults who had died in hospice over the past year. Sitting in a circle, on a signal from Frank, we passed the photographs to the right. These moving portraits, taken at different stages in the dying process, generated a range of emotions in everyone. On the faces of the dying were expressions of serenity, anger, acceptance, fear, pain, wonder, and relief. The purpose of the exercise was to have each of us explore what feelings we were having both about the people we were given the privilege to see, and ourselves. The reactions ranged the full gamut of emotions. Some painfully recalled the deaths of family members, friends, and lovers. Others wrestled with ways they were either drawn towards or repelled from something in the photographs. As someone who has been involved in helping children develop new skills for over 30 years, my first reaction was to want to "fix" everyone's problem. Whatever was going on in the life of that person, I wanted to use my skills to change it. But after looking at the fiftieth photograph, I realized there are some things in life I can't fix. No matter what I would have done if I was at the hospice center when these people were alive, I couldn't fix it. Everyone still would have died in spite of my best efforts.

Being unable to fix something is not limited to terminal diseases. Throughout our lives, we're constantly thrust into similar situations. How we react affects our lives and the lives of our family members. I worked with a very disfluent young child who had various learning problems. I approached her as if she was no different from any of the other children I've treated for stuttering. She had a problem, and I would fix it. After all, I've successfully treated over 500 kids who stuttered, why not Annie? As I used the strategies in Chapter 5, I expected the same type of positive results I had with other children. But it didn't happen. When I would try to implement a program and it didn't work, I'd blame myself. I thought I just didn't have the right components. I would either "tune-up" what I did, or substitute a completely different program. At no time did I ever think the problem was "unfixable." Three months into therapy, her speech continued to deteriorate. Disfluencies became longer, the hesitations increased, and her ability to use the strategies I taught her decreased. No matter what I did, her ability to communicate continued to go downhill. I kept blaming myself for her lack of progress—in spite of knowing an inoperable tumor was compressing an area of the brain controlling speech. In my *head* I couldn't let go of the belief that this problem was fixable. It almost was as if a personal challenge had been given. The gauntlet was thrown down, and if I didn't pick it up and win, it would be a personal loss. Only when I understood in my heart I couldn't control the situation, did I stop being a "fixer." It no longer was about my competence as a speech-language pathologist. Annie's life could no longer be cast into concepts of clinical successes or failures. It became an issue of me being able to accept what I couldn't fix. Ostaseski makes an interesting distinction between "fixing," "helping," and "serving." [15] When you fix, you assume something is broken. When you help, you see the person as weak. But when you serve, you see the person as intrinsically whole. You create a relationship in which both parties gain. Annie's mother and I moved from being "fixers" to "servers." Her speech and other parts of her ability to function would never get better. As long as her mother and I kept trying to fix them, all three of us continued to fail. When we shifted our focus from fixing to serving, Annie's life became better, in spite of her deteriorating health and ability to verbally communicate. The tumor didn't win, though it ended her life. By serving, it gave both Annie's mother and me new insights into who we were and what we could become. Just like the pictures of the dying during the hospice training, this too became a gift.

There's an old saying that beautifully captures this story: Many of the things bothering us are like empty boats; you can yell at them and get upset, but there's nobody there to do anything about it. [16] It also applies to being angry about those things in our children's lives that are unfixable. Accepting a limitation in what your child is capable of doing now and in the future can be one of the hardest things you may be asked to do as a parent. Yet, for things that are unchangeable, acceptance may be the most beneficial thing you can do for your child, family, and yourself. Accepting means letting go of expectations and unfulfilled dreams. Acceptance means loving your children for who they are and finding joy in their capabilities.

I worked with a single working mother whose daughter was severely autistic. At twelve, she couldn't communicate, dress herself, or use the toilet. This mother, who never completed high school, had more insights into acceptance than any person I've ever met. For her, every new thing her daughter did was worthy of a Noble Prize. I remember one session, when we were working on simple self-help skills.

"Stan, did you see that?" she excitedly said to me.

"No, I'm sorry Grace. What did Andrea do?"

The mother's face glowed as if her child just graduated with honors from a prestigious university. "She raised her hand so I could put on her coat. She's never done that," she said with tears in her eyes.

The mother had accepted Andrea's unfixable limitations as things that were all right. Anything new was just icing on the cake. Over one thousand years ago, the great Buddhist monk Shantideva asked the question: "Why be upset about something if it cannot be remedied?"[17]

As I watched this mother lovingly serve her daughter, I saw a twentieth-century Shantideva. Her child would never get better, but it wouldn't lessen the amount of love and compassion she gave her. This mother grew, learning lessons about life her daughter would teach her daily. It's been over 15 years since I worked with Andrea. She still lives at home, Grace still serves her, and her development is only slightly better than it was when I worked with her. But as for her mother, that's a different story. As her daughter kept teaching her new things about life, she realized she had things to offer other parents of autistic children. She became a resource for them, and today is considered a godsend by people who are just beginning to struggle with the same issues she began dealing with 15 years ago.

As you look at what your child is capable of doing and what isn't fixable, think about this incredible mother who could receive immense joy just by her daughter's simple hand movement, and who allowed her daughter to be a source of teaching and self-discovery.

COLLEGE?

You're probably wondering why I am bringing up the topic of college in the same sentence with a child who is 4 years old. Many things can happen in 15 years, most of which are unpredictable. However, there are some things you should know about college. First, it's accessible to most children with learning problems. Your child may not be able to make it into Stanford, but the choices are greater than you may think. Second, once in college, there are many services available that will enable your child to succeed. And third, the ability of a child to be successful in a chosen career has less to do with learning problems than other factors.

Qualifying

Most colleges and universities have the same standards for all applicants.[18] That means if it is a grade average, SAT scores, or a certain number of courses, it's the same for everyone—at least on paper. Some institutions try to make their student populations diversified. Although traditionally you might think "diversity" is limited to ethnicity, it isn't. Applicants who learn differently can also be part of the diversity mix.[19] Universities using diversity as a factor for admission have overcome legal challenges by applying complicated scoring devices giving extra credit to applicants possessing something they believe is important for the institution. Although your child should be encouraged to state his or her learning disability, they shouldn't believe it will be used to compensate for poor grades or low SAT scores. The label becomes more important after being accepted. Since colleges and universities usually only look at grades from ninth or tenth grade on, those marks become critical. By preparing early, like in elementary school, by the time children enter high school, they will have become adept at using the strategies you taught.

Visiting and Selecting

In the spring and summer before my son entered twelfth grade, we went on college road trips. Although I wanted him to visit schools throughout the country, he preferred to stay on the West Coast where he had always lived. We visited over ten schools between Seattle and San Diego, and as far east as Arizona. Before visiting the schools, I first read books describing colleges with programs for students who had learning problems. Every year, there are new updates. Instead of recommending one book, you can type in "college" and "learning disability" on any of the online bookseller websites. The books displayed describe features of colleges, including learning accommodations made for students. Some schools, like the University of Arizona, have a comprehensive program where students are provided with tutors, workshops, special technological devices, and even note takers. Other universities have minimal programs in which the learning disability program's sole function is to let instructors know the test-taking accommodations needed for students. By the time your child is ready for college, I would imagine the number of schools accommodating students with learning differences and ranges of services will have increased substantially. The news is good and getting better.

Getting Support

Even if the school your child selects doesn't have an extensive learning disabilities program, it will have, at minimum, an office that can coordinate contacts with professors. They'll be told if a student has a learning problem and what they can do to accommodate it. When I was teaching graduate courses, the office of Disability Services would take care of all the paperwork necessary for qualifying a student as "learning disabled." Once the student received that designation, I was allowed to let them use a computer to take tests, use spell-check devices if a computer wasn't used, take the test in a separate room, and on occasion, I even gave oral exams for students who had writing problems. The key to receiving support is the willingness of student to identify him or herself. For many, this is difficult. I had a graduate student who identified herself as having a learning problem on the first day of class.

"Dr. Goldberg, I have a learning disorder."

"What do I need to do to accommodate you?" I asked.

"Well, not very much. I'd like to tape record your lectures if you don't mind?"

"No problem."

"I also have difficulty taking tests with time limits."

"We can set you up in one of the clinic rooms and you can use all the time you need."

"Would I be able to use a computer for the exams?" she asked. "It's much easier for me to compose my thoughts."

"That's not a problem," I responded.

She did marvelously throughout her graduate program. True, the faculty had to make accommodations to meet her needs, but few were difficult to do. And those reluctant to make accommodations were required to do so by law. Even though it required an extra effort, the faculty knew they were involved in the development of an exemplary clinician. As wonderful as this story is, there's another one without a happy ending.

A few years later, I had a student in my class who never identified herself to the faculty or the disability office as someone who needed any learning accommodations. My exams were always three hours long and involved expository writing based on facts and hypothetical clinical cases. For Marcia, it was more than she could handle. At the end of her first semester she failed my class and two others. With three F's, it would be impossible to get her grade point average up to a B in only one semester. After receiving a disqualifying letter from the department chair between semesters, she came to see me, finally confiding that she had a learning difference.

"Why didn't you say anything?" I asked.

"When I was a child, I felt very different. Where my friends could do things quickly and accurately, it took me a lot of time. And when I had to do something within a set amount of time, I would panic. Usually I did poorly then. By the time I was in high school, I tried to hide the fact I had a learning disability. I vowed never to let anyone know about it in college."

As compelling as the story was, we as a faculty couldn't do very much after the fact. The Learning Disability Office also had their hands tied. According to the requirements of the university, accommodations could not be made after the fact. This student tried to hide her problem, whereas the first student didn't, believing there was nothing disordered about her abilities—they were just different. Throughout her life, her parents and teachers had been supportive. She never tried to hide her problems, and instead looked at them as something to learn from. I'm not sure there was any difference between the intelligence of these two students. What separated them was their attitude towards their problem. In large part, the attitude of each as a young adult was shaped early in life. One had supportive parents and teachers; the other had parents and teachers who made her feel like a failure. We know receiving support is important for success in college.[20] But rarely is support provided without someone asking for it. It may not be too early to think about college for your child. Not necessarily looking for colleges, but rather in knowing that how you address your child's learning differences now will affect their ability to ask for help later.

CAREERS AND LEARNING DIFFERENCES

Choosing a career can be a difficult process for anyone, whether or not someone has a learning problem. There really aren't any conclusive studies that show some careers are better for people with learning problems than others. There are too many things to consider: the type of problem, the severity, the treatment history, and the person's interests. It appears, if a learning problem does make a difference, it has more to do with a person's acceptance or denial of it, rather than anything else.[21] People who have accepted their learning problem have less difficulty with career choices than those who have not. One very positive factor in choosing careers is the support parents provide their grown children in the selection process.[22] I knew a young adult who wanted to become an actor. Doing that would require an extensive amount of memorization. His learning problem was difficulty with retrieving information. Since he was four-years-old, his parents taught him various strategies to remember things. Instead of being negative when he shared his dream of becoming an actor with his parents, they supported it, reaffirming the strategies he had used throughout his life to retrieve information. Eventually, he became very successful in Broadway shows. The more supportive parents are, the better the outcomes. However, you don't have to wait until your child is old enough to enter the world of work to provide support. Begin practicing it now with support for the activities they want to do. From these activities career choices are nurtured.

Often we just fall into careers, rather than making a conscious decision to do something. When I look back on why I became a speech-language pathologist and university professor, the reason had more to do with who I shared an office with as a graduate advisor than anything else. My office mate was completing his doctorate in speech pathology and we talked often about his thesis topic, which was stuttering. I had just started my doctoral work in political theory and strategic forecasting.

"Why don't you come up to the clinic and see what we do?" my friend asked.

"Sure, I've got nothing better to do this afternoon," I said, not realizing what I was about to do would change my life.

I had no idea what a speech pathologist did prior to observing one in the university clinic. I was fascinated. Not by the field, but by what the person I observed was doing. She was working with a young child who had difficulty using language. As the child began to use new linguistic structures, there was a glimmer in the child's eye and a tear in mine. This is what I wanted to do. My friend introduced me to the faculty after we completed our observation, and I made an application to the graduate program the next day. Deciding to become a speech pathologist wasn't based on anything other than what I had been passionate about throughout my life. Even as a child, I enjoyed helping, took pride in figuring out how to solve problems, and delighted in seeing a meaningful conclusion to hard work. "Speech Pathology" was just a convenient hole into which I was able to fit. As you watch what your child is passionate about, even as young as four, look for those things that will allow him or her to fit into their own hole.

Your child's attitudes toward a career will often be more important than any objective test of career preferences.[23] Look to see what your child enjoys doing—look at the activities. When my daughter was three, she took immense delight in painting. Today she works as an executive in a major art auction house. My son, who was always fascinated by houses and buildings, is studying to become a commercial realtor. In my wildest imagination, I couldn't have predicted either career choice. But if I really listened and watched what they did, I could have known the types of careers to which they would gravitate and excel. So, don't be too concerned with pushing or eliminating careers for your child. Encourage their passion, regardless where it takes them. Don't be too concerned about pre-choosing what they will and will not be able to do as adults. In virtually every field, you'll find highly successful people with learning differences.

Your Remarkable Journey

B eing a parent is one of the hardest things anyone will ever face. And being a parent of a child who has a problem doubles the burden. As parents we worry about everything. Things we should and things we shouldn't do. Telling parents not to worry is as silly as the proctologist telling a patient to relax right before an examination. A parent who never worries is probably someone who either lives on another planet or just doesn't care. But it's *how* you worry and *what* you do about it that can make the difference between a good life for you and your family and one that's racked with dissension and disappointment. The advice of the young monk to me is still one of the most profound messages I ever received—"You do the best you can, given the circumstances of your life."

The fact you have gotten this far in the book says you not only care about your child, but you are willing to do something about it now. Not just worry. Not abdicate responsibility to professionals. And not wait until the future. The path you've decided to take is sacred. You're assuming the role of someone who is willing to serve—to do what is necessary to make your child happy and successful. You do this, not just for purely altruistic reasons, but as a way of benefiting everyone who will have contact with your child.

As parents, we've taken this journey together. As a professional, I've been given the privilege of walking with many parents on this path. I've found the experiences and emotions of parents with children who learn differently are remarkably similar. You're not alone, nor are your feelings so strange you need to hide them. Most children, with their parent's help, develop into remarkable people, going far beyond others dreams and expectations of them. Although the journey may be long, it will contain experiences that will gratify you forever. You're off to the Emerald City. Have a good trip and be well!

Useful Resources

The organizations listed below offer important information on education and support services. Others provide a forum for parents to ask questions of experts and other parents. Since there was a considerable overlap of services, I decided to list them alphabetically. The sites are local, state-wide, and national, and cover the United States and Canada. Even if you don't live in the area served by the website, I would still visit it. Every site listed here offers valuable information. You may also wish to also visit British and Irish sites. On your Internet browser type in "Learning Disorders Great Britain (or Ireland)." The approach taken in both countries is compatible with those of the United States and Canada. I've not listed the web addresses for the organizations, as it's easier to just type the organization's name into any search engine. It will take you directly to the site.

ADD ADHD Family Support Group of Parry Sound
ADDERs.ORG
ADDO Foundation
ADHD Support Website
AD-IN (Attention Deficit Information Network)
All Kinds of Minds
ARC of Baltimore Community Center
Association for Retarded Citizens (ARC)
Baltimore's Child
Berkeley Parent's Group
Boling Center for Developmental Disabilities
Canadian CEC
Canadian Hyperlexia Organization
Center for Families of Children with Disabilities
Children and Adults with Attention Deficit Disorder (CHADD)
The Children's Institute
Children with Disabilities
Connecticut Birth to Three Program
Consultative Group on Early Childhood Care and Development
Coordinated Campaign for Learning Disabilities

Council of Exceptional Children
Cumbria Learning Disabilities Partnership Website
Division of Early Childhood Missoula
Division TEACCH
East Bay Learning Disabilities Association
Education-a-Must
Ennis William Cosby Foundation
Etta Israel Center
Exceptional Parent Magazine
Family Alliance of Ontario
Family Support and Resource Network
Family Support Center of New Jersey
The Family Support Network of North Carolina
Family Village
Family Voices
Father's Network
Federation for Children With Special Needs
Federation of Invisible Disabilities
Foundation for People with Learning Disabilities
Gifted with Learning Disabilities Educational Network, Inc.
Greater Laconia Community Services
Indiana Institute of Disability and Community
Indiana Parent Information Network
International Dyslexia Association
Kennedy Krieger Institute
Kitty Petty ADD/LD Institute
Layered Curriculum
LD Online
LD Resources
Learning Disabilities Association of America
Learning Disabilities Association of Canada
Learning Disabilities Association of Maryland
Learning Disabilities Association of Massachusetts Commonwealth
Learning Center
Learning Disabilities Association of Montgomery County
Learning Disabilities Association of Ontario
Learning Disabilities Association of South Vancouver Island
Learning Disabilities Resource Community
Maternal Child Health Library
Melvin Smith Learning Center

Merrill Advanced Studies Center
Nathhan News
National ADDA (Attention Deficit Disorder Association)
National Association for the Education of African American Children with Learning Disabilities
National Center for Learning Disabilities
National Dissemination Center for Children with Disabilities
National Parent Network on Disabilities
National Parent to Parent Support and Information System
Nevada Parent Network
Nevada PEP
NLD (Nonverbal Learning Disability)
NLDA/Share Support (Nonverbal Learning Disorder Association)
Pacer Center
Pacer Center Minneapolis
Parent Educational Advocacy Training Center
Parent Network-Parent Information and Training Center of New York
The Parent Report.com
Parents
Parents Exchange
Parents Helping Parents
Parents Reaching Out
Parent's Unite for Kids
Parent to Parent of Georgia
Parent to Parent Support Group of Thurston County
Parent Training and Information Center of North Dakota
Partners Resource Network—Parent Training and Information Center
Peak Parent Center
Pediatric Services, Early Intervention
People with Attitudinal and Developmental Disabilities Association (PADDA)
Protection and Advocacy
Roehrer Institute
SmartKidswithLD.org
South Dakota Parent Connection
The Star Center
Stern Center
Support for Families of Children with Disabilities
Technical Assistance Alliance for Parent Centers
Tufts University Child & Family Web Guide

University Center for the Development of Language and Disability
Utah Parent Center
Whole Family.com
WINS Foundation
Wisconsin Council on Developmental Disabilities
World Association of Persons with Disabilities
YAI-National Institute for People with Disabilities

Developmental Milestones

Developmental milestones are *approximations* of when children should start using certain behaviors and understanding concepts. Just as all things in the beginning, these behaviors gradually develop. Often in children who are developing normally, you might have as much as a three-month difference on either side of the milestone. As you look at the milestones and compare your children with them, don't be too concerned if some skills appear to be missing. However, if a large number of behaviors are missing, you should contact the appropriate professional for a thorough assessment. The behaviors listed below have been compiled from The National Network for Child Care, Plainsense, the American Speech-Language-Hearing Association, and NICD. There was considerable overlap in the milestones for these four lists. Also, more importantly, they differed as when the behaviors should appear in children. To reduce the confusion, I arbitrarily used the latest date the behaviors should appear. Usually, it was only a gap of three to six months.

MOTOR SKILLS

3 months
Lifts head when held on shoulder
Lifts head and chest when lying on stomach
Turns head when lying on stomach
Follows person or object with eyes
Grasps rattle when offered
Moves, kicks arms and legs

6 months
Holds head steady when sitting with help
Vision is fully developed
Reaches for, grasps objects
Plays with toes
Helps hold bottle during feeding
Shakes rattle
Pulls to sitting position with help

Sits with support
Sits in high chair
Bounces when held in standing position
Rolls over
Good head control

9 months

Moves toys from hand to hand
Likes to be tickled

12 months

Drinks with cup with help
Feeds finger foods to self
Grasps small objects with thumb and index or forefinger
Uses finger to poke or point
Puts small objects into and out of container
Shows fear of falling from high places
Sits without support
Crawls
Pulls self up by holding onto furniture
Stands alone for short time
Walks with one hand held
Helps with dressing
Shakes, bangs, drops, and throws objects

18 months

Walks well
Stacks two blocks
Likes to push, pull, and dump objects
Likes to poke, twist, and squeeze
Enjoys flushing toilet and closing doors
Carries small objects in one hand while walking
Scribbles with crayon with little control
Waves bye-bye and claps hands
Rolls a ball to adult when requested
Pulls off hat, socks, and mittens
Turns pages in book
Carries a stuffed animal or doll

24 months

Drinks from cup
Stoops or squats
Drinks from a straw
Feeds self with spoon
Helps wash hands

Stacks two to four blocks
Tosses large ball
Opens cabinets, drawers, and boxes
Bends over to pick up toy without falling
Shows affection by returning kiss or hug
May become attached to a toy or blanket
Can take step backward
Enjoys sitting on and moving small-wheeled riding toys
Begins some bladder and bowel control
Walks up stairs
Likes to run, but can't always stop

2 ½ years

Does simple dressing
Kicks a ball

3 years

Stacks five to seven blocks
Feeds self
Climbs up and down slides by self
Opens doors
Uses toilet with help
Puts on shoes but can't tie them
Folds paper if shown
Hold glass in one hand
Pedals a tricycle
Dresses self with some help
Washes and dries hands
Walks on a line
Can jump over a six-inch barrier
Feeds self with some spilling
Walks short distances on tip toes
Can balance on one foot
Can jump in place
Able to draw circle and cross

4 years

Uses fork, knife, and spoon skillfully
Can hold pencil
Tries to write name
Draws with arm, but not small hand movements
Draws face
Tries to cut paper with blunt scissors
Sometimes unbuttons buttons

Tries to buckle, button, and lace
Completely undresses self
Brushes teeth with help
Dresses self with only a little help
Walks in a straight line
Pedals and steers a tricycle skillfully
Jumps over objects five to six inches high
Runs, jumps, hops, and skips around obstacles easily
Stacks ten or more blocks
Forms shapes and objects out of clay or Playdough, sometimes human or animal

5 years

Dresses without help
Draws triangles and squares
Can draw person with head, body, arms, and legs
Can print some letters
Learns to skip
Throws ball overhand
Catches bounced balls
Rides tricycle skillfully, likes bicycle with training wheels
Balances on either foot for five to ten seconds
Uses fork and knife well
Cuts on a line with scissors
Left- or right-hand dominance is established
Walks down stairs, alternating feet without using handrail
Jumps over low objects
Runs, gallops, and tumbles
Can skip and run on tiptoes
Can jump rope
Interested in performing tricks like standing on performing dance steps
Can learn complex body coordination (e.g., swimming, roller-skating, etc.)
May be able to tie shoelaces
May be able to copy simple designs and shapes

COGNITIVE/SENSORY SKILLS

3 months

Makes cooing sounds
Smiles when smiled to
Uses crying to indicate basic needs

Can be soothed by familiar voice
Anticipates being lifted
Reacts to "peek-a-boo" games

6 months
Opens mouth for a spoon
Imitates parent's familiar actions
Forgets items that can't be seen
Explores things with mouth

12 months
Copies sounds and actions
Moves body to sound of music
Has simple goal-directed behaviors
Looks for object moved out of sight

18 months
Scribbles with crayon
Attends to toy or book for two minutes
Follows simple directions accompanied by gestures
Answers simple questions nonverbally
Identifies object in book
Likes to take things apart

24 months
Points to familiar objects
Shows preference for certain toys
Likes to choose
Hums or tries to sing
Solves problems through simple trial and error
Says *please* and *thank you* with prompting
Laughs at silly actions
Enjoys familiar songs
Turns pages in book
Can put a round lid on a round pot
Needs time to change activities
Explores surroundings
Interested in learning how to use common objects

3 years
Enjoys playing with clay, Playdough
Pays attention for three minutes
Follows simple one-step commands
Can put together six-piece puzzle
Can count two to three objects
Identifies common colors

Remembers what happen yesterday
Knows what is and what is not food
Matches objects to pictures
Can solve simple problems
Interested in things that are similar and different
Can say age
Knows where things belong

4 years

Groups objects (e.g., foods, clothes, etc...)
Identifies colors
Feeds self with little spilling
Continues activity for ten to fifteen minutes
Names six to eight colors and three shapes
Counts one to seven objects out loud but not necessarily in right order
Asks many questions, especially about birth and death
Follows two unrelated questions
Understands big, little, tall, short, textures, distance, position, and time
Can place objects in line from largest to smallest
Understands immediate passage of time (e.g., before, but not calendar time)
Wants to know what happens next
Sorts by shape and color
Follows three instructions
Identifies situations leading to happiness, sadness, or anger
Can recognize some letters
Understands order of daily routines (e.g., breakfast before lunch, etc...)
Sings songs
Takes turns without always being reminded
Finishes activities
Has gender awareness
Put together puzzle of four to twelve pieces
Pours from small pitcher
Uses toilet alone
Catches a bouncing ball
Walks downstairs using a handrail and alternating feet
Swings, starting by self and keeping self going
Understand difference between fantasy and reality
Knows first and last names
Verbalizes daily activities and experiences
Can stack ten blocks
Able to hop
Can throw ball overhand

5 years

Has address and telephone number memorized

Counts on fingers

Likes to argue and reason

Knows basic colors

Understands story has beginning, middle, and end

Can remember stories and repeat them

Understands that books are read from left to right and top to bottom

Enjoys riddles and jokes

Draws pictures that represent animals, people, and objects

Enjoys tracing or copying letters

Counts up to ten objects

Interested in cause and effect

LANGUAGE AND SOCIAL SKILLS

3 months

Smiles

Vocalizes

Loves to be touched, held

Reacts to loud sounds

Cries differently for different needs

6 months

Babbling/sing-song sounds

Watches face when family member speaks

Tries to converse using babbling

Turns head to sound

Identifies familiar faces

Laughs

Screams if annoyed or angry

Smiles at self in mirror

9 months

Responds to name

Shows distress when toy is taken away

12 months

Babbles, almost sounds like language

Says first word

Offers toys to others but wants them back

Pushes away things not wanted

Uses one to three words

Recognizes words for common objects
Recognizes family members names
Talks to self
Tries to talk
Responds to another's emotion by imitation
Shows affection to familiar adults
Shows separation anxiety
Shows apprehension of strangers
Raises arm when wanting to be picked up
Listens when spoken to
Understands simple commands

18 months

Imitates words
Plays alone with tops on the floor
Enjoys audience and applause
Asks specifically for mother or father
Seeks attention

24 months

Plays alongside others more than with them
Sometimes takes turns with other children
Uses single-word utterances
Develops a sense of humor
Acts shy around strangers
Treats doll or stuffed animal as though it was alive
Applies pretend actions to others (e.g., feeding a doll)
Difficulty in expressing self
Possessive about caregiver's attention
Shows interest in dressing, brushing hair and teeth
Aware of parent's approval or disapproval
Enjoys repeatedly looking at same book
Has fears or nightmares
Likes make-believe games
Likes to be read to
Begins saying *no* to indicate independence
Has difficulty sharing
Very possessive
May not have patience
Gets angry, has temper tantrums
Shy around strangers
Refers to self by name
Tries to do things by self

Enjoys simple pretend games
Points to simple body parts
Needs constant supervision, gets into things
Hard time remembering rules
Can become physically aggressive
Understands simple verbs (eat, sleep, etc.)
Correctly pronounces most vowels
Correctly pronounces "n," "m," "ph," and "h" in beginning of words
Uses eight to ten words
Asks for common foods by name
Makes animal sounds
Begins using pronouns (e.g., mine)
Continually adds new words

2 ½ years

Uses two word utterances
Follows two-step commands without gestures

3 years

Uses fifty different words
Uses three-word combinations
Speech is understandable to strangers
Enjoys singing
Repeats simple rhymes
Knows one to three body parts
Knows simple spatial concepts (e.g., in, on)
Uses more pronouns (e.g., you, me, her, etc.)
Knows descriptive words (e.g., big, happy, etc.)
Can name at least one color correctly
Self-Centered
Asks to use toilet
Speech becoming clearer
May leave off endings of words
Answers simple questions
Demonstrates shame for wrongdoing
Imitates housework
Uses question inflections (e.g., My doll?)
Begins using plurals (dolls) and regular past tense (jumped)
75-80 percent of speech is intelligible
Uses three to five words in sentence
Has some normal stumbling over words
Follows simple directions
Enjoys repeating certain words or sounds

May show preference for one parent
Likes listening to rhymes
Enjoys helping with household tasks
Likes being silly and making others laugh
Enjoys hearing stories about self
Understands time concepts (e.g., now, soon, later, etc.)
Accepts suggestions
Can tell stories by looking at pictures in book

4 years

Uses most speech sounds, but distorts some
Able to describe use of objects
Has fun with language
Uses regular past tenses (e.g., pulled, etc.)
Expresses ideas and feelings
Uses verbs ending in "ing" (e.g., sitting, talking, etc.)
Repeats sentences
Boastful
Use articles when speaking (e.g., a, an, the, etc.)
Begins to understand danger
Asks direct questions (e.g., "May I?")
Wants explanations
Easier separation from parents
Begins bargaining
Tries to change rules in middle of game
Likes to shock by using forbidden words
Expresses anger verbally rather than physically
Talks about action
Enjoys dramatic play and role playing
Sentences are complex (e.g., "I broke the jar after I had a cookie")
Recognizes familiar words in books or signs (e.g., stop)

5 years

Understands more complex spatial concepts (e.g., behind, next to)
Understands 13,000 words
Understands complex questions
Uses five to eight words in a sentence
May have articulation problems with long words
Uses some irregular past tense verbs (e.g., ran, fell, etc.)
Describes how to do things
Defines words
Lists items belonging to a category (e.g., animals, etc.)
Invents games with simple rules

Sometimes confuses fantasy with reality
Fearful of loud noises, the dark, animals, and some people
Likes to try new things and take risks
Likes to make own decisions
Becomes sensitive to feelings of others
Prefers company of one to two children
Likes to feel grown-up
Begins developing understanding of right and wrong
Plays contentedly and independently
Understands rules
Enjoys giving and receiving
Likes to collect things
Sometimes need to be alone
Can understand relationships
Sometimes takes turns and shares
Tests motor skills and muscular strength
Carries on conversations with children and adults
Excludes some children from play
May be bossy
Answers *why* questions.
Understands more than 2,000 words
Understands time sequences (e.g., what happened first, second, etc.)
Carries out a series of three directions
Understands rhyming
Can carry on a conversation
Sentences of up to eight or more words
Uses imagination to create stories

Notes

CHAPTER ONE

1. Jennifer P. Zickel & Ellen Arnold, "Connecting Brain Research with Dimensions of Learning," *Educational Leadership* 59 (Sept. 2001): 38–41.

2. Beena Johnson, "Behavior Problems in Children and Adolescents with Learning Disabilities," *Internet Journal of Mental Health*, (June 2002): 45–54.

3. Roper Starch Worldwide,. *Measuring Progress in Public & Parental Understanding of Learning Disabilities,* Prepared for the Emily Hall Tremaine Foundation (March 2000).

4. Howard S. Adelman & Linda Taylor, "Classifying Students by Inferred Motivation to Learn," *Learning Disability Quarterly* 6 (Spring 1983): 201–6.

5. Emanuel Tirosh, Ayala Cohen, Joseph Berger, Michael Davidovitch, & Michal Cohen-Ophir, "Neurodevelopmental and Behavioral Characteristics in Learning Disabilities and Attention Deficit Disorder," *European Journal of Pediatric Neurology* 5 (June 2001): 253–58.

6. Mel Levine, *A Mind at a Time* (New York: Simon & Schuster, 2002).

7. Roger J. Ingham, Peter J. Fox, Janis Costello Ingham, & Frank Zamarripa, "Is Overt-Stuttered Speech a Prerequisite for the Neural Activations Associated with Chronic Developmental Stuttering?," *Brain & Language* 75 (Nov. 2000): 163–94.

8. Sally E. Shaywitz & Bennett. A. Shaywitz, "Unlocking Learning Disabilities: The Neurological Basis," in *Preventing Reading Difficulties in Children*, ed. S. C. Cramer & W. Ellis (Washington, D. C.: National Academy Press, 1998), p. 98.

9. E. A. Hayes, C. M. Warrier, T. G. Nicol, S. G. Zecker, & N. Kraus, "Neural Plasticity Following Auditory Training in Children with Learning Problems," *Clinical Neurophysiology* 114 (Apr. 2003): 673–84

10. Ibid.

11. Sally Shaywitz, *Overcoming Dyslexia* (New York: Alfred Knopf, 2003).

12. Yoshio Imahori, Ryou Fujii,, Masaki Yoshio Ohmori, and Kenji Nakajima, "Neural Features of Recovery from CNS Injury Revealed by PET in Human Brain," *Neuroreport* 18 (Jan. 1999): 117–21.

13. See note 11.

14. Axel Riecker, Dirk Wildgruber, & Hermann Ackermann. "Reorganization of Speech Production Oat the Motor Cortex and Cerebellum Following Capsular Infarction: a Follow-up Functional Magnetic Resonance Imaging Study," *Neurocase* 8 (Dec. 2002): 417–23.

15. W. Murrell, G. R. Bushell, J. Livesey, J. McGrath, K. P. MacDonald, P. R. Bates, & S A. Macay, "Neurogenesis in Adult Human," *Neuroreport* 26 (Apr. 1996): 1189–94.

16. J. D. Churchill, R. Balvez, S. Colcombe, R. A. Swain, & A. F. Kramer, "Exercise, Experience and the Aging Brain," *Neurobiology of Aging* 23 (Sept.–Oct. 2002): 941–55.

17. Blas Espinoza-Varas, "Perception of Complex Auditory Patterns by Humans," in *The Comparative Psychology of Audition: Perceiving Complex Sounds,* ed. Robert J. Dooling &Stewart Hulse, (Mahwah, N. J.: Lawrence Erlbaum Assoc, 1989), 67–94.

18. Dale H. Schunk. *Learning Theories: An Educational Perspective*,3rd ed. (Englewood Cliffs, N. J.: Prentice-Hall, 1999).

19. Mark R. Rosenzweig, S. Marc Breedlove, & Arnold L. Leiman, *Biological Psychology: An Introduction to Behavioral, Cognitive, and Clinical Neuroscience,* 3rd ed. (Sunderland, MA: Sinauer Associates, 2001).

20. Dustin F. Sentz, Matthew W. Kirkhar, Charles LoPresto, & Steven Sobelman, "Intrusive Effects of Implicitly Processed Information on Explicit Memory," *Perceptual & Motor Skills* 94 (Feb. 2002): 241–50.

21. Nikos K. Logothetis, David A. Leopold, & David L. Sheinberg, "Neural Mechanisms of Perceptual Organization," in *Neural Basis of Consciousness. Advances in Consciousness Research,* ed. Naoyuki Osaka (Amsterdam: John Benjamin Publishing Company, 2003), 87–103.

22. Peter W. Halligan, Gereon R. Fink, John C. Marshall, & Giuseppe Vallar, "Spatial Cognition: Evidence From Visual Neglect," *Trends in Cognitive Sciences* 7 (Mar. 2003): 125–33.

23. Raymond W. Gibbs, Jr., "Embodied Experience and Linguistic Meaning," *Brain & Language* 84 (Jan. 2003): 1–15.

24. K. Richard Ridderinkhof, "Attention and Selection in the Growing Child: Views Derived from Developmental Psychophysiology," *Biological Psychology* 54 (Oct. 2000) 55–106.

25. Marcia J. Scherer, "Individual Learner Preferences and Needs," in *Connecting to Learn: Educational and Assistive Technology for People with Disabilities,* ed. Marica J. Scherer (Washington, D. C.: American Psychological Association, 2004), 161–81.

26. Howard Eichenbaum, *The Cognitive Neuroscience of Memory* (New York: Oxford University Press, 2002).

27. Nelson Cowan, John N. Towse, Zoe Hamilton, S. Scott Saults, Emily M. Elliott, Jebby F. Lacey, Matthew V. Moreno, & Graham J. Hitch, "Children's Working-Memory Processes: A Response-Timing Analysis," *Journal of Experimental Psychology* 132 (Mar. 2003): 113–32.

28. Una M. Z. Hutton and John N. Towse, "Short-Term Memory and Working Memory as Indices of Children's Cognitive Skills," *Memory* 9 (July 2001): 383–94.

29. Patricia J. Bauer, "Building Toward a Past: Construction of a Reliable Long-Term Recall Memory System," in *Representation, Memory, and Development: Essays in Honor of Jean Mandler,* ed. Nancy L. Stein, Patricia Bauer, et al. (Mahwah, N. J.: Lawrence Erlbaum Associates, 2002) 17–42.

30. Charles Hulme and Susie Mackenzie, *Working Memory and Severe Learning Difficulties* (Mahwah, N. J.: Lawrence Erlbaum Associates, 1992).

31. Howard Eichenbaum, *The Cognitive Neuroscience of Memory* (New York: Oxford University Press, 2002).

32. Larry R. Squire & Eric R. Kandel, *Memory: From Mind to Molecules* (New York: Scientific American Library, 1999).

33. Pramod K. Dash, Sara A. Mach, & Sonja Blum, "Intrahippocampal Wortmann in Infusion Enhances Long-Term Spatial and Contextual Memories," *Learning & Memory* 9 (July–Aug. 2002): 167–77.

34. Anita R. Bowles & Alice F. Healy, "The Effects of Grouping on the Learning and Long-Term Retention of Spatial and Temporal Information," *Journal of Memory & Language* 48 (Jan. 2003): 92–102.

35. Scott C. Brown & Fergus I. M. Craik, "Encoding and Retrieval of Information," in *The Oxford Handbook of Memory,* eds. Endel Tulving & Fergus I. M. Craik (New York: Oxford University Press 2000), p. 93–107.

36. Bradley J. Morris & Vladimir Sloutsky, "Children's Solutions of Logical Versus Empirical Problems: What's Missing and What Develops?" *Cognitive Development* 16 (Oct.–Dec. 2001): 907–28.

37. J. N. Towse, G. J. Hitch, & U. Hutton, "On the Nature of the Relationship Between Processing Activity and Item Retention in Children," *Journal of Experimental Child Psychology* 82 (2002): 156–84.

38. P. J. Bauer, "Long-Term Recall Memory: Behavioral and Neuro-developmental Changes in the First 2 Years of Life," *Current Directions in Psychological Science* 11(Aug. 2002): 137–41.

39. H. L. Swanson & L. Siegel, "Learning Disabilities as a Working Memory Deficit," *Issues in Education* 7 (Spring 2001): 1–47.

40. Dabie Nabuzoka, "Teacher Ratings and Peer Nominations of Bullying and Other Behavior of Children With and Without Learning Difficulties," *Educational Psychology* 23 (Jun. 2003): 307–22.

41. Pia Williams, "Preschool Routines, Peer Learning, and Participation," *Scandinavian Journal of Educational Research* 45 (Dec. 2001): 317–39.

42. Nancy Nordman, "The marginalization of students with learning disabilities as a function of school philosophy and practice," *Journal of Moral Education* 30 (Sept. 2001): 273–86.

43. Pema Chodron, *When Things Fall Apart* (Boston: Shambhala Publications, 2000).

44. California Department of Education, No. J-7CSR (01/02)—Special Instruction. Report on Enrollment for Kindergarten and Grades 1 through 3 for Districts in Class Size Reduction Program, 2001–02.

45. Douglas Mitchell, Sara Ann Beach, & Gary Dadarak, "Modeling the Relationship Between Achievement and Class Size: A Re-Analysis of the Tennessee Project STAR Data," *Peabody Journal of Education* 67 (1992).

46. Bureau of Labor Statistics, U. S. Department of Labor, *Occupational Outlook Handbook*, 2002–03 Edition for Teacher Assistants.

47. Ibid.

48. Nancy K. French & Robin H. Lock, "Maximize paraprofessional services for students with learning disabilities," *Intervention in School & Clinic* 38 (Sept. 2002): 50–55.

49. Richard Culatta & Stanley A. Goldberg, *Stuttering Therapy: An Integrated Approach to Theory and Practice* (Needham Height, Mass.: Allyn & Bacon, 1997).

50. Thomas. E. Scruggs & Marge. A. Mastropieri, "On Babies and Bathwater: Addressing the Problems of Identification Characterization of Learning Disabilities," *Learning Disability Quarterly* 25 (Summer 2002): 155–68.

51. Laura E. Berk, *Child Development* (Needham Heights, Mass.: Pearson Allyn & Bacon, 2002).

52. Stanley A. Goldberg, *Clinical Skills for Speech-Language Pathologists* (San Diego: Singular Publishing Group, 1997).

53. See note 11.

54. Mel Levine, *A Mind at a Time* (New York: Simon & Schuster, 2002).

55. Chad Hamilton, Douglas Fuchs, Lynn S. Fuchs, & Robert Holley, "Rates of Classroom Participation and the Validity of Sociometry," *School Psychology Review* 29 (Special Issue 2000): 251–76.

56. National Network for Child Care (www. nncc. org/Child. Dev/dc25) (2003).

57. Plainsense (www. plainsense. com/Health/Childrens/milestones) (2003).

58. American Speech Language Hearing Association (www. asha. org/speech/development/child) (2003).

59. National Institute of Child Health and Human Development (NICHD) (http://secc. rti. org).

60. Glenn J. Doman, *How to Multiply Your Baby's Intelligence* (New York: Doubleday, 1984).

61. Cindy C. Moseman, "Primary Teachers' Beliefs about Family Competence to Influence Classroom Practices," *Early Education & Development* 14 (Apr. 2003): 125–53.

62. Edward G. Feil, Hill Walker, Herbert Severson, & Alison Ball, "Proactive Screen for Emotional/Behavioral Concerns in Head Start Preschools: Promising Practices and Challenges in Applied Research," *Behavioral Disorders* 26 (Nov. 2000): 13–25.

63. See note 52.

CHAPTER TWO

1. Lily L. Dyson, "Children with Learning Disabilities Within the Family Context: A Comparison with Siblings in Global Self-Concept, Academic Self-Perception, and Social Competence," *Learning Disabilities Research & Practice* 18 (Feb. 2003): 1–9.

2. James William Higgins, Randy Lee Williams, & T. F. McLaughlin, "The Effects of a Token Economy Employing Instructional Consequences for a Third-Grade Student with Learning Disabilities: A Data-Based Case Study," *Education & Treatment of Children* 24 (Feb. 2001): 99–106.

3. *The Wizard of Oz*, Metro-Goldwyn-Mayer, Produced by Mervyn LeRoy, Directed by Victor Fleming, Screenplay by Noel Langley, Forence Ryerson, Edgar Allan Woolf, & John Lee Mahin, 1939.

4. *Shall We Dance?*, Produced by Allainira Pictures, Directed by Masayuki Suo, Screenplay by Masayuki Suo, 1996.

5. Bob Gates, Robert Newell, and Jane Wray, "Behavior Modification and Gentle Teaching Workshops: Management of Children with Learning Problems," *Journal of Advanced Nursing* 34 (Apr. 2001): 86–95.

6. Al Pocock, Stan Lambros, Meagan Karvonen, David W. Test, Bob Algozzine, Wendy Wood, & James E. Martin, "Successful Strategies for Promoting Self-Advocacy Among Students with LD: The Lead Group," *Intervention in School & Clinic* 37 (Mar. 2002): 209–16.

7. Keith Park, "Oliver Twist: An Exploration of Interactive Storytelling and Object Use in Communication," *British Journal of Special Education* 28 (Mar. 2001): 18–23.

8. J. Heidi Gralinski & Claire B. Kopp, "Everyday Rules for Behavior: Mothers' Requests to Young Children," *Developmental Psychology* 29 (May 1993): 573–84.

9. Gerald R. Adams, Bruce A. Ryan, Maria Ketsetzis, & Leo Keating, "Rule Compliance and Peer Sociability: A Study of Family Process, School-Focused Parent-Child Interactions, and Children's Classroom Behavior," *Journal of Family Psychology* 14 (June 2000): 237–50.

10. Nancy Eisenberg, Carlos Valiete, Richard A. Fabes, Cynthia L. Smith, Mark Reiser, Stephanie A. Shepard, Sandra H. Losoya, Ivanna K. Guthrie, Bridget C. Murphy, & Amanda J. Cumberland, "The Relations of Effortful Control and Ego Control to Children's Resiliency and Social Functioning," *Developmental Psychology* 39 (July 2003): 761–76.

11. Batya Elbaum & Sharon Vaughn, "For Which Students with Learning Disabilities are Self-Concept Interventions Effective?" *Journal of Learning Disabili*ties 36 (Mar. /Apr. 2003): 101–8.

12. George G. Bear, Kathleen M. Minke, & Maureen A. Manning, "Self-Concept of Students with Learning Disabilities: A Meta-Analysis," *School Psychology Review* 31, Issue 3 (2002): 405–27.

13. Paul Ramcharan & Gordon Grant, "Views and Experiences of People with Intellectual Disabilities and Their Families," *Journal of Applied Research in Intellectual Disabilities* 14, Issue 4 (2001): 348–63

14. Ellen A. Skinner, James G. Wellborn, & James P. Connel, "What it Takes to Do Well in School and Whether I've Got It: A Process Model of Perceived Control and Children's Engagement and Achievement in School," *Journal of Educational Psychology* 82 (March 1990): 22–32.

15. Karen S. Kirk, "Relations Between Measures of Attention and Memory in the Assessment of Children with Attentional Difficulties," Ph. D. diss., West Virginia University, (2001).

16. Richard P. Feynman, *Surely You're Joking Mr. Feynman* (New York: Bantam Books, 1989).

17. Kenneth E. Moyer, "Attention Spans of Children for Experimentally Designed Toys," *Journal of Genetic Psychology* 87 (1955): 187–201.

18. Chogyam Trungpa, *Great Eastern Sun* (Boston: Shambhala, 1999).

19. D. M. Kivlighan, D. D. Mullison, D. F. Flohr, & S. Proudman, et al., "The Interpersonal Structure of 'Good' Versus 'Bad' Group Counseling Sessions: A Multiple-Case Study" *Psychotherapy* 29 (Mar. 1992): 500–8.

20. Pema Chodron, *When Things Fall Apart* (Boston: Shambhala, 2000).

21. Madhavi Jayanthi & Marilyn Friend, "Interpersonal Problem Solving: A Selective Literature Review to Guide Practice," *Journal of Educational and Psychological Consultation* 3, Issue 1 (1992): 39–53.

22. Sharon Vaughn, Batya Elbaum, & Alison Gould Boardman, "The Social Functioning of Students with Learning Disabilities: Implications for Inclusion," *Exceptionality* 9 (June 2001): 305–10.

23. Adele Diamond, Anne Churchland, Loren Cruess, & Natasha Z. Kirkham, "Early Developments in the Ability to Understand the Relation Between Stimulus and Reward," *Developmental Psychology* 35 (Nov. 1999) 1507–17.

24. A. Sagie, D. Elizur, & M. Koslowsky, "Effect of Participation in Strategic and Tactical Decisions on Acceptance of Planned Change," *Journal of Social Psychology* 130 (September 1990): 459–65.

25. C. Ellinwood, "The Young Child in Person-Centered Family Therapy," *Journal of Counseling Psychology* 42 (June 1989): 105–15.

26. Bobbie Kalman, *Games From Long Ago* (New York: Crabtree Publications, 1995).

27. Arlette N. Braman, *Kids Around the World Play!: The Best Fun and Games From Many Lands* (New York: John Wiley & Sons, 2002).

28. Kjeld Kirk Kristiansen, *Ultimate Lego Book* (New York: Dorling Kindersley Publishing, 1999).

29. Stanley A. Goldberg, *Clinical Skills for Speech-Language Pathologists* (San Diego: Singular Publishing, 1997).

30. William R. Charlesworth, "Co-operation and Competition: Contributions to an Evolutionary and Developmental Model," *International Journal of Behavioral Development* 19 (Mar. 1996): 25–38.

CHAPTER THREE

1. Ann-Margret Rydell, Lisa Berlin, & Gunilla Bohlin, "Emotionality, Emotion Regulation, and Adaptation Among 5- to 8-Year-Old Children," *Emotion* 3 (March 2003): 30–47.

2. Garry Hornby & Roger Kidd, "Transfer From Special to Mainstream—Ten Years Later," *British Journal of Special Education* 28 (Mar. 2001): 10–17.

3. Clancy Blair, "School Readiness: Integrating Cognition and Emotion in a Neurobiological Conceptualization of Children's Functioning at School Entry," *American Psychologist* 57 (Feb. 2002): 111–27.

4. L. A. Smith & J. M. Williams, "Children's understanding of the physical, cognitive and social consequences of impairments," *Child: Care, Health & Development* 27 (Nov. 2001): 603–17.

5. NICD Early Child Care Research Network, "Does Quality of Child Care Affect Child Outcomes at Age 4 1/2?" *Developmental Psychology* 39 (May 2003): 451–69.

6. Linds Clare, Barbara A. Wilson, Gina Carter, Ilona Roth, & John R. Hadges, *"Relearning Face-Name Associations in Early Alzheimer's Disease,"* Neuropsychology 16 (October 2002): 538–47.

7. Hubert D. Zimmer, Tore Helstrup, & Johannes Engelkamp, "Pop-Out into Memory: A Retrieval Mechanism that is Enhanced with the Recall of Subject-Performed Tasks," *Journal of Experimental Psychology: Learning, Memory, and Cognition* 26 (May 2000): 658–70.

8. Eleanor E. Maccoby, "The Role of Parents in the Socialization of Children: An Historical Overview," *Developmental Psychology* 28 (Nov. 1992): 1006–17.

9. Virginia P. Richmond & James C. McCroskey, *Nonverbal Behavior in Interpersonal Relations,* 5th ed. (New York: Pearson Allyn & Bacon, 2003).

10. Kathryn E. Barnard & Georgina A. Sumner, "Promoting Awareness of the Infant's Behavioral Patterns: Elements of Anticipatory Guidance for Parents," in *The Infant and Family in the Twenty-First Century*, eds. Joao Gomes-Predro & Kevin J. Nugent (New York: Brunner-Routledge, 2002) 139–57.

11. Shalom M. Fisch, Susan K. McCann Brown, & David I. Cohen, "Young Children's Comprehension of Educational Television: The Role of Visual Information and Intonation," *Media Psychology* 3 (2001): 365–78.

12. David W. Allbritton, Gail KcKoon, & Roger Ratcliff, "Reliability of Prosodic Clues for Resolving Syntactic Ambiguity," *Journal of Experimental Psychology: Learning, Memory, and Cognition* (May 1996): 714–35.

13. David J. Lewkowicz, "Infants' Response to the Audible and Visible Properties of the Human Face: 1. Role of Lexical-Syntactic Content, Temporal Synchrony, Gender, and Manner of Speech," *Developmental Psychology* 32 (March 1996): 347–66.

14. Robert E. Owens, Jr., *Language Development* (New York: Macmillan, 1992).

15. Daniel S. Sessinger, Alan Fogel, & K. Laurie Dickson, "All Smiles Are Positive, But Some Smiles Are More Positive Than Others," *Developmental Psychology* 37 (Sept. 2001): 642–53.

16. Bonnie Jean Raingruber, "Settling into and Moving in a Climate of Care: Styles and Patterns of Interaction Between Nurse Psychotherapists and Clients," *Perspectives in Psychiatric Care* 37 (Jan.–Mar. 2001): 15–27.

17. Stanley A. Goldberg, *Clinical Intervention: A Philosophy and Methodology for Clinical Practice* (New York: Merrill, 1993).

18. Mark Selikowitz, *Down Syndrome: The Facts* (New York: Oxford University Press, 1997).

19. Terry Rizzo, Rebecca J. Woodard, & Deborah J. Buswell, "Learning Disabilities, Class Placement, and Depression," *Adapted Physical Activity Quarterly* 19 (Oct. 2002): 513–515.

20. Deborah C. Deidel, Samuel M. Turner, & Tracy L. Morris, "The Behavioral Treatment of Childhood Social Phobia," *Journal of Consulting and Clinical Psychology* 68 (December 2000): 1072–80.

21. William F. Arsenio, Sharon Cooperman, & Anthony Lover, "Affective Predictors of Preschoolers' Aggression and Peer Acceptance: Direct and Indirect Effects," *Developmental Psychology* 36 (July 2000): 438–48.

CHAPTER FOUR

1. Paul A. McDermoot, Nanette M. Leigh, & Marlo A. Perry, "Development and Validation of the Preschool Learning Behaviors Scale," *Psychology in the Schools* 39 (July 2002): 353–55.

2. Huey-Ling Lin, Frank R. Lawrence, & Jeffrey Gorrell, "Kindergarten Teachers' Views of Children's Readiness for School," *Early Childhood Research Quarterly* 18 (Summer 2003): 225–37.

3. Peter K. Smith, Helen Cowie, & Mark Blades, *Understanding Children's Development*, 4th ed. (Malden, Mass.: Blackwell Publishers, 2003).

4. Richard M. Shiffrin, "Modeling Memory and Perception," *Cognitive Science* 27 (May–June 2003): 341–378.

5. Mel Levine, *A Mind at a Time* (New York: Simon & Schuster, 2002).

6. Robert . J. Sternberg& Elena L. Grigorenko, "Learning Disabilities, Schooling, and Society," *Phi Delta Kappan* 83 (Dec. 2001): 335–38.

7. IDEAPractices, *300. 7 Child With a Disability, (b) Children Aged 3 Through 9 Experiencing Developmental Delays*, 2003, ideapractices. org.

8. National Education Association, *Special Education and the Individuals with Disabilities Education Act*, NEA Website (2003).

CHAPTER FIVE

1. D. J. Gillan & R. Lewis, "A Componential Model of Human Interaction with Graphs: I. Linear Regression Modeling," *Human Factors* 36 (Dec. 1994): 419–40.

2. J. E. Ramsay & K. Oatley, "Designing Minimal Computer Manuals from Scratch: Computers and Writing: Issues and Implementations," *Instructional Science*, Special Issue 21 (1992): 85–98.

3. *City Slickers*, Produced by Columbia, Directed by Ron Howard, Screenplay by Lowell Ganz & Babaloo Mandel, 1991.

4. Peter. A. Frensch & Carolyn S. Miner, "Effects of Presentation Rate and Individual Differences in Short-Term Memory Capacity on an Indirect Measure of Serial Learning," *Memory and Cognition* 22 (Jan. 1994): 95–110.

5. Jean C. Krause, "Investigating Alternative Forms of Clear Speech: The Effects of Speaking Rate and Speaking Mode on Intelligibility," *Journal of the Acoustical Society of America* 112 (Nov. 2002): 2165–72.

6. Frank E. Musiek, Jane A. Baran, & Elaine Schochat, "Selected Management Approaches to Central Auditory Processing Disorders," *Scandinavian Audiology* 28, Supplement 51(1999): 63–75.

7. Tracy A. Lanvin & D. Geoffrey Hall, "Domain Effects in Lexical Development: Learning Words for Foods and Toys," *Cognitive Development* 16 (Oct.–Dec. 2001): 929–50.

8. Peter. A. Frensch & Axel Buchner, "Implicit Learning of Unique and Ambiguous Serial Transitions in the Presence and Absence of a Distractor Task," *Journal of Experimental Psychology Learning, Memory, and Cognition* 20 (May 1994): 567–84.

9. John J. Chelonis, Jennifer L. Daniels-Shaw, Donna J. Blake, & Merle G. Paule, "Developmental Aspects of Delayed Matching-to-Sample Task Performance in Children," *Neurotoxicology & Teratology* 22 (Sept.–Oct 2000) 683–94.

10. M. E. Toplak, J. J. Rucklidge, R. Hetherinton, S. C. F. John, & Rosemary Tannock, "Time Perception Deficits in Attention-Deficit/Heractivity Disorder and Comorbid Reading Difficulties in Children and Adolescent Samples," *Journal of Child Psychology & Psychiatry & Allied Disciplines* 44 (Sept. 2003): 888–903.

11. D. E. Broadbent, "Listening to One of Two Synchronous Messages," *Journal of Experimental Psychology General* 121 (Aug. 1992): 125–27.

12. J. D. Klein & E. Freitag, "Effects of Using an Instructional Game on Motivation and Performance," *Journal of Educational Research* 84 (Oct. 1991): 303–8.

13. H. L. Dortch & C. A. Trombly, "The Effects of Education on Hand Use with Industrial Workers in Repetitive Jobs," *American Journal of Occupational Therapy* 44 (Oct. 1990): 777–82.

14. Lawrence M. Ward, "Supramodal and Modality-Specific Mechanisms for Stimulus-Driven Shifts of Auditory and Visual Attention: Shifts of Visual Attention," *Canadian Journal of Experimental Psychology*, Special Issue 48 (June 1994): 242–59.

15. Ibid.

16. Vonnie M. DeCecco & Mary M. Gleason, "Using Graphic Organizers to Attain Relational Knowledge from Expository Text," *Journal of Learning Disabilities* 35 (July–Aug. 2002) 306–20.

17. J. Sweller & P. Chandler, "Why Some Material is Difficult to Learn," *Cognition and Instruction* 12 (Apr. 1994): 185–233.

18. Jean Piaget, *The Origins of Intelligence in Children* (New York: The Norton Library, 1963).

19. D. Gopher, M. Weil & D. Siegel, "Practice Under Changing Priorities: An Approach to the Training of Complex Skills: The Learning Strategies Program: An examination of the Strategies in Skill Acquisition," *Acta Psychologica*, Special Issue 71 (Feb. 1989): 147–77.

20. C. Frankish, "Intonation and Auditory Grouping in Immediate Serial Recall: Donald Broadbent and Applied Cognitive Psychology," *Applied Cognitive Psychology*, Special Issue 9 (Jan. 1995) 14–58.

21. David C. Riccio & Jennifer K. Ackil, "Forgetting of Stimulus Attributes: Methodological Implications for Assessing Associative Phenomena," *Psychological Bulletin* 112 (December 1992): 433–45.

22. Rita . C. Naremore & Deborah R. Harman, *Language Intervention with School-Aged Children* (San Diego, Calif.: Singular Publishing, 1995).

23. J. L. Shefelbine, "Student Factors Related to Variability in Learning Word Meanings From Context," *Journal of Reading Behavior* 22 (Feb. 1990): 71–97.

24. E. Wood, D. R. Needham, J. Williams, & R. Roberts, "Evaluating the Quality and Impact of Mediators for Learning When Using Associative Memory Strategies," *Applied Cognitive Psychology* 7 (Dec. 1994): 679–92.

25. N. Balluerka, "The Influence of Instructions, Outlines, and Illustrations on the Comprehension and Recall of Scientific Texts," *Contemporary Educational Psychology* 20 (Dec. 1995): 369–75.

26. D. B. Willingham, W. J. Koroshetz, J. R. Treadwell, and J. P. Bennett, "Comparison of Huntington's and Parkinson's Disease Patients' Use of Advanced Information," *Neuropsychology* 9 (Jan. 1995): 39–46.

27. J. C. Snapp and J. A. Glover, "Advance Organizers and Study Questions," Journal of Educational Research 83 (May/Jun 1990): 266–71.

28. A. Gillstrom and J. Ronnberg, "Prediction Accuracy of Text Recall: Ease, Effort, and Familiarity," *Scandinavian Journal of Psychology* 35 (Winter 1994): 367–85.

29. H. R. Miller & S. F. Davis, "Recall of Boxed Material in Textbooks," *Bulletin of the Psychonomic Society* 31 (Jan 1993): 31–32.

30. Lawrence M. Ward, "Supramodal and Modality-Specific Mechanisms for Stimulus-Driven Shifts of Auditory and Visual Attention: Shifts of Visual Attention," *Canadian Journal of Experimental Psychology,* Special Issue 48 (June 1994): 242–59.

31. Joseph Biederman, "Diagnostic Continuity Between Child and Adolescent ADHD: Findings from a Longitudinal Clinical Sample," *Journal of the American Academy of Child & Adolescent Psychiatry* 37 (Mar. 1998): 305–13.

32. A. Bandura, *Principles of Behavior Modification* (New York: Holt, Rinehart & Winston, 1969).

33. Ursula K. Le Guin, *The Left Hand of Darkness* (New York: Ace Books, 1991), p. 220.

34. Deborah J. Stipek, "Motivation and Instruction," in *Handbook of Educational Psychology*, eds. David C. Berliner & Robert C. Calfee (New York: John Wiley & Sons, 1996) 85–113.

35. G. T. Wilson, "Behavior Therapy," in *Current Psychotherapies*, eds. Raymond J. Corsini & Danny Wedding (Itasca, Ill.: Peacock, 1989), pp. 241–82.

36. Stanley A. Goldberg, *Clinical Skills* (San Diego: Singular Publishing Group, 1997).

37. Kirby Deater-Deckard, Jennifer E. Lansford, Kenneth A. Doge, Gregory S. Pettit, & John E. Bates, "The Development of Attitudes About Physical Punishment: An 8-Year Longitudinal Study," *Journal of Family Psychology* 17 (Sept. 2003): 351–360.

38. C. B. Ferster, "Withdrawal of Positive Reinforcement as Punishment," *Science* 126 (1957): 509.

39. George W. Holden, "Perspectives on the Effects of Corporal Punishment: Comment on Gershoff," *Psychological Bulletin* 128 (July 2002): 590–95.

40. Howard N. Sloane, Jr. & Bruce D. Mac Aulay, eds., *Operant Procedures in Remedial Speech and Language Training* (New York: Houghton Mifflin Co., 1968).

41. T. Rowand Robinson, Stephen W. Smith, M. David Miller, Mary T. Brownell, "Cognitive Behavior Modification of Hyperactivity-Impulsivity and Aggression: A Meta-Analysis of School-Based Studies," *Journal of Educational Psychology* 91 (June 1999): 195–203.

42. B. F. Skinner, *Science and Human Behavior* (New York: Macmillian, 1957).

43. See note 40.

44. Henry C. Rickard, Carl B. Clements, & Jerry W. Willis, "The Effects of Contingent and Noncontingent Token Reinforcement Upon Classroom Performance," *Psychological Reports* 27 (Dec. 1970): 903–8.

45. George von Hilsheimer, "The Teacher as a Human Engineer," *Academic Therapy* 6 (Winter 1970–1971): 135–149.

46. Amy Zenzel, Lydia C. Jackson, Jennifer R. Brendle, & Keri Penna, "Autobiographical Memories Associated with Feared Stimuli in Fearful and Nonfearful Individuals," *Anxiety, Stress & Cooping: An International Journal* 16 (Mar. 2003): 1–15.

47. Michael H. Palmer, "A Description of a Rapid Desensitization Procedure," *Behavior Therapist* 25 (Oct. 2002): 171

48. Willem A. Hoffmann, "The Effect of Behavioral Therapy on Dog Phobia Response Patterns," *Anthrozoos* 14 (2001): 29–37.

49. Louise Maxfield, "Single Session Treatment of Test Anxiety with Eye Movement Desensitization and Reprocessing (EMDR)," *International Journal of Stress Management* 7 (Apr. 2000): 87–101.

50. LeAlelle Phelps, Deborah Coc, & Ellen Bajorek, "School Phobia and Separation Anxiety: Diagnostic and Treatment Comparisons," *Psychology in the Schools* 29 (Oct. 1992): 384–94.

51. Adebowale Akande, "Treating Anger: The Misunderstood Emotion in Children," *Early Child Development & Care* 132 (1996): 75–91.

52. Judith A. Cohen, Lucy Berliner, & John S. March, "Treatment of Children and Adolescents," eds. Edna B. Foa, Terence M. Keane, et al. (New York: Guilford Press, 2000), pp. 106–38.

53. Cynthia A. Erdley, "A Social Goals Perspective on Children's Social Competence," *Journal of Emotional & Behavioral Disorders* 7 (Fall 1999): 156–67.

54. Robbie Case and Michael P. Mueller, "Differentiation, Integration, and Covariance Mapping as Fundamental Processes in Cognitive and Neurological Growth," in *The Mechanisms of Cognitive Development*, eds. James McClelland & Robert Siegler (Mahwah, N. J.: Lawrence Erlbaum Associates, 2001), pp. 185–219.

55. W. Diedrich & J. Bangert, *Articulation Learning*, (San Diego: College Hill, 1980).

56. Janis Costello, "Techniques of Therapy Based Operant Conditioning" in *General Principles of Therapy*, ed. William Perkins (New York: Thieme-Stratton, 1980).

57. Pierre Maquet, "The Role of Sleep in Learning and Memory," *Science* 294 (Nov. 2001): 1048–2.

58. Stanley A. Goldberg, *Clinical Skills for Speech-Language Pathologists* (San Diego: Singular Publishing Group, 1997).

59. B. J. Zimmerman, "Self-Regulating Academic Learning and Achievement: The Emergence of a Social Cognitive Perspective," *Educational Psychology Review* 2 (Feb. 1990): 173–201.

60. R. M. Bernard, "The Effects of Processing Instructions on the Usefulness of a Graphic Organizer and Structural Cuing in Text," *Instructional Science* 19 (Mar. 1990): 207–17.

61. R. M. Jubis, "Coding Effects on Performance in a Process Control Task with Uniparameter and Multiparameter Displays" *Human Factors* 32 (Mar. 1990): 287–97).

62. See note 4.

63. R. Kinnunen & M. Vauras, "Comprehension monitoring and the level of comprehension in high- and low-achieving primary school children's reading," *Learning and Instruction*, 5 (Fall 1995): 143–65.

64. Adam Winsler, Martha P. Carlton, & Maryann J. Barry, "Age-Related Changes in Preschool Children's Systematic Use of Private Speech in a Natural Setting," *Journal of Child Language* 27 (Oct. 2000): 665–87.

65. J. A. Biven & L. E. Berk, "A Longitudinal Study of the Development of Elementary School Children's Private Speech," *Merrill Palmer Quarterly* 36 (1990): 443–63.

66. Adam Winsler & Jack Naglieri, "Overt and Covert Verbal Problem-Solving Strategies: Developmental Trends in Use, Awareness, and Relations with Task Performance in Children aged 5 to 17," *Child Development* 74 (May 2003): 659–78.

67. J. R. Lloyd, D. F. Batemena, Y. J. Landrum, & D. P. Hallahan, "Self-Recording of Attention Versus Productivity," *Journal of Applied Behavior Analysis* 22 (Aug. 1989): 315–23.

68. Anthony. J. Cuvo & Kevin P. Klatt, "Effects of Community-Based, Videotaped, and Flash Card Instruction of Community-Referenced Sight Words on Students with Mental Retardation," *Journal of Applied Behavior Analysis* 25 (Summer 1992): 499–512.

69. S. B. Salas & D. J. Dickinson, "The Effect of Feedback and Three Different Types of Corrections on Student Learning," *Journal of Human Behavior and Learning* 7 (Jan. 1990): 13–19.

70. M. H. Kernis, J. Brockner, & B. S. Frankel, "Self-esteem and Reactions to Failure: The Mediating Role of Overgeneralization," *Journal of Personality and Social Psychology* 57 (June 1991): 707–14.

71. A. D. Miller, S. W. Hall, & W. L. Heard, "Effects of sequential 1-minute time trials with and without inter-trial feedback and self-correlation on general and special education students' fluency with math facts," *Journal of Behavioral Education* 5 (Aug. 1995): 319–45.

CHAPTER SIX

1. Holly A. Ruff & Mary C. Capozzoli, "Development of Attention and Distractibility in the First 4 Years of Life," *Developmental Psychology* 39 (Sept. 2003): 877–90.

2. Norbert Boerger & Jaap van der Meere, "Visual Behavior of ADHD Children During an Attention Test: An Almost Forgotten Variable," *Journal of Child Psychology & Psychiatry & Allied Disciplines* 41 (May 2000): 525–32.

3. Stanley A. Goldberg, *Clinical Intervention: A Philosophy and Methodology of Clinical Practice* (New York: Macmillan, 1993).

4. Ira Krumholtz, "Results From a Pediatric Vision Screening and It's Ability to Predict Academic Performance," *Optometry: Journal of the American Optometric Association* 71 (July 2000): 426–30.

5. Sally Shaywitz, *Overcoming Dyslexia* (New York: Alfred A. Knopf, 2003).

6. Julie Simon, Carrie Larson, & Richard Lehrer, "Preschool Screening: Relations Among Audiometric and Developmental Measures," *Journal of Applied Developmental Psychology* 9 (Jan.–Mar. 1988): 107–23.

7. Arthur E. Dobos, Paul H. Dworkin, & Bruce A. Bernstein, "Pediatricians' Approaches to Developmental Problems: Has the Gap Been Narrowed?" *Journal of Developmental & Behavioral Pediatrics* 15 (Feb. 1994): 34–38.

8. William R. Hodgson, "Audiometric Screening and Threshold Norms," *Journal of School Health* 38 (1968): 373–76.

9. E. A. Lunzer, "Deficits in Attention in Young Children with Specific Reference to Down's Syndrome and Other Mentally Handicapped Children," *Early Child Development & Care* 17 (Nov. 1984): 131–54.

10. K. Richard Ridderinkhof, "Attention and Selection in the Growing Child: Views Derived from Developmental Psychophysiology," *Biological Psychology* 54 (Oct. 2000): 55–106.

11. Nirlipta Patnaik, "Selective Attention in Normal and Learning Disabled Children," *Psychological Studies* 47 (Jan. 2002) 113–20.

12. Martin Hanford, *Where's Waldo?: The Fantastic Journey,* 2nd ed. (Cambridge, Mass.: Candlewick Press, 1997).

13. Laila Luoma, Eila Herrgard, Perttu Sipilae, Heidi Yppaerlilae, Juhani Partanen, & Jari Karhu, "Distractible Children Show Abnormal Orienting to Non-Attended Auditory Stimuli," *Neuroreport: For Rapid Communication of Neuroscience Research* 10 (June 1999): 1869–74.

14. Francina Salavert, Manuel Pelegrina, & Fransesc S. Beltran, "Figure-Ground Perceptual Organization and Learning by Three-Year-Old Children," *Perceptual & Motor Skills* 86 (Apr. 1998) 488–90.

15. Johanna K. Kaakinen, Jukka Hyoenae, & Janice M. Keenan, "How Prior Knowledge, WMC, and Relevance of Information Affect Eye Fixations in Expository Text," *Journal of Experimental Psychology: Learning, Memory & Cognition* 29 (May 2003): 447–57.

16. Emily Marie Elliott, "Developmental Differences in the Effects of Distracting Sounds on Performance," Ph. D. diss., University of Missouri (2001).

17. J. F. Defrance, S. Smith, F. C. Schweitzer, L. Ginsberg, & S. Sands, "Topographical Analyses of Attention Disorders of Childhood," *International Journal of Neuroscience* 87 (Jan. 1996): 41–61.

18. *The House of Wax,* Produced by Brian Foy and Warner Brothers, Directed by Andre de Toth, Screenplay by Charles Belden and Crane Wilbur, 1953.

19. Horst Arndt and Richard W. Janney, "Verbal, Prosodic, and Kinesic Emotive Contrasts in Speech," *Journal of Pragmatics* 15 (June 1991): 521–49.

20. Paul Ekman, Wallace V. Friesen, & Natalie Angler. "Kinesic Cues: The Body, Eyes and Face" in *The Nonverbal Communication Reader: Classic and Contemporary Readings,* 2nd ed., ed. Joseph A. Devito (Prospect Heights, Ill.: Waveland Press, 1999), pp. 48–89

21. Joerg D. Jescheniak, Herbert Schriefers, & Ansgar Hantsch, "Utterance Format Effects Phonological Priming in the Picture-Word Task: Implications for Models of Phonological Encoding in Speech Production," *Journal of Experimental Psychology: Human Perception & Performance* 29 (Apr. 2003): 441–54.

22. Emiel Krahmer, Marc Swerts, Mariet Theune, & Mieke Weegels, "The Dual of Denial: The Uses of Disconfirmations in Dialogue and Their Prosodic Correlates," *Speech Communication* 36 (Jan. 2002) 133–45.

23. George J. DuPaul & Russell A. Barkley, "Attention-Deficit Hyperactivity Disorder" in *The Practice of Child Therapy* 3rd ed., eds. Richard J. Morris & Thomas R. Kratochwill (Needham Heights, Mass.: Pearson Allyn & Bacon, 1998), pp. 132–66.

24. Jill Cari Gitten, "Shifting and Sustained Attention in Children with Attention-Deficit/Hyperactivity Disorder," Ph. D. diss., University of Florida, (2002).

25. Natasha Z. Kirkham, "Helping Children Apply Their Knowledge to Their Behavior on a Dimension-Switching Task," *Developmental Science* 6 (Nov 2003): 449–76.

26. Nettie R. Bartel, J. Jeffrey Grill, & Helmut W. Bartel, "The Syntactic-Paradigmatic Shirt in Learning Disabled and Normal Children," *Journal of Learning Disabilities* 6 (Oct. 1973): 518–23

27. Natasha Z. Kirkham, "Helping Children Apply Their Knowledge to Their Behavior on a Dimension-Switching Task," *Developmental Science* 6 (Nov 2003): 449–76

28. Jules C. Abrams, "The Affective Component: Emotional Needs of Individuals with Reading and Related Learning Disorders," *Journal of Reading, Writing, & Learning Disabilities International* 7 (July–Sept. 1991): 171–82.

29. Tim Dalgleish, "Patterns of Processing Bias for Emotional Information Across Clinical Disorders: A Comparison of Attention, Memory, and Prospective Cognition in Children and Adolescents with Depression, Generalized Anxiety, and Posttraumatic Stress Disorder," *Journal of Clinical Child & Adolescent Psychology* 32 (Mar. 2003): 10–21.

30. Joan L. Luby, Amy K. Heffelfinger, Christine Mrakotsky, Kathy M. Brown, Martha J. Hessler, Jeffrey M. Wallis, & Edward L. Spitznagel, "The Clinical Picture of Depression in Preschool Children," *Journal of the American Academy of Child & Adolescent Psychiatry* 42 (Mar. 2003): 340–48.

31. Jerry Wilde, "Interventions of Children with Anger Problems," *Journal of Rational-Emotive & Cognitive Behavior Therapy* 19 (Fall 2001): 191–97.

32. Pamela M. Cole, Carolyn Zahn-Waxler, & K. Danielle Smith, "Expressive Control During a Disappointment: Variations Related to Preschoolers' Behavior Problems," *Development Psychology* 30 (Nov. 1994): 835–46.

33. Beverly J. Wilson, "The Role of Attentional Processes in Children's Prosocial Behavior With Peers: Attention Shifting and Emotion," *Development & Psychopathology* 15 (June 2003): 313–29.

CHAPTER SEVEN

1. Cesare Cornoldi, Gian Marco Marzocchi, Melania Belotti, et al., "Working Memory Interference Control Deficit in Children Referred by Teachers by ADHD Symptoms," *Child Neuropsychology* 7 (Dec 2001): 230–40.

2. Charles Hulme & Suzie Mackenzie, *Working Memory and Severe Learning Difficulties* (Mahwah, N. J.: Lawrence Erlbaum Associates, 1992).

3. Natasha Z. Kirkham & Loren Cruess, "Helping Children Apply Their Knowledge to Their Behavior on a Dimension-Switching Task," *Developmental Science* 6 (Nov 2003): 449–76.

4. Rossna De Beni, "Intrusion Errors in Working Memory Tasks: Are They Related to Reading Comprehension Ability?" *Learning & Individual Differences* 12 (June 2000): 131–43.

5. Dragnet, Directed by Jack Web, 1952–1959, 1967–1970, NBC Syndication Title: Badge 714.

6. Lisa Gershkoff-Stowe, "Object Naming, Vocabulary Growth, and the Development of Word Retrieval Abilities," *Journal of Memory & Language* 46 (May 2002): 665–87.

7. Wayne W. Reeves, *Cognition and Complexity: The Cognitive Science of Managing Complexity* (Lanham, Md.: Scarecrow Press, 1996).

8. Francois Vigneau, Lise Blancet, Michel Loranger, and Michel Pepin, "Response Latencies Measured on IQ Tests: Dimensionality of Speed Indices and the Relationship Between Speed and Level," *Personality & Individual Differences* 33 (July 2002): 165–82.

9. Stanley A. Goldberg, *Clinical Skills* (San Diego: Singular Publishing Group, 1997).

10. Diane Pedrotty Bryant, Marilyn Goodwin, Brian R. Bryant, & Kellie Higgins, "Vocabulary Instruction for Students with Learning Disabilities: A Review of the Research," *Learning Disability Quarterly* 26 (Spring 2003): 117–128.

11. Ellen M. Markman, Judith L. Waslow, & Mikkel B. Hansen, "The Use of the Mutual Exclusivity Assumption by Young Word Learners," *Cognitive Psychology* 47 (Nov 2003): 241–75.

12. Robert Owens, Jr., *Language Development* (New York: Macmillan, 1992).

13. Allyssa McCabe & Carole Peterson, "A Comparison of Adult's Versus Children's Spontaneous Use of Because and So," *Journal of Genetic Psychology* 149 (June 1988): 257–68.

14. Lois Bloom, *Language Development from Two to Three* (New York: Cambridge University Press, 1993).

15. Mel Levine, *A Mind at a Time* (New York: Simon & Schuster, 2002).

16. The original *Who's on First?* routine can be heard at http://www. baseball-almanac. com/humor4. shtml. It also was record by On the Air Records as an audio CD titled *Who's On First: A Collection of Classic Routines,* recorded by On The Air Records, 2000.

17. Laura E. Berk, *Awakening Children's Minds* (New York: Oxford University Press, 2001).

18. Vladimir M. Sloutsky, "Is a Picture Worth a Thousand Words? Preference for Auditory Modality in Young Children," *Child Development* 74 (May 2003): 822–33.

19. James R. Booth, Douglas D. Burman, Joel R. Meyer, Zhang Lei, Janet Choy, Darren R. Gitelman, Todd B. Parrish, & M. Marsel Mesulam, "Modality-Specific and -Independent Differences in the Neural Substrate for Lexical Processing," *Journal of Neurolinguistics* 16 (July–Sept. 2003): 383–405.

20. D. E. Broadbent, "Listening to One of Two Synchronous Messages," *Journal of Experimental Psychology General* 121 (Spring 1992): 125–27.

21. H. L. Dortch & C. A. Trombly, "The Effects of Education on Hand Use with Industrial Workers in Repetitive Jobs," *American Journal of Occupational Therapy* 44 (Dec. 1990): 777–82.

22. J. D. Klein & E. Freitag, "Effects of Using an Instructional Game on Motivation and Performance," *Journal of Educational Research* 84 (Dec. 1991): 303–8.

23. L. M. J. De Sonneville, C. A. Vershoor, C. Njiokiktjien, V. Veld, N. Toorenaar, & M. Vranken, "Facial Identify and Facial Emotions: Speed, Accuracy and Processing Strategies in Children and Adults," *Journal of Clinical & Experimental Neuropsychology* 24 (Apr. 2002): 200–213.

24. Felicia Dawn Hurewitz, "Developing the Ability to Resolve Syntactic Ambiguity," Ph. D. diss., University of Pennsylvania (2002).

CHAPTER EIGHT

1. Martin L. Lonky, "Human Consciousness: A Systems Approach to the Mind/Brain Interaction," *Journal of Mind & Behavior* 24 (Winter 2003): 91–118.

2. Brian A. Goolsby & Satoru Suzuki, "Understanding Priming of Color-Singleton Search: Roles of Attention at Encoding and Retrieval," *Perception & Psychophysics* 63 (Aug. 2001): 929–44.

3. Elizabeth May Serig, "Evaluating Organizational Response to a Cognitive Problem: A Human Factors Approach," Ph. D. diss., Rice University(2002).

4. Gavin Nobes & Chris Pawson, " Children's Understanding of Social Rules and Social Status," *Merrill-Palmer Quarterly* 49 (Jan. 2003): 77–99.

5. William V. Fabricius & Henry M. Wellman, "Children's Understanding of Retrieval Cue Utilization," *Developmental Psychology* 19 (Jan. 1983): 15–21.

6. Joseph T. Lawton and Jill Burk, "Effects of Advance Organizer Instruction on Preshcool Children's Prosocial Behavior," *Journal of Structural Learning* 10 (June 1990): 215–26.

7. Stanley A. Goldberg, *Clinical Intervention* (San Diego: Singular Publishing Group, 1997).

8. Rachel Sutherland, Margaret-Ellen Pipe, Katherine Schick, Janice Murray, &Camilla Gobbo, "Knowing in Advance: The Impact of Prior Event Information on Memory and Event," *Journal of Experimental Child Psychology* 84 (Mar. 2003): 244–63.

9. Dierdre Brown & Margaet-Ellen Pipe, "Variations on a Technique: Enhancing Children's Recall Using Narrative Elaboration Training," *Applied Cognitive Psychology* 17 (May 2002): 377–99.

10. Keiko Nakamura, "The Acquisition of Polite Language by Japanese Children," in *Children's Language: Developing Narrative and Discourse Competence*, ed. Keith E. Nelson & Ayhan Aksu-Koc (Mahwah, N. J.: Lawrence Erlbaum Associates, 2001), 93–112.

11. Shaw-Jing Chao, "The Emergence of Inferential Rules: The Use of Pragmatic Reasoning Schemas by Preschoolers," *Cognitive Development* 15 (Jan.–Mar. 2000): 39–62.

12. Paul P. W. Chang, Susan Levine, and Philip Benson, "Children's Recognition of Caricatures," *Developmental Psychology* 38 (Nov. 2002): 1038–51.

13. Donna R. Carroll, "Age-Differences in Source-Memory and Source Attributions," Ph. D. diss., University of North Carolina at Greensboro (2002).

14. Karen Hildreth, Becky Sweeney, & Carolyn Rovee-Collier, "Differential Memory—Preserving Effects of Reminders at 6 Months," *Journal of Experimental Child Psychology* 84 (Jan. 2003): 41–62.

15. Lisa M. Nimmo, "Syllable Frequency Effects on Phonological Short-Term Memory Tasks," *Applied Psycholinguistics* 23 (Dec. 2002): 643–59.

16. Judith A. Hudson & Ronald B. Gillam, "'Oh, I Remember Now!': Facilitating Children's Long-Term Memory for Events," *Topics in Language Disorders* 18 (Nov. 1997): 1–15.

17. Susan Landry, Cynthia L. Miller-Loncar, Karen E. Smith, & Paul R. Swank, "The Role of Early Parenting in Children's Development of Executive Processes," *Developmental Neuropsychology* 21 (Feb. 2002): 15–41.

18. Teena Willoughby, Eileen Wood, & Erin R. Kraftcheck, "When Can a Lack of Structure Facilitate Strategic Processing of Information?" *British Journal of Educational Psychology* 73 (Mar. 2003): 59–69.

19. Javier Vila, Mucio Romero, & Juan M. Rosas, "Retroactive Interference after Discrimination Reversal Decreases Following Temporal and Physical Context Changes in Human Subjects," *Behavioural Processes* 59 (July 2002): 47–54.

CHAPTER NINE

1. Akong Tulku Rinpoche, *Taming the Tiger* (Rochester, Vt.: Inner Traditions, 1995).

2. Jacqueline Dodge, "Reducing Supervisee Anxiety: A Cognitive-Behavioral Approach," *Counselor Education & Supervision* 22 (Sept. 1982): 55–60.

3. Pamela Duchesne Handel, "Family Relationships and Perceived Competence in Students with Learning Disabilities," Ph. D. diss., University of Missouri (1999).

4. L. Haratrey & J. S. G. Wells, "The Meaning of Respite Care to Mothers of Children with Learning Disabilities: Two Irish Case Studies," *Journal of Psychiatric & Mental Health Nursing* 10 (June 2003): 335–42.

5. Robert Weis & M. Christine Lovejoy, "Information Processing in Everyday Life: Emotion-Congruent Bias in Mother's Reports of Parent-Child Interactions," *Journal of Personality & Social Psychology* 83 (July 2002): 216–30.

6. Wendy Sturgess, Judy Dunn, & Lisa Davies, "Young Children's Perceptions of Their Relationships with Family Members: Links with Family Setting, Friendships, and Adjustment," *International Journal of Behavioral Development* 25 (Nov. 2001) 521–29.

7. Sharon Myers, "Relational Healing: To Be Understood and to Understand," *Journal of Humanistic Psychology* 43 (Winter 2003): 86–104.

8. Monty Roberts *A Real Horse Whisperer*, 20th Century Fox, 1997.

9. Shirley L. Patterson, Jay L. Memmott, Eileen M. Brennan, & Carel B. Germain, "Patterns of Natural Helping in Rural Areas: Implications for Social Work Research," *Social Work Research & Abstracts* 28 (Sept. 1992): 22–28.

10. Marc Mahilios, "Matching Teaching Methods to Learning Styles" in *Children and Stress: Understanding and Helping*, eds. Beverly Hardcastle Stanford & Kaoru Yamamoto (Olney, Md.: Association for Childhood Education International, 2001), pp. 65–73.

11. Kathleen V. Hoover-Dempsey, Joan M. T. Walker, Kathleen P. Jones, and Richard P. Reed, "Teachers Involving Parents (TIP): Results From an In-Service Teacher Education Program for Enhancing Parental Involvement," *Teaching & Teacher Education* 18 (Oct. 2002): 843–67.

12. Raci Schluter & Diane Yates, "Perceptions of School-Based Competence: Parents' and Teachers' Conceptions of Parent and Teacher Competence," Ph. D. diss., University of Texas (2001).

13. Evanthia N. Patrikakou & Roger P. Weissberg, "Parents' Perceptions of Teacher Outreach and Parent Involvement in Children's Education," *Journal of Prevention & Intervention in the Community* 20 (2000) 103–19.

14. Lisa Bouillion & Louis M. Gomez, "Connecting School and Community with Science Learning: Real World Problems and School-Community Partnerships as Contextual Scaffolds," *Journal of Research in Science Teaching* 28 (Oct. 2001): 878–98.

15. Addie Ehrenstein, Bruce N. Walker, Mary Czerwinski, & Evan M. Feldman, "Some Fundamentals of Training and Transfer: Practice Benefits are not Automatic" in *Training for a Rapidly Changing Workplace: Applications of Psychological Research*, eds. Miguel A. Quinones and Addie Ehrenstein (Washington, D. C.: American Psychological Association, 1997), pp. 119–47.

16. Beverly Hardcastle Stanford, "Experienced Teachers: Seeing Children Whole," in *Children and Stress: Understanding and Helping*, eds. Beverly Hardcastle Stanford and Kaoru Yamamoto (Olney, Md.: Association for Childhood Education International, 2001), pp. 65–73.

17. John G. Homes, Dale T. Miller, & Melvin J. Lerner, "Committing Altruism Under the Cloak of Self-Interest: The Exchange Fiction," *Journal of Experimental Social Psychology* 38 (Mar. 2002): 144–151.

18. C. Daniel Batson & Adam A. Powell, "Altruism and Prosocial Behavior" in *Handbook of Psychology: Personality and Social Psychology*, Vol. 5, eds. Theodore Millon & Melvin Lerner (New York: John Wiley & Sons, 2003), pp. 463–84.

19. Stanley A. Goldberg, *Clinical Intervention* (New York: Macmillian Publishing, 1993).

20. Geshe Chekhawa, in *Glimpse After Glimpse*, Sogyal Rinpoche, (New York: Harper San Francisco 1995): Sept. 20 (no page numbers).

21. Derek Bell, "Making Science Inclusive: Providing Effective Learning Opportunities for Children With Learning Difficulties," *Support for Learning* 17 (Nov. 2002): 156–61.

22. Jack A. Naglieri & Eric B. Pickering, *Helping Children Learn: Intervention Handouts for Use in School and at Home* (Baltimore: Paul H. Brookes Publishing, 2003).

23. Antonio L. Freitas & E. Tory Higgins, "Enjoying Goal-Directed Action: The Role of Regulatory Fit," *Psychological Science* 13 (Jan. 2002): 1–6.

24. Robert Y. Schoor & Richard Lesh, "A Modeling Approach for Providing Teacher Development" in *Beyond Constructivism: Models and Modeling Perspectives on Mathematics Problem Solving, Learning, and Teaching*, eds. Richard Lesh and Helen M. Doerr (Mahwah, N. J.: Lawrence Erbaum Associates, 2003), pp. 141–57.

CHAPTER TEN

1. Akong Tulku Rinpoche, *Taming the Tiger* (Rochester, Vt.: Inner Traditions, 1995).

2. Quote from Geshe Shawopa, in Patrul Rinpoche, *The Words of My Perfect Teacher* (Boston, Mass.: Shambhala Publications, 1998).

3. His Holiness, the Dali Lama, *Ethics for a New Millennium* (New York: Riverhead Books, 1999).

4. Alison Chapple, Carl May, and Peter Campion, "Parental Guilt: The Part Placed by the Clinical Geneticist," *Journal of Genetic Counseling* 4 (Sept. 1995): 179–91.

5. Smantha Seagram & Judith C. Daniluk, "It Goes With the Territory: The Meaning and Experience of Maternal Guilt for Mothers of Preadolescent Children," *Women & Therapy* 25 (January 2002): 61–88.

6. Sue Hall & T. M. Marteau, "Causal Attributions and Blame: Associations with Mothers' Adjustment to the Birth of a Child with Down Syndrome," *Psychology, Health & Medicine* 8 (Nov. 2003): 415–23

7. Judith C. Conger, Anthony J. Conger, Christine Edmondson, Beth Tescher, & James Smolin, "The Relationship of Anger and Social Skills to Psychological Symptoms," *Assessment* 10 (Sept. 2003): 248–58.

8. M. Ferriter & N. Huband, "Experiences of Parents with a Son or Daughter Suffering From Schizophrenia," *Journal of Psychiatric & Mental Health Nursing* 10 (Oct. 2003): 552–60.

9. Thich Nhat Hanh, *The Heart of the Buddha's Teaching* (New York: Broadway Books, 1998).

10. L. Hartrey & J. S. G. Wells, "The Meaning of Respite Care to Mothers of Children with Learning Disabilities: Two Irish Case Studies," *Journal of Psychiatric & Mental Health Nursing* 10 (June 2003): 335–42.

11. David M. Fergusson, L. John Horwood, & Michael T. Lynskey, "The Childhoods of Multiple Problem Adolescents: A 15-Year Longitudinal Study," *Journal of Child Psychology & Psychiatry & Allied Disciplines*, 35 (Sept. 1994): 1123–40.

12. Chogyam Trungpa, *Shambhla: The Sacred Path of the Warrior* (Boston, Mass.: Shambhala, 1988).

13. Anna M. Tacon, Jacalyn McComb, Yvone Caldera, & Patrick Randolph, "Mindfulness Meditation, Anxiety Reduction, and Heart Disease: A Pilot Study," *Family & Community Health* 26 (Jan.–Mar. 2003): 25–33.

14. Sogyal Rinpoche, *The Tibetan Book of Living and Dying* (San Francisco: HarperSanFrancisco, 1994).

15. Teresa E. Seeman, Linda Fagan Dubin, & Melvin Seeman, "Religiosity/Spirituality and Health: A Critical Review of the Evidence for Biological Pathways," *American Psychologist* 58 (Jan. 2003): 53–63.

16. Veronika Ospina-Kammerer, "An Evaluation of the Respiratory One Method (ROM) in Reducing Emotional Exhaustion Among Family Physician Residents," *International Journal of Emergency Mental Health* 5 (Winter 2003): 29–32.

17. Elaine R. Kamara Altman, "A Brief Therapy Model to Reduce Stress by Practicing Breathing Exercises, Mindful Meditation, and Yoga Stretching" Ph. D. diss., Capella University (2001).

18. Beth Roth, "Mindfulness-Based Stress Reduction in the Inner City," *Advances* 13 (Fall 1997): 50–58.

19. Paul Ramchandani and Alan Stein, "The Impact of Parental Psychiatric Disorder on Children," *British Medical Journal* 327 (Aug. 2003): 242–43.

20. See note 9.

21. See note 3.

22. See note 1.

CHAPTER ELEVEN

1. Lisa G. Sorenson, Peter W. Forbes, Michael D. Wiler, William M. Mitcherll, & Deborah P. Waber, "Psychosocial Adjustment Over a Two-Year Period in Children Referred for Learning Problems: Risk, Resilience, and Adaptation," *Learning Disabilities Research & Practice* 18 (Feb. 2003): 10–24.

2. Maria Veronica Svetaz, Majorie Ireland, & Robert Blum, "Adolescents with Learning Disabilities: Risk and Protective Factors Associated with Emotional Well-Being: Findings from the National Longitudinal Study of Adolescent Health: Erratum" *Journal of Adolescent Health*, 27 (Nov. 2000): 340–48.

3. Akhtar Sayeda, "Parental Attitudes and Resultant Behavior of Children," *Child Psychiatry Quarterly* 11 (Apr. 1978): 37–48.

4. Dabie Nabuzoka & Janet M. Empson, "Social Cognitive Development of Children with Learning Difficulties," *Educational & Child Psychology* 19 (Jan. 1997) :16–26.

5. Elaine Fine, "Are We Preparing Adolescents with Learning Disabilities to Cope with Social Issues?" *Journal of Learning Disabilities* 20 (Dec. 1987): 633–34.

6. Helmut Remshmidt, "Evidence Concerning the Effectiveness of Psychotherapies with Children and Adolescents," *Current Opinion in Psychiatry* 16 (July 2003): 389–93.

7. *Best Boy*, Ira Wohl, Producer and Director, 1979.

8. G. H. Katz, "Should the Child Be Sent to an Institution?" *Nervous Child* 5 (1946): 172–77.

9. Paul Ramcharan, "Bridging the Divide at Transition: What Happens for Young People with Learning Difficulties and Their Families," *Journal of Learning Disabilities* 7 (Sept. 2003): 283–84.

10. Arnold L. Gilberg, "The Stress of Parenting," *Child Psychiatry & Human Development* 6 (Winter 1975): 59–67.

11. Mohammad R. Taghavi, Tim Dalgleish, Ali R. Moradi, Hamid T. Neshat-Doost, & William Yule, "Selective Processing of Negative Emotional Information in Children and Adolescents with Generalized Anxiety Disorder," *British Journal of Clinical Psychology* 42 (Sept. 2003): 221–30.

12. Sol Stein, *On Writing* (St. Martin's Griffin: New York, 1995).

13. G. K. Chesterton, *Orthodoxy* (New York: Dimensions, 1991).

14. Marisa Smyth and Roy McConkey, "Future Aspirations of Students with Severe Learning Disabilities and of Their Parents on Leaving Special Schooling," *British Journal of Learning Disabilities* 31 (Mar. 2003): 54–59.

15. Frank Ostaseski, *Being a Compassionate Companion* (San Francisco: Zen Hospice Project, 2003).

16. Pema Chodron, *When Things Fall Apart* (Boston: Shambhala Publications, 1977).

17. Shantideva, *A Guide to the Bodhisattva's Way of Life* (Dharamsala, India: Library of Tibetan Works and Archives, 1979).

18. Stephen A. Spillane, Joan M. McGuire, & Kay A. Norlander, "Undergraduate Admission Policies, Practices, and Procedures for Applicants with Learning Disabilities," *Journal of Learning Disabilities* 25 (Dec. 1992): 665–70.

19. Stephen B. Thomas, "College Students and Disability Law," *Journal of Special Education* 33 (Winter 2000): 248–57.

20. Yvonne Mary Bradshaw, "Case Studies of Postsecondary College Students with Learning Disabilities," Ph. D. diss., Virginia Polytechnical Institute (2001).

21. Abiola Dipeolu, Robert Reardon, James Sampson, & Jane Burkhead, "The Relationship Between Dysfunctional Career Thoughts and Adjustment to Disability in College Students with Learning Disabilities," *Journal of Career Assessment* 10 (Nov. 2002): 413–27.

22. Lauren E. Lindstrom & Michael R. Benz, "Phases of Career Development: Case Studies of Young Women with Learning Disabilities," *Exceptional Children* 69 (Fall 2002): 67–83.

23. Rebecca J. Panagos & David L. DuBois, "Career Self-Efficacy Development and Students with Learning Disabilities," *Learning Disabilities Research & Practice* 14 (Winter 1999): 25–34.

Index